WILL TO WIN

70

WILL TO WIN

How one young rider reached the top

RACHEL HUNT

DAVID & CHARLES
Newton Abbot · London

To M and M
and DL

The author and publishers would like to thank the following for supplying photographs for this book: Alf Baker, p. 99; John R. Corsan, p. 17; Hugo M. Czerny, pp. 81, 86, 88; Findlay Davidson, p. 11; Chris Davies, pp. 45, 46, 47; Peter Doresa, p. 24; Equestrian Services, p. 92; *Eventing* magazine, pp. 117, 122; Carol Gilson, p. 67; *Hampshire Chronicle*, p. 113; Clive Hiles, pp. 26, 60; Kit Houghton, pp. 2, 7, 28, 31, 35, 38, 43, 51, 63, 94, 97, 100, 101, 102, 104, 106, 110, 111, 116, 119, 120, 124, 125, 132, 139, 143, 146, 147, 148, 149, 158, 160, 161, 162, 168, 170, 171, 179, 190; Anne E. Hughes, pp. 1, 109; Jim Meads, pp. 13, 53; Steve Moore, endpapers; MVR Photographic, p. 55; Pleasure Prints, p. 186; Geoff Raines, p. 130; Southern Newspapers Group, p. 40.

To David Bickers for persuading me to take up the challenge of writing this book.

To Richard Bickers for all his assistance in the writing.

To Annie Lanz for her diplomatic tact, enabling me to complete the challenge.

To all those people and my sponsors who have and continue to contribute to my riding career.

Endpapers: Rachel with Friday Fox, Piglet and Aloaf

Page 1: Friday proves she is one of the best when she completes clear and is placed at Badminton

Page 2: Happy combination at Holker Hall 1988

British Library Cataloguing in Publication Data
Hunt, Rachel
Will to win.
1. Three-day eventing – Biographies
I. Title
798.2'4'0924

ISBN 0-7153-9398-7

Typeset in 11 on 12½pt Goudy by Ace Filmsetting Ltd, Frome, Somerset and printed in West Germany by Mohndruck GmbH for David & Charles Publishers plc Brunel House, Newton Abbot, Devon

Contents

To be the Badminton champion must be the ambition of every three day event rider, and to compete there at all is considered an achievement. I made my first attempt in 1984, but could hardly have expected to win—even to think of being placed in the top twenty seemed over-optimistic. It was going to be difficult enough to complete the cross-country, the most formidable part of the competition, let alone do well in the other disciplines.

Badminton was 'the big one' for me, right from the early days. I had walked the four-and-a-half-mile Badminton course for the first time when I was ten years old, and had treated my family to a display of youthful pride and confidence in my ponies: 'Oh, Charm could jump this . . . Zephie would fly over that!' However, the realities of jumping at any level of competition soon became apparent when, competing in my first Pony Club hunter trial during the next Easter holidays, I suffered the indignity of two refusals. This did not deter me from my deep-set determination to ride at Badminton one day. And now, in 1984, here I was!

1 The Badminton Challenge

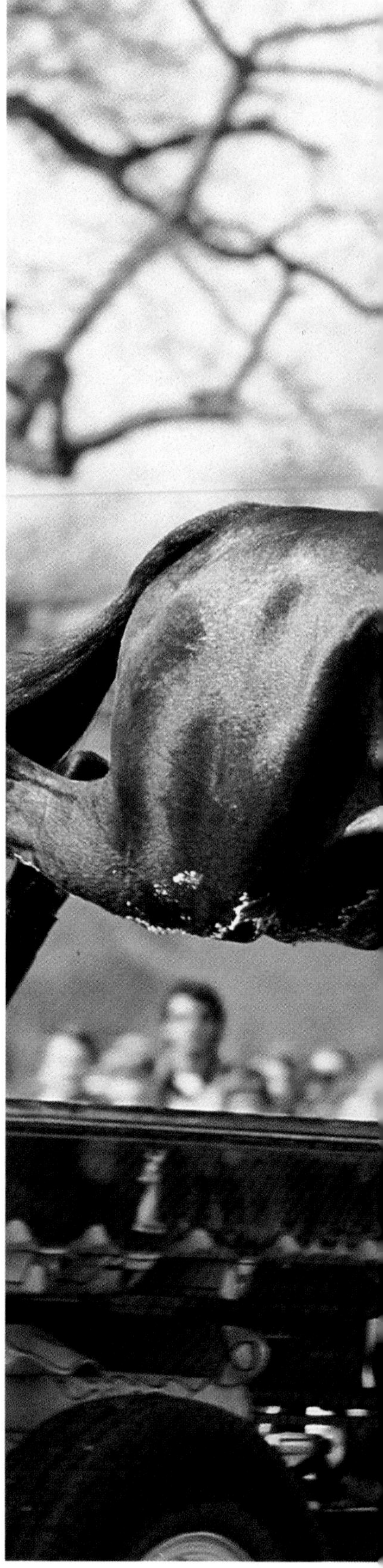

Furthermore, I had seen my stepbrother David trying to qualify his horse, Crown Wheel, and this had also impressed me. Sadly, he did not succeed; but he was a good second at Bramham in 1978 to the Strakers' George, and George later won Badminton and Burghley, ridden by Lucinda Prior-Palmer (now Mrs Green). Witnessing his determination and effort simply whetted my appetite even more.

And now, here I was, at the tender age of nineteen—with the notorious Ski-Jump in prospect, and taking the right line over tricky obstacles like the Vicarage Ditch and the Pigsty, the immediate future was in fact a trifle daunting. It wasn't that I was afraid of any of the jumps: I was simply anxious to do well for the sake of my family and friends who had always had such confidence in me, and who had contributed so much affection, advice and encouragement to my getting to Badminton at all.

Anyone who takes part in any sporting event is meant to feel butterflies in the tummy; without nervous tension, they say, nobody is keyed up to the highest pitch. However, I don't suffer from this particular kind of qualm, perhaps because I began riding when I was two and went hunting soon after, and children never seem to worry much about what is on the other side of a hedge or wall, they just go for it. This press-on-regardless attitude has survived in me, and helps to keep me calm.

The actual competing is not the only cause of anxiety: any arduous, top-level event involves the careful preparation of every detail and starts weeks before, and ensuring that one's horse is in all respects ready is not simple. My first Badminton attempt was to be made with Piglet, a ten-year-old, 16.2 brown gelding, ⅞ Thoroughbred and ⅛ Exmoor pony; for this occasion he had to be groomed to perfection, too—his shampoo and

Me and Piggy—Badminton 1984

'Finding your way about when competing for the first time is puzzling: there are not many signposts, and this made me feel more an outsider ...'

set—and the horsebox loaded with particular care. Luckily I had persuaded a friend, Bonnie Robinson (née Lucas), to help me; she had been Richard Meade's groom for many years, had been to the 1976 Olympics in Montreal with him, and was familiar with Badminton.

Finding your way about when competing for the first time is puzzling: there are not many signposts and this made me feel even more an outsider—I envied all the competitors who had been there before—the insiders—who knew exactly where to find everything. Having followed the signs for 'Badminton Horse Trials', I found myself at midday on the Tuesday of Badminton week wondering where the stables were and where to find the vet. I parked on the village green and was directed to the village hall, where the vet would have to pass Piglet before I could stable him.

'Passport, please,' said the vet. Each horse intending to compete must have this document, which is a record of all the injections the horse has been given—there are special ones for going to various countries—and all the blood and dope tests that have ever been done. The annual 'flu injections are the essential ones: without the proof as contained in the passport that these are up to date, no horse is allowed into the stables at an event.

I searched my bags, but couldn't find Piglet's. 'I must have left it at home,' I told the vet. This was particularly vexing after all the trouble I had taken over preparation before setting out.

'I'm afraid your horse can't go into the stables until I've seen the passport.' Luckily we lived only sixty miles away, and a quick telephone call to Bonnie ensured that it would reach me that afternoon. The problem now was poor Piggy, but Richard Meade had heard of my predicament and kindly offered me a stable on his farm nearby, and invited me to join his family for lunch.

Later that afternoon Piggy was stabled in the grounds of Badminton House. Next to him was Pomeroy, the ride of my great friend and rival, Rodney Powell, who was also attempting his first Badminton. The passport troubles behind us, the exciting prospect of the next few days now really started to well up as I hacked Piggy out into the park—our first taste of the very special atmosphere that is unique to Badminton. That evening we watched the video of Badminton 1982, which was no help at all to us newcomers and only made us more nervous.

Next day, an early morning exercise round the park brought me to the practice arenas, where the feeling of being rather young and inexperienced soon overshadowed my eager anticipation as I made an embarrassing attempt at dressage amongst the best riders in the sport. We had a good look at the main arena from the collecting ring and returned to the stables.

Every year, all competitors have to assemble in the village hall for an initial briefing and are given programmes, maps and badges. On this occasion there were not enough seats for everyone, so latecomers had to stand at the back. Colonel Frank Weldon was still the director of this great event at the time, and introduced us to the ground jury: the three people who over-see the whole competition, including judging the dressage. He reminded us of a few rules and regulations, discussed the course, and prepared us for the initial drive over the course, emphasising that four-wheel-drive vehicles were a necessity.

All these vehicles were soon overloaded and queuing behind his Land Rover; thus we set off to drive Saturday's Phases A and C, the roads and

tracks, stopping to walk Phase B, which is the steeplechase course. Everyone has to stay behind Colonel Frank's car, but the competitive spirit in top-level sport is such that even on an exercise like this everyone vies for second place, so the guided tour soon becomes a cross-country motor rally. Rodney was driving our vehicle, and it didn't take him long to gain this prime position, although the process was more than a little nerve-racking!

This was an Olympic year, so the distances for the various phases were different from usual. Phase A was 4,400 metres, to be ridden in 20 minutes (which is a good trot). Phase B, the steeplechase over eight fences, was 2,760 metres and the optimum time 4 minutes. Phase C was 9,900 metres, to take 45 minutes—a good trot. We then arrived at the ten-minute box: on cross-country day there is a compulsory ten-minute pause for each competitor before he may tackle the cross-country course itself—6,630 metres in 11 minutes.

This is the last phase and is inspected on foot; this is the best way to register the first impression that each fence makes, which is what the horse will see. Three or four of us did this together. Out across the front of Badminton House over fences one and two, the Barrels and the Log, we chatted quite happily, but as the two-hour walk progressed the conversation waned to silence, apart from the odd groan and sigh. Famous fences that had formerly been only names to me now became reality: the Stockholm fence, Horsens Bridge, the Lake, the Quarry and, last of all, the Bar.

After weeks of looking forward to this prestigious event, we were still faced with a hectic practice schedule before our hopes and fears could find release in action. That afternoon we were to school under the watchful eye of Gill Watson, trainer of so many Young Riders; I would then have to familiarise Piggy with his new surroundings.

'I had to try to keep him as calm as possible … otherwise we would probably have failed to complete the test and been eliminated for leaping clean out of the arena.'

An hour later we were in front of Badminton House to come before the ground jury at the first vet's inspection; Piggy was looking the picture of fitness and health as we waited our turn. The crowd seemed enormous, but Piggy rose to the occasion in his normal way by stepping out with his head held high, looking fit to run for his life. Unfortunately he was feeling so well that he trotted up sideways, so we had to trot up for a second time. Thumbs up from the jury, a big sigh of relief from Bonnie and me, and we were through to the first stage of the competition.

This began the following day. Piggy was never built for dressage. His action and temperament prevent his ever performing a classy test, so despite months of training only one approach could be taken: I had to try to keep him as calm as possible so he did not become rigid in his body, by making him believe he was doing everything right—otherwise we would probably have failed to complete the test and been eliminated for leaping clean out of the arena. As always, Gill Watson's help was invaluable on that sunny Thursday morning. Unlike cross-country, dressage has always made me nervous, so Gill not only has to help with the dressage work before we go into the arena, but also has to calm *me* down.

Piggy and I, both trying very hard to relax, performed our test in front of the ground jury without major disaster, but with nothing to sing and dance about either, finishing sixty-fifth out of seventy-five starters.

On my second walk over the cross-country I joined Gill and the other Young Riders she trains. This gave us the chance to hear each other's views at the problem fences, and after discussing them it was up to each individual to decide which line would be best for his or her horse.

After the first day's dressage the Duke and Duchess of Beaufort always invite all the competitors and officials to a cocktail party. Champagne flowed as we talked about the day's events and our expectations for Saturday's endurance tests, and in fact I was unaware of my many refills until my glass slipped from my fingers and smashed on the floor—luckily we were in a marquee with a coconut matting floor. Later, as we were leaving, some unopened bottles of champagne caught my eye. What a waste! I sneaked one off the table, but where could I hide it? Rodney was wearing a blazer: why not tuck it inside? But now came a problem as we had to shake hands with Their Graces on the way out. Rodney managed not to let the bottle slip and safely outside we thought it very funny—only to feel very guilty in the morning.

Piggy felt wonderfully fresh and happy as we jumped and had a pipe-opener—this was much more his style of work than dressage. There was still plenty to do: my final cross-country walk, which I always do alone; a more serious drive round the roads and tracks; a walk round the steeplechase in peace; and preparing all the equipment required in the ten-minute box. A couple of fences were still worrying me: the corner at the famous Vicarage Ditch and a bounce at the Pigsty—though the latter shouldn't cause any concern to a piglet!

For the rest of the afternoon I was free to browse around the many trade stands. A friend persuaded me to buy a jumper that had pigs and 'DISGRUNTLED' across the front, as this was how I was feeling after my dressage, especially watching all my heroes performing expert tests—I just hoped I might be as good one day. Being the youngest competitor, my challenge was to complete the course; theirs was to win.

That night I jumped the course a hundred times in my sleep. The next morning Mike and David, my stepfather and stepbrother, arrived early, having driven from Hampshire at crack of dawn to avoid the traffic, which by 9am is solid for miles around. Mum had stayed at home, unable to nerve herself to watch or even walk the course—she had come for the dressage and that was enough, but I knew she was with me in spirit which gave me great strength. Bonnie, David and Mike were my organised backup team who did all the worrying and running about. My father had also come to watch.

Banking the Pigsty fence—our only uncomfortable moment on the way to a clear round

My last preparation was to write my times on a card and strap this to my arm, to ensure that I arrived at each phase on time. If you are too slow, you receive penalty points; too fast, and you waste your horse's energy—a few seconds just inside each time is ideal.

Waiting is the hardest part of a cross-country morning. Piggy could hear the loudspeakers and knew very well what was to happen on this day, but if only I could warn him that it was bigger than ever before. He wouldn't worry, he could do it—it was convincing myself that it wasn't going to be too bad.

We were twelfth to start, so there was no chance to watch any of the earlier riders. At last it was time for me to move up to the collecting ring at the start of Phase A. Bonnie led Piggy round while I weighed in: all riders have to carry 11 stone 11 lb. At the two-minute call I mounted, girths tightened and watches set. Piggy was now full of himself, unable to stand

still for a second. Countdown . . . We're off! It was meant to be at a trot, but whenever Piggy is in a start box and someone says *'Go!'* he never waits but takes off like a bullet. However, he settled quickly once he realised his mistake.

He cruised through the next phase, the steeplechase, feeling strong and showing off to the large crowd; then after a short walk we continued around Phase C at the mandatory trot. About three kilometres before the end of this phase is Worcester Lodge, and from here the approach and the view straight down to Badminton House is amazing. It seemed to take forever, though, to trot down that wide grass avenue, and my head was spinning with thoughts of the imminent cross-country. As we neared the park gate the spectators were a packed throng, and a mounted escort had to see us through to the ten-minute box.

'... my head was spinning with thoughts of the imminent cross country.'

Here, the vets checked Piggy over to ensure he was fit enough to continue. This stop is compulsory; riders can dismount and the horses are refreshed and walked about. Grease is put on the fronts of their legs to help them slide over a fence if they hit it. Gill had been watching the closed-circuit TV and reported on the course so far. I was still not sure what to do at the Vicarage Ditch or the Pigsty—there had been trouble at both, though I knew Piggy could do it. Then Lucinda Green, who had had a trouble-free ride on Village Gossip, told me that both fences had ridden well for her: 'Just keep kicking,' she said; and I did.

As I waited for the two-minute call, the adrenalin was really mounting, though I felt apprehensive of any mistakes I might make that could harm my courageous Piggy. It was too late, however, to ask myself why I was there.

'Three . . . Two . . . One . . . *Go!*' Piggy shot out of the box. This time it really was cross-country: we headed across the park to the first of Colonel Frank's imposing fences. Piggy attacked it—and all the rest—with his usual panache.

'As I waited for the two-minute call, the adrenalin was really mounting ... Three ... Two ... One ... Go!'

We met the Vicarage Corner on a perfect stride and he made it feel easy . . . nothing to it! The Stockholm fence has caused plenty of trouble in the past, yet he tackled it boldly and as neatly as a cat. I felt honoured to be riding such an intelligent horse as he sprang bravely off the unfinished Horsens Bridge, out over the chasm to land a few feet below. Ears pricked, he continued with tremendous vitality towards his next challenge: the Lake—the crowd was staggering, but Piggy's stride never faltered—he adored showing off, and took athletic bounds through the water; then on towards the Normandy Bank.

At the Ski Jump you feel as if you are about to hurl yourself off the end of the earth. Piggy took off courageously, then as he saw what he had to do, slid neatly down the steep bank to jump the arrowhead at the bottom. He was going so well that we tackled the straight route at the Pigsty—he banked the second part, and this was the only uncomfortable moment on the whole course. Undaunted, he sped on with the crowds giving him plenty of encouragement. He hesitated for an instant as he alighted on the platform at the Quarry, but a second later had summed up the situation and plunged down, turning and accelerating to leap powerfully over the wall: the feeling he gave me was really exhilarating.

Once again he surged on, with more praise from the crowd and his jockey. As we came out of Huntsman's Close we had a minute to get home, but I didn't know how long it would take; with Piggy still full of running, we flew down over the Lamb Creep and round the corner to the Whitbread Bar, checked cautiously as I straightened him and he jumped it beautifully, galloping through to finish well inside the time.

I just could not believe it. By the time I had slowed Piggy to a walk and come back to weigh in, a provisional third place was announced over the loudspeaker. I was so proud of my dear Piggy. He had looked after me so well, even if the speed at which he had taken some of the fences hadn't been my choice. But whatever suits him suits me.

He towed Bonnie through the crowd back to the stables while I gave Gill a quick rundown on how the course rode so that she could inform her later riders. Mike, David and I packed all the equipment into the car and fought our way back to the stables. Piggy was my next concern, though

Receiving our Badminton rosette from HM The Queen

perhaps it should have been for Bonnie, as Piggy was lashing out at the water while she washed him down. *He* knew how clever he had just been.

Once Piggy was safely snuggled up in his stable, Mike went to telephone Mum—apparently she had been gardening all morning. She was so relieved, and could now watch it all on television that afternoon.

I spent the next four hours in the ten-minute box, looking at the closed-circuit TV. Watching all the other riders it was just like any other Badminton at home, and I kept having to remind myself that *we* had actually finished that course . . . and clear. I still couldn't believe it; and didn't fully until later that evening when we celebrated.

Of the sixty-odd horses that followed us on the cross-country, only ten had done better than Piggy; this left us in thirteenth position overnight, and prompted a five-pound bet with a friend who believed we would finish in the top ten. My opinion differed: if I stayed in the top twenty I would be lucky.

Piggy trotted out that evening as if he thought he should go around the course again, which was great. Next morning I rode him out around the

park for a leg stretch. We were now allowed to ride right up to the fences that we had thought so intimidating twenty-four hours earlier. They looked a little better from a horse, especially as we were not going to have to jump them.

Piggy behaved himself at the vet's inspection this time. Showing his free, springing step to the crowd, he was passed on to the show jumping phase. Running in reverse order meant that I would be jumping in the afternoon, which gave me time to walk the course before watching the morning horses go round. It also allowed plenty of time to get nervous.

It always seems a shame that the whole competition could be won or lost on this phase, for the show jumping course is never large, and always well within the capabilities of all the horses. It is simply an exercise to test their suppleness after the rigours of the cross-country.

Mum had come to watch the show jumping, but still couldn't be persuaded to look at the enormous fences Piggy had jumped the day before. To this day she hasn't walked the cross-country at Badminton when I have been riding, even though she has done so at every other three-day event.

'... to receive one of those prestigious silver horses from the Queen ... was a moment I will never forget.'

During the parade, Piggy insisted on trotting sideways, making it most awkward for me to salute the Queen; then the last twenty-five horses began their rounds. Gill helped me loosen Piggy up over a few practice fences. He felt like an unexploded bomb, trying to jump around on the approach to every one—he can never contain himself when faced with a jump.

Waiting for my call, I knew my chances of a clear round were slim: it was now more important not to be eliminated from the competition than to go clear. I ran through the course again in my head, fence by fence. Remember to salute the Queen and don't start before the bell, I thought, as Piggy and I cantered into the arena.

He cleared each fence by his customary centimetre which was agonisingly hair-raising for my supporters (I've always preferred riding to watching!). He also finds cross-country pace more to his liking and I don't really have much say in the matter: so he skimmed quickly round the course, just touching two jumps. We might have been a little unlucky at one, as the horse three before us had hit it quite hard and dislodged a rail which had not been properly checked and replaced in its cups—we barely brushed it, but off it came.

Although a little disappointed, I was delighted to have completed my first Badminton. Piggy was my hero, despite his minor errors—it was, after all, the cross-country that mattered most.

In the end I won my five-pound bet. Lucinda Green won her sixth Badminton on Beagle Bay, with Mark Todd second on Charisma; Rodney finished eighth on Pomeroy and Piggy and I were twelfth. We had gone too fast in the cross-country, so Rodney won the Whitbread Spurs for the rider under twenty-five with the best time. But to finish Badminton in the front line and receive one of those prestigious silver horses from the Queen—always awarded to the first twelve—was a moment I will never forget.

However, I was brought back down to earth when I read my dressage sheet: one of the judges gave me only four for my riding. Obviously I still had a lot to learn! Frank Weldon's reply to my thank-you letter was also cautionary: 'Don't expect it to be so easy next time.'

From as early as I can remember my life has been inextricably bound up with horses; I owe an enormous debt of gratitude to the help and encouragement of my family, who have inspired and supported my riding career throughout every success and failure right from the very beginning. My mother's dynamic enthusiasm and tireless energy have always been a particular inspiration to me; from leading-rein class to preparing for Badminton, she has devoted herself to the interests of my career, and much of my success I am sure I owe to her.

I was born at Tidworth in Hampshire on 9 March 1965; when I was two we moved to Swains Firs, near Coombe Bissett in Wiltshire where we kept a variety of horses, and it was here that I began riding. My mother showed ponies in in-hand classes and competed in riding events, and both my parents hunted.

Mum came home from Reading horse sales one day with a 15hh cob called Domino, and a black Shetland gelding of unknown background which was to be my first mount. She had taken a fancy to him on account of 'his lovely big eye'; and she feared that if she didn't buy him he might end up in the knacker's wagon.

2 Laying the Foundations

Me aged two at my aunt's wedding

Top right: Me at school, aged four

We named him Safety Pin, after an old Shetland my father had once owned: Pinny for short. He had the perfect temperament for small children: didn't mind being pulled, pushed or climbed on and was well behaved on the leading rein. I rode him bareback until we found a saddle that fitted; when I was three he took me to my first horse shows in the leading-rein and fancy-dress classes: when my sister Lucinda—Lucy—started riding him, I had a smart, pretty little Welsh Section A pony, Trehern Margarete.

At four, I progressed to another Welsh pony, Silver—11.2hh, snowy white and with a pink muzzle and thick tail. Mum had bought him to sell on, but finally decided that he was too useful to part with. I was a confident rider by then and off the leading rein, which led to a misadventure that could have put an end to my equestrian career before it had got into its stride, and left Lucy without a sister.

My cousin Titia on her pony, Tamsin, and I were out riding with Mum after school one afternoon. We had crossed the busy Salisbury–Blandford main road on which we lived into a lane and we children wanted to canter, so Mum sent us ahead; however our ponies would not go faster than a trot so she overtook us to urge them on by giving them a lead. Titia's pony, Tamsin, wasn't having this: it wheeled about and set off for home, still at a trot. Silver immediately followed suit, but broke into a canter. Mum raced after us and reached Titia in time to stop Tamsin, but could only watch in horror as Silver and I streaked across the main road—where a car, bus or lorry could have caused us a fatal accident, but miraculously there was no

traffic in sight: a rare dispensation. Mother describes this near miss from extinction or severe injury as 'the worst moment of my life as a horsey mum'.

It was clear that Silver was too much of a handful for a small, skinny four-year-old girl, so we lent him to my cousin Titia, two years older than I, for a year or so while I reverted to dear old Pinny. Usually well behaved, Pinny did set his limits. One day when Lucy and I were riding him and her turn came up again, I was so cross at surrendering the saddle that when she was up I whacked Pinny on the bum. I had not foreseen his natural resentment: he kicked me in the tummy. My pride was hurt more than my body, and matters were not improved when Mum ignored condolences and said it served me right for being so stupid.

When Lucy and I were toddlers we used to follow the hunt in a Land Rover, but later hunted regularly ourselves. Silver was a star performer: he could jump anything, though was naughty enough to stop at ditches, something that really teaches you how to ride. My competitive riding began seriously when I was six. At first we took part in ridden pony classes and nursery stakes for working hunter ponies, and made the usual beginners' mistakes of cantering on the wrong leg and refusing the jumps—but I was learning all the time. If I didn't ride Silver with determination he would run right past a jump, which taught me to go straight and never to be complacent.

When Lucy was five and I seven, we moved to Dorset where my new stepfather, Mike, had a beautiful manor house in Buckland Newton. It stood half-way down a hill opposite the church, with a spectacular view over the village and a stream that wound through the valley. Among the friends we made were Helen and Clare Sunderland; we went to school by bus with them every day, and rode in the afternoon.

We were now too big to ride Pinny, so a local acquaintance named Scutt helped us break him to harness. We used to put him between the shafts of a small rubber-tyred, two-wheel exercise cart known as a John Willie—though driving was not without its minor perils. One day we were going along a single-track lane when Pinny took exception to a stretch of new tarmac—he whipped round and galloped off in the opposite direction; with a high bank on one side and a flint wall on the other, we would have been poorly placed had we met another horse or vehicle!

All four of us used to take liberties with Pinny. He was perfectly well behaved when on a leading rein, but as soon as this was taken off he knew that his rider was reasonably competent, so when asked to canter would disport himself by bucking. We thought it great fun to canter him round a field and make him do this, though no doubt *he* found it rather tedious.

Silver and me at Pony Club Camp in 1973

Lucy and I joined the Blackmore and Sparkford Vale Pony Club, and in addition to summer camps and rallies we competed in gymkhanas and hunter trials where Silver won a variety of first prize rosettes. Lucy recalls that 'Even at this age Rachel was far more ambitious and competitive than I, always aiming to be the best and win, while I bumbled around quite happy to gallop just anywhere and make as much noise as possible.'

The Pony Club is an organisation without equal for giving children a thorough and comprehensive equestrian education. The classes are varied and instructive but also fun, and—then as now—each gave us a different insight into the equine character: jumping, gymkhana, dressage, showing

Jo and Jane Cray, Lucy and me, out hunting on our ponies

and fancy dress, each inculcated its own discipline. In addition we learned how to care for both horse and tack. The annual week's camp entailed daily instruction in dressage and jumping, with lessons on the theory of stable management—as it still does. Similarly there were the daily tasks of mucking out the stables, cleaning tack and grooming ponies until both gleamed, and making sure our personal turnout was impeccable. Points were awarded for each activity and the competition to attain the highest score was intense.

Mike was Joint Master of the South Dorset Hunt so we rode to hounds every Saturday during the winter months. We enjoyed every minute of it, however cold and wet, jumping fences that looked gigantic to us and must have appeared equally big to our little ponies, returning home exhausted and plastered with mud. Silver would jump almost anything, but I do remember one crash at a 3ft 3in tiger trap when he hit the top rail and we 'buried ourselves' on the other side. Nonetheless, Mum always maintains that hunting is the best way for any child to learn to ride across country.

We led a strenuous life, Mum, Lucy and I. At least three days a week in the show season Mum would be up at 3am plaiting manes and generally preparing at least three ponies. She would rouse us early too, and go through a checklist of all we needed in the way of clothes and tack. The night before, she always made us a buttonhole: a yellow rose for me to wear with my brown outfit, a pink or blue flower for Lucy, who wore navy blue. We used to sleep on the way there and back: in the interim we enjoyed ourselves to the hilt. We had lots of friends who competed in the

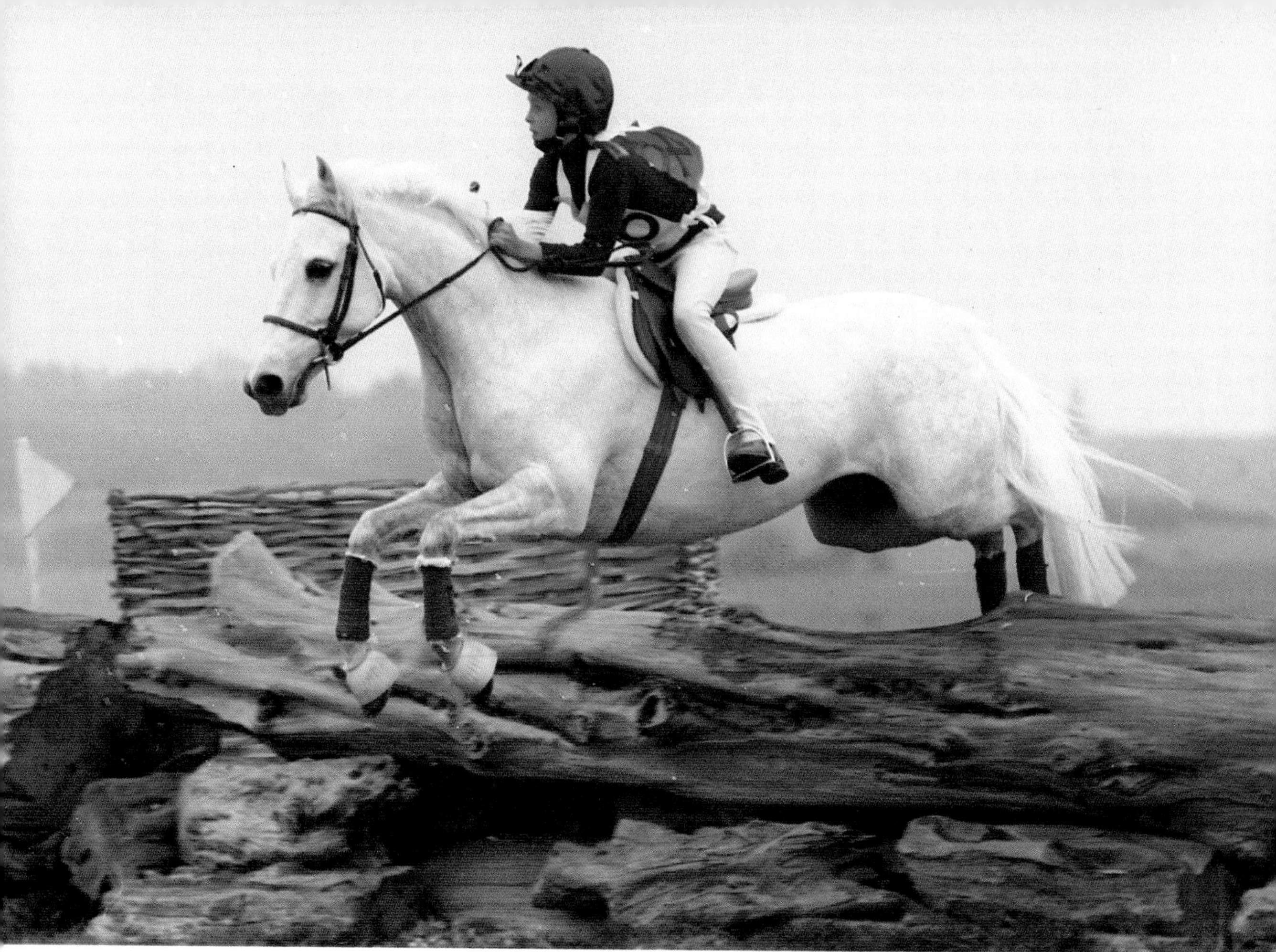

Me, aged eleven, with Zephie at a Pony Club Hunter Trial in 1976

same shows so the whole excursion was like going to a party. We seemed to live on salad sandwiches with mayonnaise and ice cream, and our ponies Silver, Zephie and later Charm accumulated a gratifying number of rosettes to justify all the effort.

Oakley Zephanella, otherwise known as Zephie, was a 13.2hh grey mare that Mum had bought as a yearling and had lent to Titia until I was big enough to compete on her. When she came back to us, I handed Silver over to Lucy; at eight I was still small for my age, and must have looked like a pea on a drum aboard my new mount. She was excitable—'gassy' in 'horsey' parlance—but safe and would jump anything; and as long as I sat quietly, was a fair performer at dressage.

On Zephie, I went in for my first junior one day event and had the added responsibility of being in my Pony Club team. Although Mum lunged Zephie for hours, the pony whizzed through the dressage test at rather more than the ideal speed. This was followed by the cross-country over a smallish twisty course that we had walked twice, with great care. I was excited, but Mum was more anxious about my eventing début than I was, and was full of useful instructions on how to hold my whip and where to remember to turn, and to kick on at a trappy little ditch which had been causing trouble.

Running round the course watching, Mum saw that while I was racing on and gaining ground, the rider before me was having trouble at that very place. As I galloped towards it, he was trying for the sixth or seventh time

to jump it; Mum yelled at the judges, who were oblivious of the situation, to 'Get that —— child out of the way'. Zephie flew over easily . . . but I was eliminated for outside assistance! Unfortunately our team was also eliminated because one rider did not complete the course.

Since then, Mum has never intervened even when my times were not correct. She doesn't even hold a stopwatch, but stays by the lorry while I ride the cross-country.

Mum was still keen on showing. In 1974 she fell for a beautiful, five-year-old 13hh liver chestnut show pony she saw at the New Forest Buckhounds Show, and bought it from the Bucknells, from Reading. Prince Charming—I dubbed him Charm—lived up to his name in looks and behaviour. He wasn't easy to handle; young, powerful, rather fast and inclined to buck at first, he dumped me quite a few times when riding at home. Alison Bucknell had qualified him for Wembley before we bought him and we had promised to let her ride him there; anyway I was rather small to cope with the Horse Of The Year Show. So whilst we were getting to know each other we entered only straight showing classes; towards the end of the season, however, we had what Mum called a 'major triumph' when he won his class and was champion against some high-powered opposition, which qualified him again for Wembley.

'Get that — child out of the way.'

Silver qualified for the nursery stakes at the British Show Pony Society's Championship Show; so in September, in great excitement, we went to the East of England show ground at Peterborough where this show was being held. We walked the course twice, to make sure I didn't go the wrong way; it comprised at least fifteen fences crammed into a narrow little ring, and the jumps made me think that I had strayed, like Gulliver, into the land of giants. There were lots of trees, black barrels filled with water, twists and turns and combination fences: in all, quite a mini-Badminton for a small girl of nine.

I didn't feel nervous, just stimulated and eager for my turn; but we were to ride in catalogue order so I had to wait—but profited by watching several other riders go round, making a mental note of how I should tackle the course. The moment came at last and Silver excelled himself: he jumped a perfect round at just the right speed, popping over the fences with good rhythm and halting square in front of the judges at the end. The most difficult phase was over.

For the showing part, the ponies were judged for conformation. First we had to show off the pony's different paces on each rein, then give a good display of its gallop and after unsaddling, trot it up in hand: that is, lead it so that the judges could see if it moved correctly. Silver did equally well here and you could see how proud he felt. He did a great gallop, demonstrating that he was a true hunting pony, then stood quietly while the judges picked up his legs and looked at his feet. There were about 150 ponies competing, so the judges took hours to arrive at a decision. When they announced the results Silver and I were third: we went home in euphoria.

After this excitement came a brief transitional period in my education. The Kemps of Withypool, on Exmoor, had employed a tutor called Madame Rickovich for their fourteen-year-old daughter Rosalind and her friend Penny O'Sullivan, who was twelve, and I joined them for a term, taking Silver with me. Leaving home for the first time and with the pros-

pect of two girls much older than me as companions might have been quite an ordeal, but in fact it turned out to be great fun. We worked in the morning and rode on Exmoor in the afternoon, and spent the mid-morning breaks jumping courses on foot, each assuming the identity of a well-known show jumper: Rosalind was Tony Newbery on Warwick III, Penny was Paddy McMahon on Pennwood Forge Mill and I was David Broome on Philco.

Not such good sport was when we had to make a public appearance at Taunton Town Hall. Madame Rickoyich loved poetry and entered us for a competition there—I had to recite a poem about a turtle, and when the dreaded hour arrived I would willingly have withdrawn into a shell of my own; for although I am bold enough in front of spectators at a riding event, I am in fact shy by nature. Madame had coached us to say our piece so that our voices reached the back of the large auditorium, but as I stumbled through my lines the people in the front row could hardly hear me. When they applauded, I froze and forgot how to walk off the stage in the way I had been taught. It was altogether a considerable embarrassment and I would rather have attempted the most daunting fence in the world on the worst pony than go through that experience.

In October we went to London for the Horse Of The Year Show. Not only was Alison Bucknell competing on Charm, Rosalind Kemp had also qualified her 14.2hh pony, Fairytale. We enjoyed the marathon trip all the more because they came third and fourth respectively.

In the spring, Lucy and I became weekly boarders at a pleasant little prep school, Knighton House, near Blandford. The school uniform was red dungarees, and in these we were even allowed to climb trees; generally, we enjoyed considerable freedom. The school kept ponies, so we had a weekly riding lesson and our P.E. teacher encouraged us to take part in primary school sports meetings; I began to take sprinting and long jumping seriously, and also liked gymnastics and swimming. In the winter holidays Mum, Mike, Lucy and I went skiing. Basically, as long as I had someone or something to compete against, I was happy.

Lucy, reminiscing about those skiing holidays, puts it this way: 'We took to the sport as most small children do, without fear, and just went hell-for-leather down whichever piste we were put on, and loved to ski without poles. Rachel was very quick and neat and was always competitive. When the general slalom race came round at the end of each week, you would see that determined face once again—her only aim was to reach the bottom before anyone else. She definitely has the killer instinct for competition and at such times can be quite ruthless. But it's essential to have this drive if you intend to reach the top.'

One of our big outings was the annual trip to the Royal Show. We used to go for the working hunter pony and the show pony classes, so we took a caravan and stayed from Sunday until Wednesday night at a nearby farm that had stables. Mum had some torrid differences of view about this with the school authorities; she insisted on telling the truth about our absence rather than faking illness for us.

At ten years old I had to make a serious decision: whether to pursue a riding career or, as I was representing Dorset at running and jumping, be sent to a school that would concentrate on my athletics. I have always been rather lazy when I find things easy, so opted for riding, as I thought

Lucy and me on a family skiing holiday in 1976

that ponies would be less work as well as more fun than track and long jump. I often wonder how far I would have got if I had made the other choice: the Olympics, maybe?

I didn't really get the hang of riding Charm for quite a while. We decided to get him jumping as he was a good type for the working pony classes, but his naughtiness caused me many troubles. His jump was titanic, but he often stopped so abruptly that I flew over his head—I used to enter him in lots of pairs classes, with friends who had good ponies to give me a lead; finally when I was eleven we started him in working pony classes, small to begin with, to encourage us both to get round. Silver and Zephie were experienced before I got them and both loved jumping, but I had to teach Charm; so he was really the pony that taught me to ride.

I was so lucky. I might have a difficult round at a hunter trial or in a working pony class with Charm, but then could get onto Zephie, fly around clear and probably win a prize. So I never became disheartened about Charm and kept persevering: he would go clear one day and make me think we were out of the wood, then misbehave in our next competition. I kept taking him in show classes and even had side-saddle lessons with Jinks Moire (Bryers); Jinks helped both Lucy and me a great deal. We went to Jinks every Friday evening after school for a lesson on Charm and Silver. She was strict but it was great fun and we learned such a lot. We did everything from no stirrups on the lunge to dressage, show jumping, side saddle and—if I was very good—even cross-country. When Mum was young she had had lessons with Mrs Betty Skelton, Jinks's mother, so this was a pleasant continuity in a family association.

My mother continued to be the driving force behind my riding career. She spent hours teaching Lucy and me, taking us for rides, driving us to Pony Club rallies, riding lessons and competitions; and while we were away at school, would lunge and school our ponies so that they would go well for us at shows. And Mike was endlessly generous in providing a variety of mounts.

My first experience of eventing above Pony Club level was through Mike's son, David. David was show jumping with Ralph Coates and had a good horse, Doctor Zhivago, which had reached Grade A; however, Zhivago wasn't quite scopey enough for the big tracks so Mum persuaded him to try eventing—he did well, and reached the final trial for the juniors. Mum had a brown horse called Big Cloud, by Little Cloud, that was quite a useful eventer. She had lent him to Mike Felton to ride for a while in juniors, then David took him on and they went round the Wylye and Bramham three day event courses. That was another week of fun when I remember playing truant from school.

In my early teens most of my spare time was spent in the garden by a clump of trees building elaborate miniature cross-country courses with every variety of jump: banks, ditches, coffins, bounces, doubles. If, having watched some big event, there had been a fence that I particularly liked, I would build one on my course the next day—attention to detail was meticulous, the poles safely secured as in the real world. I used to spend hours sitting and studying these obstacles and dreaming of how I would ride over them. Lucy found this boring and used to nag me into playing with her—so we would go into the woods and build another course, for us and our horsey girl friends to race over on foot, timing each competitor to determine the winner.

Me and Charm at the Plympton Horse Show in 1975

One day events were becoming more popular every season, so the standard was rising and dressage was beginning to dominate them. This was my weakest phase, and therefore by far the most demanding and I spent many hours having lessons, or schooling at home. I used to pray for an early dressage time because if the cross-country started before or during my test both Charm and Zephie would hear the commentary and immediately lose concentration in anticipation of the excitement to come. As Lucy says: 'You feel as though you are on a time-bomb ready to explode, yet you have to give the judges the impression that all is calm and under control. While your horse side-steps out of the arena, canters on the spot or fails to halt at the start and finish, you sit and smile and try to look relaxed.'

Always sensitive to my problems, Lucy is also generous in her praise: 'To watch Rachel on the cross-country was a different matter. Once through the start flags, the only thing on her mind was to go clear and not

to score any penalty points so as to stay in the lead or improve her chances of getting there. She very seldom took the long routes and usually jumped the biggest fences, cutting the corners wherever possible to save time. Charm had the stride of a horse and could have jumped a house, while Rachel had the style of a mini-professional and nerves of steel—no fence was too big. They were often remarkable to watch and certainly made people look twice.'

Riding Charm at South Dorset Pony Club in 1977—I was beginning to get the hang of him

Mike had always wanted to be a farmer and in 1977 bought an idyllic property, Hoplands Farm, at King's Somborne in Hampshire. Set in gently rolling countryside, its scope and situation was perfect not only for keeping, schooling and exercising our own horses, but also for holding our own one day event—though at first the horses had to live in a converted calf shed while a proper stable yard was built. At about this time a smart new horsebox arrived, fitted with a cooker, refrigerator and seats. Mike continued as Master of the South Dorset Hunt, so we still joined the field every Saturday.

We had to find another school, and preferably one that would allow enough free time for riding to maintain an adequate competitive standard. This we did: the Godolphin, in Salisbury; hitherto the school had taken only full boarders and day girls, but it agreed that I could be a weekly boarder. I was more interested in sports and games than in studying, and most of my spare time was spent practising lacrosse or running round the grounds to keep fit. If it was raining, half an hour's skipping in the gym had to do.

For both Lucy and me 1978 was a particularly good year. Lucy was winning prizes with Mano, her little grey show pony, Silver was still showing everyone the way and both Charm and Zephie were doing well in all the Pony Club junior one day events. Charm must have won at least thirty qualifying working hunter pony classes, including the 13-hand at the

Royal Show—the championship was in the main ring where the atmosphere was electric. On the same day, Chris Hunnable won the 14-hand class on a pony that Mum had bred, so there were big celebrations.

It was now my turn to borrow a pony from Titia: a 15hh dun gelding called Cossack, no stunner to look at but a great performer. Eventing was his forte, and he took me round all the senior Pony Club one day and two day events, including the championships.

I was fifteen when I competed in my first British Horse Society horse trials, a junior Novice event at Bicton, in Devon. Compared with Pony Club courses, this one looked mountainous: the timber was so large, the ditches were so wide and the drops so deep, and I quite thought dear Cossack would have to go round on his own. However, he performed accurately in the dressage and went clear in the show jumping, to lie well up in order before the cross-country. But I still felt inferior walking through the park on my little dun pony with such big, scopey horses on all sides. However, that didn't worry Cossack. He stormed off round the course, splashed through the water jump that looked ominously blood red in the Devon soil, up the hill . . . and we'd done it. My wonderful Cossack showed those big smart horses just how the course should be negotiated and with only a few time faults, we finished second.

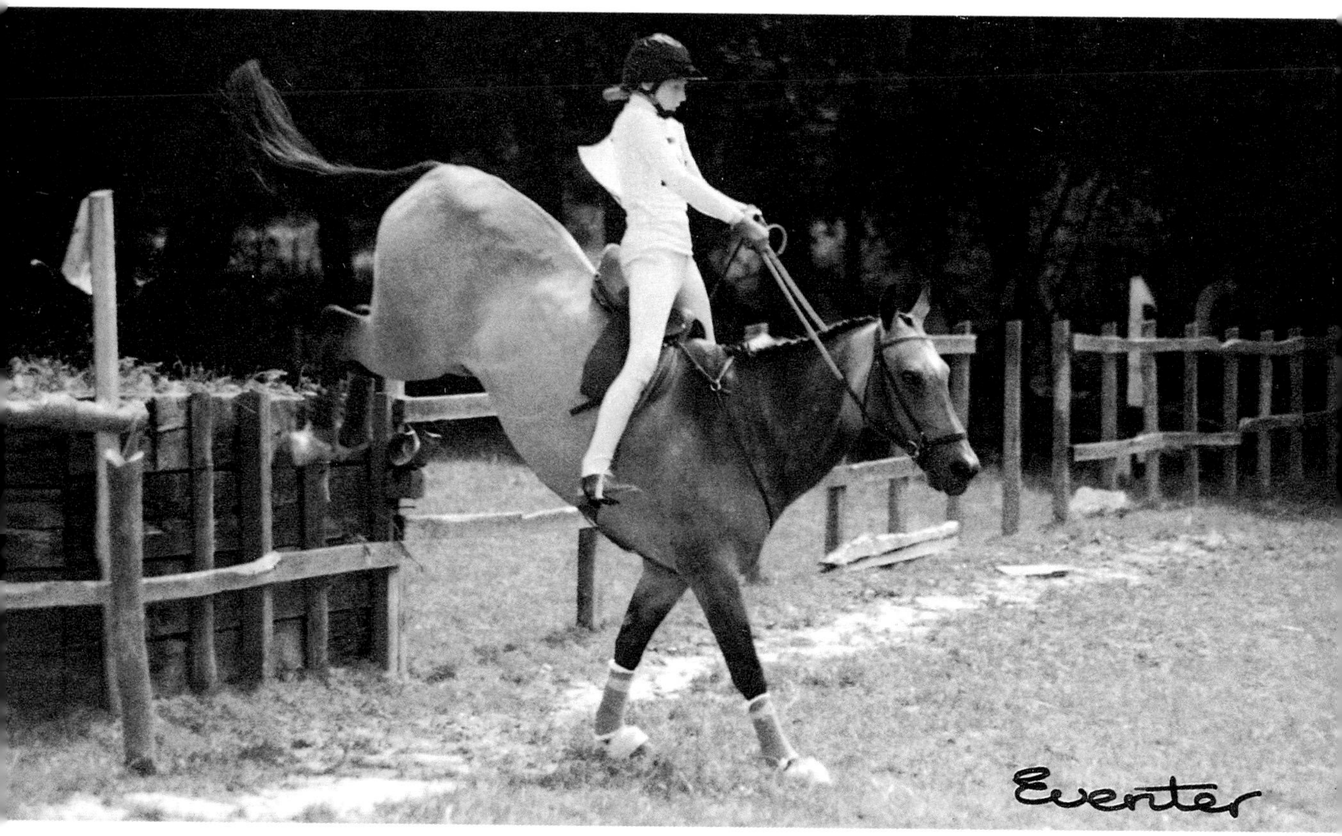

Riding Cossack—my cousin's pony who helped me in my transition from ponies to horses

At this stage in my riding career it was becoming increasingly obvious that with so much experience gained but with still so much to learn, the time had come to say goodbye to ponies and move on to serious eventing on horses.

There is no exact formula for breeding the ideal event horse. A top class three day event horse must have so many qualities if it is to perform well in all three phases: courage and steady temperament, good paces, and not least, jumping ability. Quite a lot of Thoroughbred blood is needed for speed, but horses quite different in size and type do reach the top—Charisma (Mark Todd's) is a blood pony at 15.3hh, and Murphy Himself (Ian Stark's) is huge, over 17hh, and obviously part Irish Draught. The horses we have bred have varied, too: Friday Fox not too large, very bouncy and confident; Spangle soft and cautious; Aloaf big, droopy and scared of everything—yet in their different ways they have reached the top.

'. . . horses quite different in size and type do reach the top . . .'

One of my best performance horses was Friday Fox, bred by my mother out of a 14.3hh grey Irish cob originally bought through *Horse and Hound.* Both my parents hunted her, and found she was absolutely genuine, willing to tackle anything within her scope and she had the stamina to go all day; she also competed in riding club events and hunter trials. At the end of her long and busy career she was sent to a Thoroughbred stallion, in the hope that she would produce a foal which ultimately would be bigger and of better quality than herself.

3 Finding the Event Horse

Sadly, she lost her first foal. Her second was by the Thoroughbred Fair Knight, a bay filly with very long white socks and small white patches on her neck and tail; we named her China, because the farrier used to call the dam 'my old china'. Her third foal was by the Thoroughbred HIS horse, B.P., and was undoubtedly skewbald; this one we called Friday Fox, after the day on which she was born.

Friday and China grew up with two other youngsters; Mum broke them in as four-year-olds and a year later, when I was fifteen, gave me the choice between them. I preferred five-year-old Friday and started to compete on her in Pony Club novice hunter trials, while China became Mum's hunter. I don't know why I decided on the younger one—at the time I didn't even consider her as an eventing prospect—but wish I could have ridden both, for they had similar characters. Like their mother, they revelled in jumping and generally enjoyed life to the hilt—even just hacking, they would walk off down the road as if it were a race. At this stage I was also starting to compete on Spartangle (Spangle), another five-year-old home-bred mare whose sire, Spartan General, was a Thoroughbred one would have thought more likely to produce an event horse than Friday's sire.

FRIDAY FOX

Friday had a short neck which she liked to carry high: great for jumping, not so helpful for dressage. To jump her was wonderful, all bouncy under-

Dad jumping Foxie (Friday's mother) at a Hunter Trial in 1968

Right: Friday and her sister China (Mum's hunter)

neath me and in total self balance, and her shortish stride meant that we usually met the fences right. But she found everything she did extremely exciting, so our dressage tests were always rather hurried. She was independent and never needed affection; as long as she was fed and properly looked after she was quite happy—unlike Spangle, who loved being fussed over and took life with a little more caution.

Both would get rather uptight in dressage, but a lot of their tension must have come from me—in my effort to produce the best from them I tried too hard, which upset them. I was really as green as they were, and it took me a few years to realise that if I pretended that the test didn't matter and relaxed, then the horse would also feel less tense. This doesn't always work but it helps, though for Friday this discovery was too late—she was already about nine and set in her ways. In her last two years of eventing she did settle a little more, but not consistently.

The mares I have ridden have, on the whole, been careful; they don't want to hurt themselves, so patience is needed in their early training and certainly Friday wasn't always the perfect jumping machine. Any young horse finds some fences more frightening than others when seen for the first time, and a mare's more cautious temperament accentuates this hesitation.

In our first Pony Club hunter trial Friday had two stops: one at an upside-down water trough, another at a tiny into-space. 'I can't imagine this horse ever doing Badminton', I thought. But with patience and as the Easter holidays progressed, so did Friday's courage. From the beginning she had never shown any fear of water: she loved it. Even so, just to show how unpredictable a horse can be, when she was eight and eventing successfully at Intermediate level, she suddenly decided that she didn't like water any more. She sprang this unwelcome surprise on me at the first event of the autumn season, and neither Mum nor I could understand why. At her next event she nearly stopped at a rail quite far from the water's edge, though this time I did manage to get her over first time.

Before the Novice Championships at Locko Park, we had one more run across country and again she hesitated at a log into water. By the time I rode her at Locko, however, she had got over her fear of water and never showed it again.

Friday and Spangle spent their five-year-old winter with my mother on Exmoor. Exmoor has always been my mother's favourite place to ride and hunt and I have to agree with her. It is the most beautiful country I have ever had the pleasure to ride over, spacious and free with almost unlimited access, and is surely the best training ground for young horses. The wooded combes and sharply sloping rocky paths, the streams, ditches, heather hills and even bogs all teach a horse natural self-balance—it learns to cope with wet or tricky going, to find a 'fifth leg', also that water must be crossed if it doesn't want to be left behind. Mum and Mike hunt two or three times a week, both fox- and staghunting, and many of the meets are within hacking distance.

After Christmas, with Friday and Spangle rising six, they moved back to Hoplands, in Hampshire so that I could do some indoor show jumping at the weekends and have help with my dressage before my first season in senior British Horse Society trials. It all sounded far too grand for me—having watched my stepbrother David compete for the past few years, thinking how easy it looked, it now suddenly seemed a lot more frightening.

CROSS-COUNTRY WITH LADY HUGH RUSSELL

I was to learn more about cross-country riding one cold February morning in 1981: a two-hour session on a bare and windy stretch of Salisbury Plain had been booked with Lady Hugh Russell. This sounded great fun, a good gallop round a cross-country course on top of a hill—but we soon learned better! All tacked up and ready to go, four of us walked expectantly round the indoor school. I had been warned that I should wear all the right cross-country kit, so sat on Friday feeling quite confident that all was in order. Then into the school came Lady Hugh's Mini-Moke—Lady Hugh broke her back in a hunting accident and has driven the Moke ever since. After she had found out what we had done with our horses—for me, it didn't sound much—we headed for the top of a hill. A minute later, she noticed that I had no studs in Friday's shoes and nearly sent me home for being so thoughtless—Friday could easily have slipped over and hurt herself. I felt miserably small.

However, once we were up the hill and with the fences in sight, excitement banished my shame. With the Mini-Moke following behind, I set off round a course that Lady Hugh had planned for me. I couldn't quite hear what she was saying to me while I rode, and arrived at the finish quite pleased with the way it had gone.

'Why did you trot into that drop, when I said a bounce canter?' she asked me. 'And your line was all wrong through the angled rails: you could have hurt yourself and the horse. Why didn't you jump over the string markers that were put there specially for that purpose?' She also told me that I had gone too fast in some places and had not got straight in others.

It is a bit of a shock, at first, to be told how useless you are. But by the end of two sessions, I was beginning to appreciate the importance of a

Lord and Lady Hugh Russell

good line into a fence and the pace at which it should be taken.

Lady Hugh took an immediate liking to Friday, partly because she is fond of skewbalds but also because of the mare's obvious ability and enthusiasm. Lady Hugh has been a great help to me since those February mornings, always available to give advice at the big three-day events or to discuss any problems.

SENIOR BHS TRIALS, SPRING 1981

My first senior Novice event was to be the Aldon horse trials in Somerset. In our enthusiasm, and determined not to be late, we in fact confused the date on which the clocks were to be put forward to Summer Time and arrived to find that not even the car park attendant had shown up; we had anticipated the time change by a week! However, we made the best of our mistake by taking an extra careful walk around the course, though the freshly painted fences on the deserted expanse looked enormously imposing; perhaps they might have seemed more inviting if horses had been jumping them while we strolled.

'... Mum was so cross, she sent us straight home ...'

Spangle and I negotiated the dressage without any major hiccups: in other words, we managed to stay in the arena, and walked, trotted and cantered in the right places; I had not yet mastered all the intricacies of rhythm, balance and bend. In the cross-country we went clear but incurred 30 faults for exceeding the optimum time, which should have been fairly easy to achieve. A safe round was a good start, but to win prizes we would have to go faster than the proverbial Sunday afternoon hack.

Friday and I made our début the following week at Ermington in Devon, and this time I thought I could manage to ride both horses. However, Friday's dressage was so bad that it almost became a comic turn: she would not stand still or walk, and her canter was so hurried that we bustled through in what must have been the fastest time of the day; we were last! Spangle also disgraced herself, so although they both had clear rounds in the cross-country, I decided that as yet it was not a good idea to ride two horses at the same event.

At the Portman trials, Friday was to be my only ride, so I would have no excuse for a poor performance. I felt no qualms about the cross-country but working in for the dressage, Friday was so explosive that I became flustered and by the time we entered the arena my nerves were taut. She refused to halt and then we tracked left: the peremptory hoot from the judge's car brought me to a stop. What had I done wrong? Tracked the wrong way? OK, I'd start again. I entered the arena for a second time: the horn blared at once. Surely I can't be wrong this time, I thought: I haven't done anything yet. But I had: I'd left the arena and was therefore eliminated.

Mum was furious; I sulked and blamed Friday. Never mind, I consoled myself, we should have a good cross-country. But we weren't given the chance as Mum was so cross, she sent us straight home. I am not surprised. It was enough to make anyone blow a fuse, after all the hours of work, preparation, and then driving, only to see me do something so stupid. Unfortunately my memory for learning dressage tests has never improved and I still have mental blanks quite often.

At Bicton (Devon) I did ride both Spangle and Friday in the Junior

'… we always found a funny side to every subject – when demonstrating the maintenance of lawnmowers and wheelbarrows …'

Novice trials; David was competing in the Intermediate class the next day. Friday did a reasonable dressage and her now customary fast clear round across country, and won; Spangle was still rather spooky but finished third. And now, just as we were beginning really to understand each other and get our performance together, both horses went down with flu and were off for the whole summer. And in July I left school.

The ponies still kept me busy, but it wasn't much fun being only a team supporter at the Pony Club Area Trials. We did manage to have Friday up and fit for the last couple of events in October. At Holdenby, she managed to contain herself better in the dressage, then took me round the cross-country at such a cracking pace that we were well inside the time. Greatly elated by her performance, I chatted all the way back to the horsebox, describing every turn and jump, how Friday had reacted and how utterly brilliant she was. To crown our delight, we were third and therefore won our first points (points are not awarded in Junior classes).

CHATTIS HILL, 1981/2

A week later I began a six-month course with seven other girls at the Chattis Hill riding stables near Stockbridge, a former racing yard. We had two lessons a day with Carrie Burtenshaw, and had two horses to take care of; at the weekend we helped with the instructing. For two days each week we went to the nearby Sparsholt Agricultural College, where we were taught about farm accounts, typing, cooking, animal husbandry, tractor driving, machinery maintenance and first aid.

It was sometimes extremely frustrating to ride such awkward riding school hacks; some of them refused to co-operate however hard one tried. 'Dolly' was one, a skewbald built like one of the Queen's drum horses, and any pupil that Carrie felt needed 'sorting out' would be allocated this contrary mare for a jumping lesson. Dolly would turn at the top of the school and canter slowly towards a line of fences; two strides from the first fence she would take hold of the bit and charge straight past the lot, usually continuing right out of the school before she could be stopped. Tarragon was another wayward performer, whom I seemed to have to ride rather too frequently. He always bucked after a fence and frequently put in a quick dirty stop that could land you on the ground if you were not expecting it.

We had daily lectures from our riding instructors, and occasionally from Mr Lambert who was the course organiser and the owner of the establishment and its surrounding farmland. He taught us how to maintain a horse-lorry or trailer, and how to build show jumping and cross-country fences. I'm not sure how much we took in, for we always found a funny side to every subject—when demonstrating the maintenance of lawnmowers and wheelbarrows, he was remarkably tolerant with his unruly students.

One afternoon we had a mock Pony Club 'H' test, and Dot Willis came to examine us. Dot is Ginny Leng's trainer, and impressed me as much as a frightening headmistress: I was terrified. I have never been good at exams as I don't like to get things wrong; so unless I am certain my answer is right, I never trust my instincts enough to answer anything. With the formidable Dot Willis in front of me, I became even more tongue-tied. Had I known her as I do now, I would have relaxed and even enjoyed the examination. I

Friday jumping boldly at Bicton in 1981

did actually pass my 'H' test later that year with Dot's help in exam technique.

Before our Christmas and Easter holidays we performed for our parents: musical rides and bareback madness on the ponies, together with serious dressage and jumping displays—we would spend some wild afternoons practising.

THE NEW YEAR 1982

In February I moved back home so that I could ride Friday each morning. Then I would hack Spangle over to Chattis Hill (nearly an hour), spend the day there, then ride home in the evening; in all, I was probably on a horse for five or six hours every day. One problem was finding the time to do some dressage with Spangle, so I often schooled her in my lunch break. With all that work she became too fit for a Novice six-year-old.

In March was my seventeenth birthday, and with a provisional driving licence I was let loose on the road: the start of many an anxious moment involving various vehicles. Mike allowed me to practise with our long-wheelbase Land Rover, but of course, I had to be accompanied by a qualified driver. On college days one of my fellow students would come home with me for this purpose. This was the first chance I had of an independent social life, and as we all wanted to go out, the Land Rover (which we called 'the tank') was essential—though I am sure that when one first learns to drive, ten passengers are rather too many to have in the vehicle!

'... the tank mounted the bank, burst through a hedge, tipped onto its side and grated across the tarmac to a bone-shaking sudden stop.'

On a few occasions I took the law into my own hands and drove with no co-driver, either back from Winchester or the stables—probably slightly over the limit, too, as drinking was also a new experience, though luckily I found three glasses of wine was usually enough. This was rather a casual view of driving and may have had something to do with why I failed my test three times; I eventually passed it after nearly a year. I was not, however, directly responsible for the crash with Mike's Land Rover. Friends had joined me for a couple of nights' partying, but as I still had only a learner's licence, Mike said I ought not to drive with thirteen aboard, so one of them agreed not to drink. The party in the neighbouring village in fact turned out to be rather boring, so we left early, my abstemious friend at the wheel. Unfamiliar with the tank, he took a ninety-degree corner a little too fast. It mounted the bank, burst through a hedge, tipped onto its side and grated across the tarmac to a bone-shaking sudden stop. We escaped with bruises, but when we inspected the damage to the hedge and road next day, we realised how lucky we had been.

We worked hard during those six months, and we played hard; by the end of the course I felt a lot deeper in the saddle on the flat, having spent more time riding without stirrups than with them. My ability to stick on when jumping had also improved—it would have hurt my pride too much to have let myself be seen on the ground!

SPRING TRIALS 1982

While on the course I was able to event at the weekends, riding both Spangle and Friday—and was to learn about success and failure the hard way. Arriving at the first event of the season, I was sure that Friday would now win, having been third at the end of the previous season. But when she pecked on landing at a drop fence on the cross-country and galloped back to the boxes without me, I knew that I had set off far too confidently round the course and hadn't thought enough about the deep going: I had come in to the drop too fast and she had been unable to find her feet on landing. I took more precautions when I rode again later on Spangle.

The mistakes I made in these early events taught me to adapt my attitude and ride according to the problems and conditions ahead; I learned to reflect and anticipate better, and organise my riding and approach in a more thoughtful manner. The following weekend certainly witnessed a more mature rider who gave more attention to detail when walking the course, and who still rode forward but with better preparation into each fence. It did work, for Friday won her section from one of Ginny Leng's novices, and Spangle came second in her section which gave me great joy.

Even though Friday was still a novice in point terms, I felt ready to try a Junior Open Intermediate trial. In these trials, the selectors watch all the juniors who are trying to make the Junior Championships at Windsor three day event in May. The course is of Intermediate standard, the class above Novice in which the fences are allowed to be 3ft 9in high, 3in more than Novice height. This difference doesn't sound much, but when the course builder can position the fences in more technically awkward places and can also increase the width, the whole course is considerably bigger. Having been accepted to run in the Tidworth Junior trial in Hampshire, I planned to ride Friday round two Intermediates, then two Novices (in

case she frightened herself over the bigger tracks) before my trial.

When I arrived at Downlands horse trials near Liphook in Hampshire, I was feeling rather nervous about the whole ordeal. One of the first problems was that I had not realised that a black or blue jacket was compulsory for Intermediate classes, which merely added to the panic I was already in after walking the course; however, I was able to borrow a black one. It is easy to say a course is simple when you are not going to ride round it; I had walked many courses of this height when David was competing and had found them jumpable—yet this time they suddenly looked a lot larger.

We were half-way up the order after the dressage, but I totally messed up the show jumping because I did not ride Friday into her fences with enough forward impulsion and, as a result, she had one stop and one fence down. Then, not having learned enough from this experience, I made the same mistake in the cross-country. When taking the smallest jump on the course, a rail at the top of an awkward dip, I just sat there and didn't give her any impulsion up the slope so that she could jump the fence. So there was another lesson learned: always keep up the impulsion. This doesn't necessarily mean go faster; you have to maintain the energy so that it can be used when necessary.

The following week at Frensham the cross-country was even larger but I felt more positive, for it was too big merely to sit there. Friday responded beautifully and just flew round; my head was in the clouds after we had completed the course.

Soon after I had passed my test, Mum and Mike went on holiday. Our groom Mary Mears and I were attending an Iris Kellet show jumping course at Catherston Stud, the home of Jenny Loriston-Clark, our top dressage rider. Mary should really have done the driving, but I thought I could handle things. All went well for two days, so maybe I was feeling over-confident on the third day. On this occasion, a car pulled out in front of me and I had to brake suddenly; it then swerved into the side of the road and stopped while the occupants fastened their seat belts, so our horses were again unsettled by sudden braking. The car finally moved on, but as I started to drive down the hill, the disturbed horses' movements set the trailer swinging, and this became worse until we were being flung from one side of the road to the other. In panic, I stamped on the brake and the Land Rover and trailer jack-knifed.

'We opened the trailer ramp with trepidation, fearing that we would find two mangled horses ...'

We opened the trailer ramp with trepidation, fearing that we would find two mangled horses, but neither was badly hurt. One was a home-bred youngster called Aloaf; a lot of hair had been scraped off his hind legs and some bandages were torn, the partition had broken and he looked rather like Bambi on ice—legs everywhere, including out through the roof. The other horse was Alight, his younger sister, who was squashed underneath him. The queue of cars behind us was dispersing, but a few helpful people did stop to give a hand. Amazingly, Aloaf and Alight sorted themselves out and with heads down managed to back out of the wreckage. To get them out of the way, we took them into a nearby wood, tethered them and left them—something I never normally do—while we arranged for our farm manager to drive the horsebox over. Both horses walked straight into it as though nothing had happened. A week later, Aloaf won a Novice section at Crookham horse trials, to prove he was well in himself.

The construction of an official BHS cross-country course and the organisation of a horse trial involves an unbelievably large amount of time and hard work. Yet for a long time Mike had been determined that one day he would run a BHS senior event, not simply at Novice level, but a horse trial that would attract competitors of international calibre and win a respected place in the calendar for Advanced events. When he bought Hoplands Farm, King's Somborne, in 1977, he acquired a site, situation and working team which were eminently suited to achieving this goal.

We moved to Hoplands Farm in 1978; the house had been derelict for several years so needed a lot of renovation, and it was six months before it could be occupied. Besides the main house there was a farm manager's house, and also four brick and flint cottages, formerly for the farm-workers. The land, all arable and beef, had also been neglected: the fencing needed renewal and the fields had deteriorated to weeds and rough grass. Mike had little farming experience and wanted to run mainly sheep; on his fifty acres in Dorset he had kept a flock of small, delicate brown Soays, a rare Scottish breed, which we had brought with us.

4 A Course For Horses

On the course at King's Somborne in 1986

One of the first jobs therefore was to erect new sheep fencing round most of the 500 acres, with a few cross-country type tiger-traps and rails built in, for David and me to practise over. The farmyard was just as run down and there were no stables, although there were some calf pens which had originally been a dairy, so the concrete floors were smooth. This was far from ideal, but we nonetheless converted them into an indoor yard with seven loose boxes. These were small and the passage was narrow, but since most of our horses at the time were small or ponies it didn't matter. We turned the bull pen into a stable too, and fitted three good-sized boxes into a small barn for David's horses.

David was already living in one of the cottages and Lucy and I were at school when the big removal was carried out; Mum and Mike made numerous trips with the horsebox and trailer from Buckland Newton in Dorset, and our only loss was a cat, which jumped out of the back of the trailer somewhere along the way.

Once settled in, we built a new stable yard with seven boxes—one big enough to be a foaling box—a big tack room, wash room, feed room and hay store: all forming a neat square.

The next year, Mike decided he would like to hold a Pony Club event, so we set about building a cross-country course suitable for children of twelve years and under. It included a quarry, ditches, a bank, into-space fences, and fences going into and out of a wood, and this was a great success. We held this event and a couple of Pony Club combined training programmes for two years.

My stepfather Mike—organiser of King's Somborne Horse Trials

By 1984 Mike was determined to run his British Horse Society senior event. First we had to apply to the BHS for approval—the standard procedure is to run a Novice event for at least a year before being upgraded to Intermediate or Advanced, but Mike wanted to begin with Intermediate or drop the whole project. The BHS sent a steward to inspect the site and he found it entirely suitable, so we gained our permission. We had wanted to call it 'Hoplands' Horse Trials', but all new events have to be named after a place on the map to make it easier for everybody to find their way there, so we were obliged to have 'King's Somborne'. Next came the allocation of a date. Existing events have priority, so we had to make do with a Wednesday—there wasn't even a weekend available for us—in May: the first King's Somborne horse trials were held in 1985.

Mike and I designed the course. We used the lie of the land to determine many of the fences—for instance, steps going up the hills and into-space fences to come down. The water complex posed our first problem, as there are no natural rivers or streams on the property and we had to build it from scratch. In September 1984 we had been to the Luhmühlen

'... Robin Hood had never had anything to do with horses. We gave him a book on course building and left him to it.'

Young Rider European Championships where there were two man-made water fences, both of which went in and out of water twice, and Mike had decided that this was what he would like to have. We positioned the pond in the valley bottom next to the pump house under a couple of oaks, and made it so that it could be jumped from either direction.

The design done, construction had to be tackled. This was the priority of our farm manager, Robin Hood (yes, really!), who had never had anything to do with horses. We explained in detail what we wanted done, gave him a book on course building and left him to it. He made the water complex of concrete with a sand and gravel bottom, and when it was finished we were all very proud of it; Rob was much encouraged by so triumphant a beginning.

The steps were next because they had to be constructed before December, to give the earth time to settle. The job seemed straightforward, but as work on the four angled steps advanced, we found that although originally all of the same height, by the time they had been rolled and the soil had compacted, they varied quite a bit. However, when we tried them we found they jumped well, so let them be.

To help Rob further with his task, we suggested he walk the cross-country course at nearby Brockenhurst, a one day event venue. He took his family, who enjoyed a novel outing; Rob himself learned a great deal, and also began to appreciate what I spent my whole time doing—in fact, so successful was this trip that a couple of weeks later he went off to walk the Badminton course. He couldn't believe that we actually jumped over those fences, but was quite happy to reproduce some of them at King's Somborne. He took pride in his work, justifiably—the zigzag he built over a ditch was faultless, the logs fitting into each other to produce perfect angles and finished off with rounded ends.

However, some of the fences built before Christmas weren't quite right; we told Rob to cut notches in the tops of the posts, then rest the poles in them and wire them in place. However, this kind of fence construction, although acceptable, is not the best—now, all post and rail fences use a main post with a smaller one in front of it on which to rest the top rail. If a lower rail is also required, another smaller post is put in front of the first one, to support it; this is to ensure that a horse cannot knock a rail off its post.

With the help of Anthony Ffookes, our BHS technical adviser, and all the farm workers, the whole course was at last ready and Mike asked me to ride round to make sure that it was all correct and satisfactory. Piggy was resting after Badminton, so I took Friday and Mike followed in the Land Rover; in order to inform him thoroughly about each fence, I jumped most of them twice and then stopped to discuss it with him. Because of all these necessary pauses, Friday didn't work up her usual enthusiasm—if I had ridden her right on round, she would have flown over every obstacle—and at the third last jump we had four stops. This was a big trakhener with a deep water ditch under it, and with only a single rail over the top it was quite 'gappy'. We pondered Friday's refusals and thought there must be something wrong with the fence: what we hadn't appreciated was that to get her adrenalin flowing, Friday in fact needed the atmosphere of a competition, with loudspeaker announcements and all the other stimulating noises. Anyway, we decided to put a second rail lower

down, to cover up more of the water. That was the only fence we modified, for the rest of the course had ridden well; and even that one could have been left as it was, because if Friday had been in an attacking mood it would have been fine.

Building the course was a considerable challenge for Rob. As changes have had to be made year by year and his knowledge of the subject has grown, so has his enjoyment in putting it into practice; and not only because it makes a change from farm work but also because of his acquired interest in the event.

Designing a course does not preclude the designer from competing over it, but had I intended to enter for that first event I would not have *ridden* it in advance, because that would have disqualified me for the year. In fact, I was to ride Friday in an Advanced event a few days before ours, and anyway ours was to be an Intermediate event. The rule about familiarity with a course was changed the following year (1988): now, if you have lived for more than six weeks on the same premises as the course, you are not allowed to take part in an event there. In fact, I would not have trained on it, as it is far too big.

For the additional rail at the water ditch, a tree had to be cut down. The one Robin Hood selected happened to stand in a wood right next to the dressage field, and he didn't fell it until the day before the cross-country, when the dressage phase was already under way. The roaring of the chainsaw and the crash of falling timber reverberated all over the arena, to the consternation of the startled horses and the less-than-pleased comments of their riders. But nobody remained disgruntled for long, and when the disturbance subsided everyone managed to see the funny side of Rob's mistiming—and it did add to his knowledge of what not to do in the vicinity of that often perplexing creature, the horse.

Each phase of a one or three day event presents its own difficulties when choosing terrain. Nobody likes to do a dressage test on sloping ground and at Hoplands we are fortunate to have two flat fields, both of which are entirely suitable. For the show jumping, although good level going is needed, it does not have to be absolutely flat; ours is on a slight slope, which makes it all the better a test.

The advertising of any official event is undertaken by the BHS, which publishes all relevant information for its members three times a year. Details have to be submitted by October for the season beginning in the following March and must include the place, date, name, address and telephone number of the secretary, the various classes, the timetable, and every other item that intending entrants may need to know. We also relied on word of mouth for news of our new event to get around. Holding it in mid-week that first year did not suit everybody, but the calendar was short of Intermediate classes, so it attracted a big enough entry to fill five sections.

'Inevitably we overlooked some essential details, and learned a lot about organising an event on the day itself.'

Inevitably we overlooked some essential details, and learned a lot about organising an event on the day itself. Some dressage was to be run on the day before the cross-country, but we had forgotten to arrange the distribution of numbers; we used my horsebox as the secretary's 'tent', but I didn't have it ready in the right place at the right time, or ensure that a table and chair were in it. Then some whose dressage had come early in the day were leaving at the same time as others with a later time were arriving, and as the

My sponsors kindly supporting the King's Somborne Horse Trials 1989

Right: The Mercedes Star

Below (l to r): R. Mickelburgh and Come Alive at the British Wool fence; Rodney Powell and The Irishman on their way to winning an Advanced section at the Driza-Bone Farmyard; Claire Mason and Dreadnought at the MacConnel Mason Masterpiece; Vanessa Ashbourne on Hector James at the Bailey's Rails.

drive is almost a mile long and too narrow for two-way traffic, there was chaos for a while. However, this was the only major snag, and everyone who took part considered that it had been worthwhile.

Each year all the farm workers are involved in the preparations. During January and February, the slackest period in a farmer's year, they help to build the obstacles. Two or three days before the competition, the hundred sheep are moved to a far corner out of sight and fencing is temporarily taken down to allow general access. At the first event we held, the seriousness with which our people took their duties was not without its humorous side: the gamekeeper, for example, was put in charge of the car park and instructed not to admit anyone without receiving payment. When my stepsister, Judy, and her husband arrived without a car pass, he was impervious to their claim of the right to free admission as members of the family, and wouldn't let them in until they forked out the cash!

For our second year we were allocated a weekend, although we had to hold it in May again; the disadvantage of this time of year for us is that the chalk soil tends to be dry and hard, and as we had to sow grass on land that had been arable only two years before, it had not had time to grow thick so the going was rather stony. However, Bruce Davidson and Torrance Fleischman came over from America to ride, and Bruce won; I was second and third.

In 1987 Badminton was cancelled, so the entries for King's Somborne doubled; we laid on extra classes and held the event over two days. Many riders were so impressed by our course after the first year that it became regarded as a potentially good pre-Badminton event. We therefore asked the relevant committee if we could hold our event in March or April; furthermore, in most parts of the country the ground is too wet then, whereas ours is in perfect condition. So in 1988 we were allotted March. This is also convenient because it interferes less with the farming and the event is out of the way before hay-making.

Incidentally, just prior to the King's Somborne Horse Trials in 1988 I had heard from IMG that, despite having successfully negotiated a number of sponsorship agreements on my behalf, they had made a policy decision to decrease their interest in individual event riders and stay with the actual events. I therefore needed to find a new agent and was introduced to David Bickers, who has a marketing company based in Andover, by my stepbrother David's wife Annie, who works with him, since when David Bickers has been my agent.

Captain Mark Phillips, Ginny Leng and Mark Todd are among the many top riders who have ridden at King's Somborne regularly. Karen Straker has ridden there twice and Ian Stark made the trip from Scotland to take part in 1988 and 1989. Everybody knows now that ours is a big track that needs a bold horse; it is not at all trappy, and competitors can jump big fences off nice going to land on nice going, and the course follows straight lines as much as possible. This is what they like: a track that allows horses to stand back and jump really big.

For the spectators it is equally attractive, laid out in a beautiful chalk valley in such a way that, whichever side of the course they stand, they can enjoy an extensive view and see virtually all of it.

One of our most notorious fences was the **Mercedes star**, in a circle of rails, which we designed in 1985. The circle stands half-way down the hill

Mum and Teazle jumping during the 1989 King's Somborne Horse Trials—'From a good line of jumpers'

near the end of the course and looks most imposing, and the star was perfectly all right if ridden correctly. In its first year, the good riders jumped it easily, but others didn't appreciate what it involved and came in far too fast. The next year, these were apprehensive, but if they watched it being ridden well they saw how to take a better line and this halved the number of falls: demonstrating that you can jump anything if you *ride* it properly. Technically, it was only three fences in a row, but because of the circle, you had to get your line absolutely right both going in and coming out—if you drifted one way or the other and made it short or long you were in trouble. Because of the circle it was difficult to keep a line, but if you established one after walking the course and knew exactly where to jump each part, the distances were perfect. There have been some spectacular falls, but no one has been badly hurt; the star has in fact been superseded by bullfinches.

We make a few changes each year. For an Intermediate event there have to be between eighteen and twenty-four fences, although we find it difficult to keep to this limit because we get carried away by enthusiasm and usually end up having to cut some out! An Advanced course has from twenty-six to thirty fences.

The 1989 Advanced course is as follows: it starts up a slight slope over two straightforward fences to get the horses going on a good gallop. The third fence goes into a wood, still up the hill—this is a good sort of start because it checks any undue freshness in the horses. In the wood is a **wooden house** with a tiled roof, followed by a **log-pile** at the base of a bank.

The **palisade** out of the wood is an innovation this year. We used to have an ascending spread, two rails filled with bales and brush, but there were a few falls here and we could not really understand why. I think it was rather awkward to get straight at it, and so a lot of people ended up riding it at an angle which meant that the horses were not setting up properly and then tried to bank it. This time people will be able to set up better for this fence and the horses should therefore jump it well. It was mostly rider error that caused the falls: the horses made mistakes because their riders did not ride it properly.

The first **water fence** for the Advanced involves a small log with a big drop of six feet into the water, two strides in the water, then onto an island with a stride, to a rail and a stride back into the water, two short strides, up a step out of the water and bounce over an arrowhead to jump the narrow part. The longer route is up the step, swing right or left and jump the rail on the side. Soon after comes the **chair fence** (last year it was a bullfinch), so there are several fences close together to entertain the spectators.

After a good gallop comes the **Pardubice** fence, a very impressive solid brush with a ground rail quite far out, to fake a ditch—this is a lovely fence to jump and dramatic because it looks so big. The jump beyond is an **upright**, put there to set up for the **farmyard complex** that follows: a bounce over two gates, one stride to a haywain and another stride to a hayrack; the alternative is an S-shaped route through the combination. Then on to a **telegraph pole** with a **natural hedge** underneath (in the fence line), to a big solid **tree-trunk** (it had come down in a gale, and we dragged it down the hill to this spot). Then uphill before turning back down to jump a **palisade into space**; steeply downhill to a narrow

upright at the bottom; left and downhill once more, to level off and over the **steeplechase fence**. Then right-handed and slightly downhill into the **second water fence**: the quick way is a bounce of rails into about three strides of water, up a step out of the water, then two strides to an upright; the alternative is long and wiggly.

Gallop on to a **plain parallel**, a 'let-up fence' before the **coffin combination**: a rail, one stride to a trakhener and a bounce over another rail. This looks quite technical, but when the horses are set up properly it rides very well and there have been no problems.

Carry on to a **triple brush**, a lovely fence to let a horse go on at. Next up a steep bank and a **stone trough** with a rail over it; gently uphill to a **corner fence** at the top, then down to Friday's famous **trakhener**, a big water ditch with (this year only) a single rail over it. At the bottom of the valley is the **Mercedes star**, with a new look this year: the circle of rails is still there, but now it is a bullfinch both in and out, with three long or four short strides between. The last fence is a narrow **table**, adorned with several baskets of flowers.

The distance over all BHS courses is measured with a wheel and the speed for each class category is calculated in metres per minute. On ours, there are always a lot of time faults—riders often have to slow down as it is so hilly and because there are quite a few technically difficult fences. If the time is set at six minutes, some riders might take seven or eight.

The event has grown quickly. It was held over Easter weekend last year and attended by about six thousand spectators, and that was with no advertising other than from within the horse trials network. There is always a great number of trade stands selling a variety of products.

This is the only event we hold, and I don't practise over the course. On the day after the event we leave it open for one day for cross-country schooling, and I might go round then if I have a horse that needs it. In 1988 I went round because other people were having problems and they wanted a lead. So, rather rashly, I took my novice horse through the Advanced water several times, although he had not even done an Intermediate; he coped well and I was very pleased with him. The Intermediate is quite difficult, too, with the big rail straight into water. Somebody was having a lot of trouble there and I must have jumped my novice over this rail about fifteen times, each time thinking that sooner or later I was bound to fall!

When it is all over, all of us involved in running these trials flake out completely—we suddenly realise how tired we are, not only from the physical exertion but also from constantly worrying about the multitude of details we have to think about while the show is going on. The first year we forgot to arrange for a doctor to be present, so there was panic telephoning at the last moment; another time we didn't have a horse ambulance, so our trailer stood by while we hoped fervently that no accidents would happen. Luckily, none did.

Each year brings different problems, new ideas, unforeseen difficulties, but always a fresh challenge to do better than the last time. And if everything always went perfectly every year, I don't think it would be nearly so much fun.

Piggy and me competing *hors concours* at King's Somborne Horse Trials 1988

The event horse must be just about the most demanding and time-consuming leisure animal in the country, and to get ready and keep a number of competition horses at near peak fitness means keeping to one of the most strenuous daily routines imaginable. Feeding and grooming, schooling and exercising, breaking, training and competing all entail a full and extremely hard-working day, especially if you are anywhere near the top (and want to stay there!). It is a rigorous yearly round, but one I must admit I would never wish to change.

5 Full Cycle: the Eventing Year

The event horse's year could be said to start in December, when they will all have their flu injections; this dictates two or three days with no work at all, or anyway only basic, quiet work, so it has always seemed sensible to have these done while horses are still in the field. Over the Christmas holiday I attend some of the local hunt balls with many hunting friends, and then work starts in earnest: my first priority is to prepare the horses that are going to Badminton. The first event of the season is held in the second week of March, so all the horses that need to come in for this, together with the Badminton ones—probably four or five in all—are wormed and shod ready to resume work after New Year. They all start together so they can follow the same exercise programme, beginning with a month's walking on the roads.

RUNNING A YARD: THE DAILY ROUTINE

In January I take on an extra helper to stay until after Badminton. We don't need so much help in the stables as the year wears on, since the novice horses can live out in the summer, and inevitably there are the odd ones that go lame and have to have a holiday. By October I have only my head girl—Alex Evans at the moment—and one other. Alex has been with me for three years now and has passed her HGV test so she can take a turn at driving the lorry, which is most useful. I have a working pupil to whom I give lessons, and a girl from Warwickshire College whose three-year course entails the middle year being spent working in a yard. She has been with me since last June and will stay until the coming July.

In spite of so much help, I can spend as many as six or seven hours in the saddle on most days, and my average over the year must be two or three. My helpers spend several hours in the saddle each day, too. When the advanced horses are in full work in March and April they have about an hour and a half's hacking daily; the novice horses have an hour.

In the stable management and general running of my yard I know exactly what is going on, and equally Alex knows too, so I can leave a great deal to her. I do check the feeds that the horses are getting and tell her when they are to be changed, but she has plenty of initiative and I don't

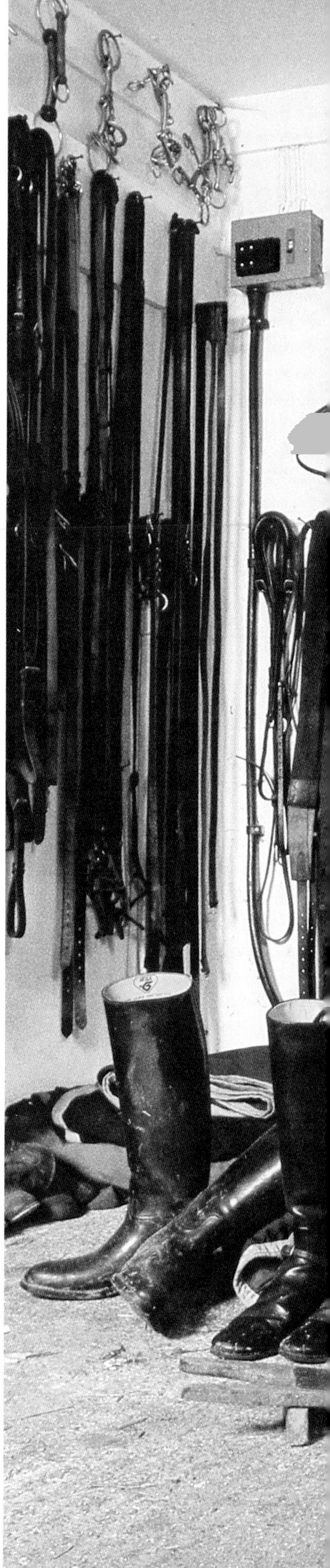

R.M.HUN
LUHMÜHLEN
EM
1987
LUHMÜHLEN
CCI
EM
30.8.-2.9.1984
INTERNATIONALE
MILITARY
1984
de grote prijs van Enschede
11 t/m 14 oktober
Boekelo
INTERNATIONALE MILITARY
1985
BOEKELO
15 JAAR
Heineken
HORSE
TRIALS
AT
PUNCHESTOWN
MAY 15TH-18TH 1987

have to know, for instance, if a horse has cut itself: she will see that it is treated and come to me only if she is particularly worried.

In the evening I write a list setting out each horse's routine for the next day. On an average day the routine is as follows:

7am	Horses are fed. I may have schooled one or two before that.
8.30am	Stables are finished.
9am–1pm	Hacking out; all exercise is done in the morning. I school or jump whichever horses require it.
2pm–5pm	Grooming, any odd jobs.

As a rule I don't ride in the afternoon unless I've run out of time in the morning: in which case the breaking in of young horses might be done then. The timetable on competition days is determined by when I have to leave, how many horses have to be plaited, how many people are left in the yard. If I am going to an event two hours' drive away, I would probably need to leave at 7am, which means rising at 5.30 and sometimes not getting back until 10pm. But the tack will probably have been cleaned on the homeward journey, so all we have to do is unload and put the horses to bed; unless we get home really late we muck out the lorry immediately. If two helpers are coming with me we have to be up extra early to finish stables before the three of us set off. On a hunting day, however, I seldom leave before 9am, and have time to school one or two horses first. I like to have the yard finished and the horses fed by 5pm, but if I return from hunting later with a muddy horse and tack, the girls will come down and help me with these.

On a normal day lunch is from 1 to 2pm, then we groom. We spend half an hour on each horse, so with eleven in the yard we sometimes have to move rather quickly. The farrier comes once a week, but the vet is called out only when really necessary.

We still have the row of four cottages on the farm. My head girl, Alex, and the working pupils all live in one—I used to share the cottage with Alex when there were only the two of us, but four is crowded, so when my stepbrother moved out of his, I moved in and am now on my own. Robin Hood and his family live in a third and Mrs Street, Robin's mother-in-law who cooks for my grooms in the evening, has the fourth. I provide all the grooms' food and they cook their own breakfast and lunch.

If we did not enjoy the good fortune of living on a farm, there would be even more to look after. As it is, Robin Hood and his merry men take care of many jobs for us: they maintain the post-and-rail fencing of the fields surrounding the yard; they do the harrowing, hay-making and rolling and they spread the nitrogen; they fetch straw and hay and unload it for us; and they roll the school and deal with the muck heap. The water troughs are usually cleaned out during the summer as well.

Robin also relieves us of numerous other tasks: mending windows in the stables and replacing rings that have come out of the wall; if the lorry won't start, his men will come out with a tractor, whatever the time of day; if the battery goes flat, they are always there with a tractor and jump leads; they even take the rubbish up to the farm dump for us. Robin's help extends to the houses, too: chopping logs, mending burst pipes, unblocking drains and loos. We depend heavily on him. In fact the whole community at Hoplands, farm and stables, works together in harmony.

Exercising at home accompanied by Teazle

JANUARY

Busy with the paperwork

In January, work with the horses starts with road walking, which continues for a month or so. We begin with about three-quarters of an hour, and gradually increase it by a quarter of an hour a day until the horses are doing two hours. For the first two weeks they will walk on the flat, and for the next two some hills will be included to help clear their wind. Their woolly coats are left on, because they can then be turned out afterwards without having to worry about rugging them up—nor do they need exercise rugs on very cold mornings while we ride them, as they would if they were clipped. January is also registration—I have to think about registering all the horses for the coming season. The horse trials office becomes busy at this time of year, since entries start in the middle of February.

The young horses are still competing, and some of the horses that have been hunting will be fit and might be show jumping a little. However, those that have been hunting for most of the winter but are also going eventing will have an easy January; they will be let down a bit and be given a short holiday, otherwise they would be in for too long a season and become stale. They are clipped, so will be not be fully turned away because the weather is too cold and wet. They have about an hour a day in the field, otherwise they will be too fit for the beginning of the season.

As their work increases their food changes. They start off with as much hay as they like and as they do more work they get more hard feed; as their fitness increases they eat less hay. A dentist comes regularly to attend to their teeth, the older horses only once at the beginning of the year, but the five- or six-year-olds will be seen again in June or July.

FEBRUARY

By February they are ready to start some flat work. For the first couple of days this will be just fifteen or twenty minutes at a working trot to loosen them up and get their muscles working. They will also do some trotting on the road. While walking, their progress will all have been the same, but once they start trotting some horses will need more hill work than others, depending on how clean they are in their wind. Thoroughbreds need less work than half- or threequarter-breds.

At the end of February they will have their first good canter in preparation for the first events the following month; they also have some hill work to make them blow. Schooling for dressage starts as soon as they have done a month's walking. They are schooled daily, building them up by asking a little more each day. They have to be brought into all this work very slowly, to allow their muscles time to build up again after the winter rest.

I will not let them even attempt to jump until six weeks after I have brought them up. Then they will jump twice a week until their first jumping competition, then once a week in between show jumping competitions—I will probably compete in these from the third week of February; as a preliminary I take them for some jumping lessons.

The novices will have been busy for most of November and December, and the four-year-olds will probably go on holiday in the middle of February when I get busy with the horses that have just finished walking, to leave me more time for the main horses. We ride five-year-olds in this month;

they will then have a holiday until I bring them up again after Badminton when things are a bit quieter once more, and hopefully will do a few events in the autumn.

February is also team chasing. I took up this sport two years ago when my hunting friends in the Portman invited me to join their teams. Each team has four members, all wearing the same number but each a different colour so that the commentator can identify them individually. The whole team sets off together, each team on its own, and the fastest team round the course wins. Only the three fastest times count, so if one member is much slower or fails to complete the course this doesn't spoil the team's chances. It is not a plain circuit as in a three day cross-country or steeplechase, but has quite a few tricky hazards—for instance, there is usually a section, probably with two fences, which must be jumped as a team, all taking off together; or a pen into which we all have to go, shutting the gate before we leave it.

'Team chasing is an excellent way to show young horses what cross-country fences are…'

Team chasing is an excellent way to show young horses what cross-country fences are, and following other horses usually encourages them. I take the horses that I have been hunting; it is good practice for their first event and gets them thinking about jumping different kinds of fence. In team chasing the organisers try to keep the fences as natural as possible—in the Portman country, in Dorset, we have lots of hedges—but competitors must be prepared for artificial ones, including combinations, banks and steps.

MARCH

In March is the King's Somborne horse trials, which means urgent final work on the course. By this time I am also thinking about which horses I shall take to which events. I try to keep to a maximum of three horses at any event, so I have to pick and choose to ensure that all my horses have good outings. Badminton horses have to go to the events that are most suitable for them and I give these horses preference so that I can spend plenty of time with them. I would try to run them in at least two one day Advanced events, but would enter them for at least four in case weather or some other reason caused any to be cancelled. The courses need to be big, bold and imposing, the sort of fences one meets at Badminton, and in fact there are only about five one day events in the spring that meet this requirement.

We blood test the horses in March, before they start cantering, to find out how their health is. Then if anything is wrong, we hopefully have time to cure it before a horse begins to feel really unwell; we repeat these tests throughout the year.

In the middle of March we start letting down the horses that are to be roughed off. When the younger horses have finished team chasing they will also be on holiday, which leaves only the event horses in full work.

APRIL AND MAY

April is a busy time: jumping and dressage lessons, and eventing twice a week. Pat Burgess holds sessions once a week at Mark Todd's yard in Cholderton, only twenty minutes from where I live. I take two horses to

jump, and ride others either before I go or when I come home. Dressage lessons with Paul Fielder are forty-five minutes' drive away, and I take two Advanced horses early in the morning.

The Badminton horses start cantering six weeks before the event, so if it is held in May, they will have been cantering since mid-March and by April this is a major part of their work. We canter them twice a week, with short stretches at the gallop, to build up their stamina and clear their windpipes. Out hacking we increase the amount of hill work, and before Badminton they do some mile or mile-and-a-half gallops. We do the cantering on our own farm when the ground is suitable, but if the weather makes the going either too hard or too soft, we have to take them by lorry to all-weather gallops or to some other place where the ground is good.

The competitions themselves bring on their fitness more than anything else, because jumping fences demands such a lot from a horse. Competitors at Badminton have to do a 4½-minute steeplechase with eight fences at a good gallop, followed by a 12½-minute cross-country with thirty-five fences, and a horse must be exceptionally fit to cope with all this.

The other horses need not do so much cantering, but any three day event horse must be thoroughly fit before each competition. The going at Badminton is not particularly tough because it is quite flat—at some events it is quite hilly—but it is the biggest test over fences and also covers more distance than most three days. Horses should be at peak fitness a week before they go cross-country and then brought down slowly after the competition to bring their condition back to normal.

'Horses should be at peak fitness a week before they go cross-country ...'

After Badminton, a three-star event, the horses have a small rest, how long depending on what they will be doing in the autumn. Riders lucky enough to be on the shortlist for the European, World or Olympic Championships—whichever is being held that particular year—have a final trial either in July, which means three weeks' holiday for the horses, or August, after which they can have four weeks.

Windsor Intermediate three day event probably comes a fortnight after Badminton, with an Advanced two-star three day at Bramham a week later.

JUNE

In the second week of June, after the last three day event of the spring, we start bringing up the Badminton horses again. They will not have lost much fitness, so can go straight into light work on the flat, walking and trotting, no cantering. After two weeks they may start jumping. June is quiet, so I have time to go out, if necessary, and look at horses to buy.

My five-year-olds will by now have been brought up from their holiday and will start eventing. Their first appearances will be at Pre-Novice competitions, where the fences are 3ft 3in instead of the Novice standard of 3ft 6in.

JULY

July finds the Badminton horses hacking for 1½ hours, nearly all trotting uphill and down. By the middle of the month we are back in full swing, with perhaps two events a week, novices one day, older horses on another,

Main picture: Interval training Aloaf before Burghley 1984. This picture shows just how big and strong he is for me to ride

Left: Taking Aloaf through the showjumping phase at Burghley in 1984

and the normal dressage and jumping lessons in between. Those shortlisted for a British team will usually have the first team training at Badminton at about this time, a four to six day period. We usually take only three horses and have as much tuition as we like. Ferdie Eilberg teaches us dressage, and depending on how many of us there are, we have one or two lessons each day he is there, which might be three times in a week. Pat Burgess is also there three days a week to give us jumping training; this can include cross-country if we wish, but the horses are probably eventing at the weekend so might need only a little cross-country jumping before their first competition of the autumn season. We are more likely to be schooling our younger horses than our team horses.

Team training is wonderful for the horses that are there, but the horses left behind are not getting any help from us if we live too far away to ride them each day. They keep fit and are lunged, but one cannot bring them on in their work.

AUGUST

August brings the bigger one day events such as the National Open Championships at Gatcombe, where we all want to ride our top horses. The three day event everyone aims for is Burghley, in September. Other three day events include Boekelo in Holland, a popular two-star; and Rotherfield, which is putting on an Advanced one this autumn; Chatsworth used to be the two-star three day event in England, but had to be abandoned.

Normally there are about seventy British horses at Burghley, but this year the European Championships are being held there, so only twelve will be allowed to compete. There are, therefore, a great number of riders with top class horses who will not be able to take part and will have to go to Rotherfield. The Intermediate and Novice Championships at Locko Park are usually in August, and to qualify for these you have to be placed in the regional finals. Rotherfield will finish the British season this year and Le Lion d'Angers, in October, is the final event on the Continent.

SEPTEMBER

Most people's advanced horses have their holiday after the autumn three day events, though there are a few more events that go on until the middle of October. After Burghley, which is at the beginning of September, mine usually go out in the field for about three months, are fed there, and don't come in until the weather becomes too bad in December. They are roughed off slowly. To start with, the rugs are taken off each day and the horses brought in every night; their feed is lessened, though we continue to ride them for a few days so their fitness tapers off gradually. The rugs are left off altogether when they are used to the colder weather. We leave front shoes on, but take off their hind shoes in case of kicking; they are checked daily when we feed them, to make sure that they are in all respects well.

AND OCTOBER

With some of the horses on holiday, I have more time for the novices and for teaching, so the pupils get more lessons at this time than at any other. I also like to get out and about looking for young horses. The novices stay in, and I spend a lot of time schooling them; they go hunting in October and November as it is such a good experience for them, and makes them brave and careful. Sometimes I take retired event horses because they enjoy it and there is nothing else for them to do out in the field all day; their schedule is therefore the reverse of that for the competition horses, in for the winter and out in summer.

During the winter we do some indoor show jumping, and spend time training the young horses and breaking in the three-year-olds, some of which are home-bred and some bought in. I like to start each winter with both three- and four-year-olds, preferably two or three of each, to work with. Thus the amount of work does not really get any less, but it is not so important as in spring and summer, and I can sometimes take afternoons off to look at prospective purchases.

In October the Horse Of The Year Show is held at Wembley. I have show jumped there once, in 1985, having managed to qualify Friday Fox for the Foxhunter championship, although she was first and foremost a three day eventer and not a show jumper. To qualify, a horse has to be in the first two in a regional finals, which is a very high standard. All the other horses were top novice show jumpers, so even though Friday's eventing category was Advanced, she was not accustomed to this type of competition and was up against the best at their own game.

She really acquitted herself very well on that occasion. We did a practice round on the first morning and the first round of the competition in the afternoon, followed by the second round in the evening for all those who had gone clear. We were among these and when I walked the course

Mum (right) and me on Piggy and Nightwatch leading the Cattistock Hunt followers with Tessa Jackson (centre), wife of the joint master and huntsman

Friday and me jumping in the Foxhunter showjumping competition at the Horse Of The Year Show 1984—the biggest show jumps I have ever jumped. Friday finished fifth

Piggy and Friday on a well-deserved holiday

for the second round I found that it consisted of the tallest show jumping fences—I couldn't even see over the top—and the widest parallels I had ever seen. But Friday's good jumping in the first round had given me confidence. A lot of my friends had come to watch and it was encouraging to hear them cheering me on.

The Wembley atmosphere is electrifying. The spectators in tiered seats closely surrounding the arena, the bright lights, the public address system so much louder than at an outdoor event, the sense of occasion, all combine to heighten the tension and animation. The spotlight then falls on each rider and horse as they are about to start their round, and the commentator's voice booms around the huge roofed enclosure, introducing them. It is a garish contrast with the quiet, the fresh air and the familiar scenery at a country event. On the course, you can feel the crowd's expec-

tancy, eagerly awaiting a good performance or with equal enthusiasm some bone-shaking spill. Riding indoors is totally different from riding outside. You really do have to come off the corners with lots of impulsion, as the fences are bigger than the normal 3ft 11in of Advanced courses and there is not nearly so much room to get to them, so the horses need the impulsion to clear them. This demands a slightly different style of riding, which I am not used to.

We went round well until we reached the fence related to the ultimate treble. I jumped a single fence off the turn, then with only one more fence to do, sat up, confident that we were going to have a clear round. But because I sat up between those last two penultimate fences, Friday immediately slowed a fraction: so, when we got to the treble, although we were not too far off it we had lost the impulsion to get over the parallel and she bounced the back rail. She jumped the other two parts faultlessly, but my inexperience had cost us one fence down. There were only three clears, so we finished equal with four others that had also put one fence down. I haven't jumped as big a track since, but valued the experience and would like to qualify again sometime.

NOVEMBER

At this time of year, of course, we start work on our King's Somborne course. In October and November we attend to any major fences which need steps; these must be constructed early enough so the ground has time to settle. Building with rails is done after the Christmas holiday if the weather is good and we can still get the tractors into the fields. Work on the course generally continues throughout the winter.

November and December tend to be less busy and I can have a holiday! If I can organise the horses they can usually have a couple of weeks off, too. I always used to go skiing, but for the last three years have chased the sun; I like to travel, but the more of the world you want to see, the more expensive it is. My holidays have included scuba diving on the Barrier Reef and a safari in Kenya in 1988, and I would like to return to both, especially as I spent only fifteen days in Australia, so didn't see much of the country—although the scuba diving was fabulous. I would love to go skiing again, too, but haven't been able to fit it in for the past four years. In November I also have more time than usual for promotional work, which necessitates visits to London.

I don't seem to need any extra fitness work in the winter for myself, because I hunt with the Portman twice a week and team chase in February. The longest time that I have been off a horse was when I went to the Caribbean for two months in 1982. When I resumed riding I was most uncomfortably stiff, which made me reluctant, for a while, to work as hard as I usually do. Even when I went to Kenya for three and a half weeks I stayed with friends who had horses, which I schooled for a few hours.

At home, family and friends will be celebrating Christmas. The young horses are hopefully finding their feet in the hunting field, and we will soon be thinking of bringing up the competition horses again in preparation for the coming season. And so the equestrian year will have come full circle once more.

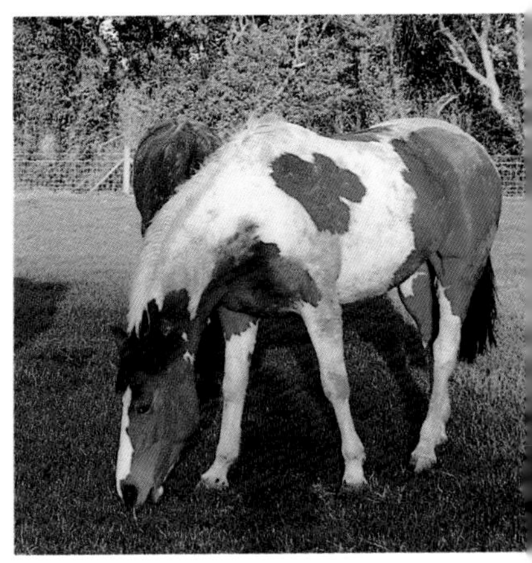

The horses that win through to the top of the eventing ladder are truly courageous—the sport is increasingly competitive and year by year demands a higher standard of ability and talent. We have bred some good horses and bought some, but in every case look for that special something—that extra presence and bold outlook—which hopefully will mean extra toughness and courage. Under the stress of top level competition this may make all the difference between a good horse, and a great one.

'In Piglet, we thought we had found the wonder horse ...'

PIGLET

In Piglet, we thought we had found a wonder horse. He was for sale only because Carol Rowcliffe, who owned and rode him, had had a bad fall in which she suffered several broken ribs, a broken collarbone and a punctured lung, and so had decided to give up eventing. Piggy was the only horse she had ever considered safe enough to risk riding in Advanced classes, and ironically the accident happened at Downlands in the spring when she tried him in his first Advanced event. They had a late cross-country start time and the sun was low. As Carol rode out of a wood they were faced with a Normandy bank type of obstacle with a drop, but the sun was in Piglet's eyes and he galloped straight into the bank.

6 The Brave and the Bold

We had followed this horse's career the year before. First, his name amused us. He had often competed against one of David's Intermediate horses, Hotelier, so we had seen how well he could go. David had been trying for years to qualify for Burghley or Badminton on his old horse, Crown Wheel, but had never succeeded because Crown Wheel's dressage was so bad that he never gained enough points to upgrade him to Advanced. So when in early May 1982 we saw Piglet advertised in *Horse and Hound*, we thought it would be a good opportunity to buy a horse capable of Badminton or Burghley for David and that could possibly do Juniors with me. We went to see him the day after reading the advertisement, and Mum, Mike and David watched me ride him. Carol had bought him as a foal at one of the Hunter Improvement Society sales that are held every spring and autumn—she is a wonderful person and Piglet obviously had an excellent home. Several people wanted to lease him, but later Carol told us that she had decided she liked us and knew that we would give him as good a home as the one he was leaving.

We went home to discuss it and concluded that we probably could not afford such an expensive horse and perhaps did not really deserve one. Mum insisted that we ring Carol straightaway, as it would be unfair to leave her in the dark, so Mike disappeared into his office. When he rejoined us he didn't say much, but presently astonished us with the news that he had made an offer subject to veterinary examination, which Carol had accepted. It was a sublime surprise for us all. The next day we took David Watson, our vet, to look Piggy over; and two days later we brought our new horse home.

He had been kept fit because Carol had entered him for Bramham in case a new owner should want to take him there, but to try him out we first took him to a Novice event at Tweseldown, where David rode him HC. He did well in the dressage and show jumping, but having had him only a few days, we were not sure about the cross-country and were apprehensive. Rightly so, it seemed: he stopped at some steps down the hill. This was a Novice fence and we had just spent a lot of money on an advanced horse. Had we made an appalling blunder? He was about to compete at Bramham and apparently wouldn't even tackle a Novice course without stopping. We decided to risk it, so trundled up to Yorkshire to take part in this event.

BRAMHAM

In the spring of 1982 Spangle was still carrying on with her Novices, and we had recently started competing with a home-bred horse called Aloaf. With Piglet entered for the Advanced three day event at Bramham, David put Aloaf in for the Novice two day, which I entered as well with Spangle. It was a hot, sunny weekend and we had a wonderful time, although it was a trifle too hot for some of the horses, especially in the three day, and a lot of them were exhausted after the cross-country.

Piglet performed atrociously in the dressage (as he continued to do for the rest of his career!) because he couldn't contain his excitement; and after his bad showing at Tweseldown we were uneasy about the cross-country. However, we need not have worried: he gave David a wonderful ride and took all the fences with consummate ease, and we understood now why he had let us down that first time—what cheek, he must have thought, taking me to a Novice event that is far below my ability. To be thought of as a novice was an insult. This was typical of him, and taught us that big cross-country fences are what suit him best. Furthermore, he finished perfectly fit although the day was hot, and we went back to the stables feeling pleased, for all three horses had gone extremely well—Spangle upgraded to Intermediate on the final day, and Aloaf only just missed a place.

We returned for the show jumping next day in a heatwave punctuated by thunderstorms and rain. One sharp downpour burst upon us while Piglet and two other horses were waiting to go into the arena, and continued for their rounds. Piglet put his ears out sideways and indicated that he wasn't going to go. He had two stops at the water jump and when David managed to get him over the little hedge at the third attempt he landed in the water. He completed the round, but we were all rather put out because we felt the organisers should have stopped the action until the rain squall was over—none of those three horses jumped a clear round. Bramham concluded the spring season.

SPRING TRIALS 1982: FRIDAY FOX

Friday Fox had also had a fairly successful spring in 1982; having had a good run round one Intermediate trial with her, I wanted to tackle a

PIGLET
Owned by Mr Mike Lanz and my mother, bred by Mr Tom Gage
Born 1974, Devon
16.2hh brown gelding
By: Newlinacre (Thoroughbred)
Ex: Pampus (¾ Thoroughbred, ¼ Exmoor pony)

Major placings
1983: 9th Wylye CCI** (England)
1984: 12th Badminton CCI*** (England)
1984: 8th British Open Championships Locko Park
1984: 2nd Boekelo CCI** (Holland)
1985: 1st Gatcombe (England)
1985: 5th Rotherfield 3 day
1985: 11th Boekelo CCI** (Holland)
1986: 2nd Badminton CCI*** (England)
1986: 1st Gatcombe (England)
1986: 8th and team win Alternative World Championships Bialy Bor (Poland)

Does not include the many one day event wins and placings achieved.

FRIDAY FOX
Owned and bred by my mother
Born 1975, Dorset
16.0hh skewbald mare
By: BP (HIS Thoroughbred)
Ex: Foxglove (14.3hh Irish cob) hunted by my parents

Major placings
1982: 3rd Novice Championships (British)
1983: Member of gold medal team, Junior European Championships Rome (Italy)
1984: Individual bronze and team gold medal at Young Rider European Championships Luhmühlen (West Germany)
1985: Individual 4th and team gold, Young Riders European Championships Le Lion D'Anger (France)
1986: National Young Rider Champion
1986: Individual bronze and team gold Young Rider European Championships Rotherfield (England)
1987: 5th at Stockholm, CCI* (Sweden)
1988: 7th at Badminton, CCI*** (England)
1988: 7th at Gatcombe British Open Championships

Does not include the many one day event wins and placings achieved.

Junior Open Intermediate trial; this meant I would be riding in front of all the Junior selectors, an important opportunity for both Friday and me. Another new experience was that we would have to do the FEI test, which takes ten minutes instead of the usual four or so and entails some movements that were then unfamiliar to me, such as canter to halt, rein-backs, medium trots and 10 metre circles—much more than Friday and I were capable of at this stage. Debbie Johnson was helping me with dressage and we spent a lot of time practising these in an arena we built in the field.

By the time we went to the trial at Tidworth we thought that Friday and I had improved considerably; this emboldened me to ride her in a double bridle for the first time, as a last-minute resort to try and get her to concentrate. She didn't like it, but it helped because it did give me more control. She has always been difficult to keep in a round outline, and I would have preferred to use a snaffle, if only she would go into the bit—it took me years to get her to take the bit in a snaffle. Although we were not in the lead after the dressage, we were quite pleased and thought that Friday had tried hard. She took the show jumping with her usual ease.

The cross-country was not as big as at the Frensham event where we had come sixth the previous week, so I had no worries—except for one big jump over a river that looked impossibly wide. I didn't know how we were going to get over it; I would just have to keep going forward in the hope that Friday would leap far enough. Actually, that sort of fence, when it is only a ditch or open water, always looks much worse than it is; in fact it is merely a canter stride. It was my third Intermediate and Friday had gone really well at Frensham, which I thought was huge; I knew now that if I kept kicking she could jump anything.

She made a good start, but at the third fence it was clear that she was not going forward like her normal self. At the fifth fence, up a step and a rail, she stopped. I was so incredulous that I gave her a good whack, which galvanised her into jumping it; but she stopped again at another fence. She managed to clear the big river, but she wasn't going a yard and I should really have pulled her up and abandoned the run, found out what was wrong with her and come out for the next day. But because it was a trial and so important, my pride would not let me give up: I felt I had to finish the course. At the water fence she was eliminated. I walked her back to the lorry amid general astonishment that this had happened to Friday, who had never before stopped like this; nor could I understand why, when she was perfectly fit—although it was strange that she was blowing so hard. When the vet came to see her the next day he diagnosed that she had been suffering from some form of twenty-four-hour virus. My brave mare must have been feeling wretchedly ill while trying to struggle round the course. Although I had not known this, I repented deeply my insistence on forcing her on when she was obviously not running with her usual zest.

This put paid to my hopes of going to Windsor for the Juniors in May that year. I was not entered for any other trial and the selectors had not seen Friday at Frensham, so were unaware of her capabilities. When she had fully recovered I took her to a Novice event where she went so well that she was upgraded to Intermediate. After that she went to Exmoor for Mum to take hunting (the season there lasts until May), which we thought would make her feel a bit happier after her rough time at Tidworth.

After our summer break, I had Spangle and Friday to ride, David had

Aloaf and Piglet. However, David was running the Sports Centre at Bournemouth, and a week before Heckfield horse trials he phoned to say he was too busy to spare the time for this event, and that I could take his place on his horses. I was seventeen. We decided that four horses—two Intermediates, one Advanced and one big Novice—were too much for me to cope with, so we semi-retired Spangle and confined her to a few Junior trials and Pony Club events. To have an Advanced horse and a classy Novice was a big step in my riding career. I was still on the Chattis Hill course during the week, so until I left in June and could spend all my time at home, competing at the weekends meant schooling my four horses early in the morning or late in the evening.

Aloaf at his first party, (Exford Show), as a four-year-old whilst being educated on Exmoor. Ridden by Jennett, groom for my mother's hunters—lovely-bodied horse, shame about the head!

Aloaf as a foal with mother

ALOAF

I spent most of the summer with Aloaf. He was a big horse for me to ride: 16.2hh, which isn't very tall, but he was always really a man's horse on account of his long stride. We took part in many Pony Club one and two day events, and he also won the area trials and therefore qualified for the championships. However, until I knew him better I did not want him to upgrade; I rode him in a few Novices but twice had to withdraw him after the dressage and show jumping because he was usually in the top three and I could not go slowly enough round the cross-country to avoid scoring the points that would have earned him an upgrading (this practice, is, of course, not a popular course of action).

Mum had bred Aloaf. He was by Sam Barr's Welton Louis, a seven-eighths Thoroughbred, out of a mare called Mother's Pride on which David used to show jump at Grade A and in Young Riders' competitions. Aloaf is a good stamp of horse but by no means handsome, with a big, rather ugly head. After he turned three we were thinking of breaking him in, when David noticed one morning that he was not in his own field, but in the adjacent one—something must have frightened him and made him jump the post-and-rail fence, and he had impaled himself on a six-inch post. One foreleg was almost severed, and the wound needed 150 internal and 200 external stitches, which left a scar from the middle of his chest to his girth and up the girth line. This accident delayed breaking him in for another year. We tried unsuccessfully to sell him as a show jumper because his dam had been so good, and his prodigious leap from field to field suggested that he had inherited her talent; we offered him first to John Whittaker, and then to Andy Croft who said he would never be big enough.

Sarah Fenwick was helping us in the stables at the time, and when Aloaf was four, she did all the school work on him and lots of minor competitions. She rode him in his first Novice event when he was five and three more that same autumn, where he did well—he won the second one, which earned him six points towards the sixteen needed in those days for upgrading to Intermediate. The following year, David took over the ride until Bramham, when I carried on.

Aloaf's dam, Mother's Pride, at Hickstead with David in 1973

Aloaf was the most difficult character I have owned, and I don't think we would have persevered with him if he had not been home-bred, even though we soon realised that he had talent. He was not vicious, he was just frightened of so many things—not only unaccustomed sights and sounds, but even his everyday surroundings would sometimes terrorise him. And he was big, which added to the problems of handling him.

As a yearling and two-year-old he always had to be bridled before we led him anywhere, even in surroundings with which he was familiar. He could be thoroughly hazardous—one of our working pupils was one day leading him into his field when something scared him and he reared, knocking her to the ground and breaking her jaw. This was the first seriously alarming display of Aloaf's uncertain temperament and warned us that we would have to watch him most carefully.

None of my other horses has a nature remotely like his. He is a worrier and life thoroughly puzzles him. But if he understands what you want him to do, he tries his hardest. I would never let any of the girls ride out on him unaccompanied, because he is so nappy—a mere upside-down leaf is enough to make him jink and whip round. We have tried everything we can think of to cure him of this, but know now that he will never change. He is quite happy when plodding along behind another horse: it is when he is on his own or out in front that he seems to find life so frightening.

As a novice he was notably laid back and did not get excited about a cross-country, I think because he could not really understand why we were doing it: but being anxious to please, he obeyed. He never really enjoyed a cross-country or any sort of competition, merely put up with it because he was instructed to, but tried extremely hard just the same. By the time he was eight and Advanced, he was a seasoned competitor but he was still reluctant to leave the start box for a cross-country: I had to kick him out every time. His conduct changed suddenly at Locko, in the Open Championships, when he evidently decided that the occasion was excessively worrying—while we were waiting to start he astonished me by going up in the air. Ever since then I have had trouble settling him at the start of a cross-country, or the steeplechase or the roads and tracks in a three day event—it is because he tries so hard to do everything right that he works himself into a state of nervous anxiety each time he enters a start box.

Oddly enough, he doesn't mind being clipped, a less frequent and worrying experience which one would expect him to dislike. But he does not like men at all, and particularly vets until he gets to know them, although at thirteen he is slightly more amenable in this aversion. As a young horse he was stubbornly intractable about it; perhaps because of the huge number of stitches he had to have after his accident as a three-year-old. But still, if a strange man appears Aloaf will retreat to the back of his box and snort and worry, as though to say 'Who are you? I don't like you.'

In the stable he usually looks dopey and soft, his lower lip droops and his deportment is sleepy. But he can be the complete opposite, and this is where he is dangerous, because when he does get frightened he simply runs away—all he thinks about is getting away, quite regardless of the risk of hurting himself or his rider; he is just as likely to swerve under a low branch so his rider is swept off, or he might go straight through a fence instead of over it. He is unable to work out whether there really is anything to be frightened of, and just dashes off. If a lorry came past, he would buck

ALOAF

Owned and bred by my mother
Born 1976, Dorset
16.2hh chestnut gelding
By: Welton Louis (7/8 Thoroughbred eventing stallion)
Ex: Mother's Pride III (Grade A show jumper)

Major placings

1983: 3rd British Novice Championships
1984: 4th British Open Championship Locko Park
1984: 4th Burghley CCI*** (England)
1986: 10th Burghley CCI***
1987: 4th individual and team gold European Championships Luhmühlen (West Germany)

Does not include the many one day event wins and placings achieved.

'Aloaf ... would have thrown himself to the ground, he was in such a panic ...'

and rear and skitter sideways; so would Piglet, but whereas Piglet would not be at all frightened, just mischievously playing around with his rider, Aloaf would genuinely be in abject terror.

If Aloaf is left in the lorry on his own he bangs and crashes like fury. I remember one show when he was five, and we had also taken Friday and Spangle. Hardly had these two gone when we heard over the tannoy that some horse was upside down in its box. That was Aloaf, and since then we have always left another horse with him. Nowadays we can leave him on his own, but for the first ten minutes he will thrash around and make a resounding din. And when we return he carries on in a most extravagantly welcoming manner, which at the same time is rebuking us for having deserted him, and implying that it is high time the other horses were put back in the lorry with him. Nor will he travel in the front of the lorry, only on the back. And he objects to being out in the field on his own—he likes to have his friends with him. He really is a big soft baby!

I am sure Aloaf would be quite happy never to compete again, even though his ample scope and abundant talent, coupled with his willingness to do what I ask him, have brought him great success. He would be content to stay at home being schooled every day. Nor does he mind being on holiday as long as his friends are with him, so his annual three months in the field do not bother him at all—Friday and Piglet, on the contrary, would find life unbearably dull without the challenge and excitement of competition.

Usually a horse only goes across country because it enjoys it, but Aloaf goes because he is told to. He finds it easy physically but mentally a strain—it is therefore just as well that he has always had the ardent wish to please and try his utmost, because no amount of natural ability will ever compensate for a horse's lack of effort. Even now he is nervous of cross-country. He finds three day events easier, because the roads and tracks and the steeplechase calm him down, so that by the time we have to do the cross-country phase he is relaxed and going well.

He hates crowds, as we found out at his first Burghley in 1984. During the cross-country he does not notice them, because he is concentrating on the fences. Similarly in his dressage test, he concentrates intensely on the dressage and ignores the spectators—but as soon as we leave the arena I am lucky if he is not on his hind legs, for he hates the sound of clapping. At Burghley, all the horses parade before the prize-giving: competitors circle the outside of the ring and the crowd is clapping the whole time. I was lucky to stay in the saddle. Aloaf did not know what to do with himself and would have thrown himself on the ground, he was in such a panic; he wouldn't approach the prize-giving stand, and we had to wait away out of line. And if a band starts to play, his antics reach their most frantic and I have to sit mighty tight!

Riding him into the arena for the show jumping phase of a three day event is a problem in itself: 'I can't do it,' he seems to be telling himself, 'it's too frightening.' But once we are in the ring and cantering through the start he focuses all his attention on the jumps and is fine—until the clapping starts, when he goes absolutely loopy again. He is the only one of our horses which has ever had problems of this sort. All the others enjoy their work—maybe they get a bit excited when there are people watching the dressage, but they are not actually worried.

Aloaf in the Burghley Parade, 1984

39

TRIALS WITH PIGLET

At the same time as I was persevering with Aloaf and competing with Friday, I was doing my best to get to know Piglet. In July 1982 Piglet and I competed together for the first time at an official BHS event (Heckfield), when I took over David's ride. Shortly before this we had in fact been eliminated from a Pony Club trial because I went wrong four times in the dressage, but at Heckfield we both managed better, and he performed well in this test.

Piglet stands the same height as Aloaf, 16.2hh, but is short-striding and easier to ride. But it took me a long time to get used to his show jumping. I had always gone round at a good medium length show-jumping canter and taken each fence smoothly; but Piglet tended to bounce on the spot and then go for the fence in the last three strides. This totally confused me that first time, with the result that we had one stop and one fence down. We took the cross-country slowly but he performed really well.

'... when asked to weigh in, I was too light, and was disqualified!'

Our first Advanced together was at the beginning of August at Molland, in Devon. He disgraced himself in the dressage by coming last and had one fence down in the show jumping, but in the cross-country he zoomed round at his normal rate and finished with the fourth fastest time. This put us ninth overall, but Molland was to result in yet another frustrating outcome: I had not realised that in Advanced classes I had to carry a weight cloth, so when asked to weigh in, I was too light, and was disqualified! David had never had to carry weight, so it had never occurred to us that I needed to. We went straight out and bought a weight cloth.

AUTUMN TRIALS 1982

Before Molland, I had ridden Friday in the Novice regional final at Dauntsey, which she won—having hesitated at the water—and thus qualified for the Novice championship at Locko, in Derbyshire. This was our next big outing.

Friday went quite well in the dressage, where we performed in a smart arena surrounded by white railings and flowers, and pleased me by coming twentieth out of seventy-seven horses. She went clear in the show jumping. Although this was a Novice championship, the cross-country was Intermediate standard and looked most imposing; however, by now I was realising that everything was within Friday's scope, so I had no qualms except for the water because of her spookiness about it at Dauntsey in July. This obstacle entailed jumping down into a river and out the other side. When we came to jump it, she did hesitate a bit; once we were through there, however, I felt totally confident and we carried on to finish with only one time fault and were third, over the biggest course Friday had yet jumped. This was highly encouraging, and she thoroughly deserved the handsome rug she won from the Midland Bank, sponsors of the event.

Piglet and I did a couple of Open Intermediates while I was getting to know him, and got our first placing at Kyre horse trials in Worcestershire; he was lying second after the show jumping, in which I had my first clear round. On the cross-country, about three fences from home, were some steps downhill; I had been taught to trot into steps down, but Piglet never jumped out of a trot, which I didn't at first know—perhaps in his early training with Carol he had never been asked to trot into his fences. He had whizzed round with no problems, then I brought him back to a trot for the steps—and he stopped. I turned round and brought him back at a canter, and he popped straight down: I was learning the ins and outs of Piggy's character the hard way.

The following event for him was the Advanced at Taunton Vale, where I turned up with my new weight cloth and what seemed like tons of lead—I didn't weigh much, at seventeen. All the family were there in support, because I was also riding Aloaf in the Novice. Piglet did not do badly in his dressage, went clear in the show jumping and had the fastest time in the cross-country, to win the whole event and qualify us for Locko Open Championships the following year. This was very gratifying, though I was fast realising that I must start slowing him down, if necessary—the going had been so hard that taking him round so fast was not the best way to keep him fit and sound.

'... intoxicating news!'

That autumn I had intended to ride both Piglet and Friday in the Junior Autumn Cup at Crondall. However, Friday again gave me an unexpected disappointment: at about fence five, the officials stopped me for some reason and there was quite a long wait; when they finally let me continue I went straight at the fence—and she stopped. She does not like refusing, and to have done so shook her confidence so badly that she refused again at our second attempt. We then finished the course without further trouble, but I had certainly learned the lesson that when stopped and kept standing around, it is essential to take a horse far enough away from the fence and wake it up with a good gallop, to encourage it to forget that there has been an interruption. Furthermore, this fence—a drop into a quarry—was a particularly nasty one to expect her to tackle after she had 'gone cold'.

Piglet went well and finished fifth, but next day I found that he must have banged his leg going round the cross-country; after the necessary lay-off he wouldn't be ready for Wylye so, disappointed, I put him out on holiday and reconciled myself to taking only Friday to Wylye.

WYLYE 1982

Held at the end of September, or beginning of October, Wylye used to be an international event which also ran a friendly junior international class. This year there were competitors from Germany and Ireland, so it was decided to run an unofficial team competition. Much to our delight Friday and I were picked to compete because we had gone so well at Locko, which was intoxicating news! At the time I didn't know any of the others in the team, or the trainer, Gill Watson. Five of us were considered. After the vets' inspection the team was Jessica Atkin on Prairie Wind (another skewbald), who had been in the Junior team at Kalmthout in Belgium; Jackie Toogood, in the Junior team at Rotherfield in August, on Superstar; Fenella Fawcus, who had also done Rotherfield, on Blue Max, which had also won this Junior three day event last year; and Friday and me. I felt proud to belong to such a good team, in which Friday was the only horse that had not yet made its reputation. At the briefing I was told to sit with the selectors and see Gill Watson, which did make me nervous as I didn't know anybody. I remember feeling most embarrassed when,

seated at the table with them, I heard Gill Watson ask Colonel Alfrey and Colonel Nicoll 'Where is Rachel Hunt?'

In July I had been to a Pony Club associates' camp at Chattis Hill, at which Annabel Scrimgeour was my trainer. We got on so well that I asked her to help me with a few more events during the autumn, including Wylye. Lady Hugh used to run a three day event course for juniors at Wylye in the spring of each year; but the one in which I took part in 1982 was her last. She taught us all the basics: how to write up our times, speeds for roads and tracks, and the speed to ride a steeplechase; and we had plenty of cross-country practice. This was a great preparation for my three day eventing career.

With Annabel's help, Friday and I worked hard on our dressage, trying to improve our performance in this FEI test, but at Wylye she disappointed us badly by not behaving well in her test on the first day; I think it was Wylye's rousing atmosphere, as it stands high on Salisbury Plain and is open and windy, with lots of flags snapping in the breeze. On the second day, however, I felt quite at my ease when we set off on the roads and tracks section. After all the road and tracks practice I had had with Lady Hugh in the spring, I was well used to trotting around it at the proper pace; and when we came to the steeplechase section, Friday went round it well, and inside the time. Although this was meant to be a Novice three day event, the cross-country course was of Intermediate standard, which meant that no one would enter a horse that had not already competed in an Intermediate event.

'He had never seen such badly broken knees, and was much distressed ...'

The cross-country course was most impressive. I had walked it carefully with the rest of the team and Gill, who had helped us to decide where we would jump each obstacle; two of the most tricky were a big corner at a coffin and a water jump. I think my colleagues were worried that I was not quite up to the team standard; but there was no question of that, for Friday flew round with no time faults. On the following day when we trotted up at the vets' inspection, she was full of beans and went on to finish seventh in the whole competition. Prairie Wind was sixth, so we won the team prize, with Germany second and Ireland third. This was my first team win, albeit the team was only a friendly unofficial one.

Wylye was the last event of the season. By this time I felt that at last I was getting to know Aloaf, and that Piglet and I, too, were coming to terms with each other. And Friday, of course, was going like a star. So I was now looking to do Windsor Junior Championships the next year with Friday and Piglet, and thinking about upgrading to Intermediate with Aloaf.

Spangle had done some Pony Club events and shows that autumn and was due to compete in one of the later Novice events. But while I was at Wylye she tripped and fell on the road, and as she was not wearing knee boots, she broke her knees and could not walk. Normally when we ride and lead horses, they always have knee boots on but we do not use them on all the horses every time they leave the yard. Mary Meares was our groom at the time and, showing her usual good sense, rode back and fetched the trailer, loaded Spangle aboard, returned to the yard and sent for the vet.

He had never seen such badly broken knees, and was much distressed by the serious possibility of having to put Spangle down. She is beautifully bred, by Spartan General out of a Tangle mare, and was potentially a

Friday and me competing in the Juniors at Wylye in 1982, the first time I represented Great Britain

highly valuable brood mare. Not only would her destruction have caused us great grief, it would also have been a waste of a fine horse, even if she were never sound enough to compete again. All we asked of the vet was that he would try to save her knees so at least she could be used for breeding.

He operated on her and put her knees together. Thereafter she spent six months standing in a stable, and the first eight weeks tied to a hay net with a water bucket close by it. In July she came back to work, and when she was fit enough I rode her in a couple of Pony Club competitions, but although one knee was perfect, the other, despite having healed well, had a big bump on it and when she jumped she could not bend it enough. This meant the end of her eventing career, but since then she has borne some lovely foals.

By the end of 1982, therefore, I was well on the way to a good partnership with my three performance horses, Friday, Aloaf and Piglet. Aloaf went on holiday after I had done some Novice events, and after Friday had done Wylye and with Piglet turned away on account of his injury, I was free for my next experience: the Caribbean!

WIDENING HORIZONS

Sometimes a holiday one has really looked forward to, and thought would bring excitement and novelty, turns out to be an anticlimax; just as certain periods in one's normal working routine—perhaps a change of scene—are often far more satisfying than anticipated. My two months' sailing in the Caribbean were rather disappointing, whereas the time I spent working with the Scrimgeours was thoroughly rewarding and pleasurable. The wonderful experience of being selected to represent Great Britain was similar: training with the other members was extremely hard work but infinitely rewarding, particularly if there was the added glamour of travelling and competing abroad.

7 ◊ Widening Horizons

'Mum and Mike keep a boat in St Lucia … so that they can escape the British climate …'

Mum and Mike keep a boat at St Lucia in the West Indies so that they can escape the British climate in the first three months of the year. A few months earlier their skipper, a Swede named Stefan, had been asked to bring a boat of the same design from Rhode Island, USA, to the Caribbean. He had asked Mum if she would like to crew on this trip but she declined, and suggested that I might like to. I had already sailed a little and loved it, and this offer sounded great fun. At my stepsister's restaurant in Lymington, I discussed arrangements with Mum and Mike, Stefan, a Swedish friend of his who was in the crew, and the fourth member, Richard Morgan who was the son of the owner of the charter company with whom our own boat was moored. It meant that I had to leave for America on the day after the 1982 Wylye three day event, where Friday had been so good; this I did, leaving Mary to let her down and put her on holiday, which made me feel a bit guilty, although I was keenly looking forward to the adventure.

This began with what could have been a small disaster. When we got to the airport we found that the airline had double-booked and that our tickets were not valid for the flight we had intended to take. Eventually we did rather well out of it, because we were all given stand-by seats and travelled first class for half the proper fare, except for Stefan's friend, who had to stay overnight. He caught us up at Boston; from here we went by taxi to Newport, where the boat was supposed to be ready for us. In fact, she had been in dry dock and wasn't put back in the water until the day we arrived, which meant there was still quite a lot of work to do on her. We had six days before we could sail. It was rainy, cold and miserable, and Newport is not the most exciting place to be with nothing to do. We lived on board, but could not use the refrigerator, stove or lights because the electricity wasn't working, so had to have all our meals out; and I found myself using a lot of the money I had brought in a way that I had not expected to.

When we did set sail, it was into heavy weather. The four-day passage to Bermuda through rough seas made us all soaking wet, and some of us did not feel too good. I was all right when I was lying down or at the helm, but trying to keep my balance in the galley while getting food, or staggering to my bunk—right in the bows, the most tossed-about part of a sailing yacht—made me feel so seasick that I could scarcely peel off my oilies. However, despite being encrusted with salt and uncomfortable, sailing in stormy conditions was much more fun than on calm waters.

We kept four-hour watches, which was a tiring routine, snatching sleep while we were off watch and feeling torpid and unrefreshed when we were on. One night when I was on watch at 4am I found it difficult to stay awake. The wind had dropped, the sea was scarcely ruffled and the boat was hardly moving, all of which made it even harder to keep alert. I fell asleep. The wind freshened and shifted. I woke with a start as the boat gybed and the boom slammed across with a thunderous reverberation that woke everyone. Stefan, who was due to relieve me at 8am, was furious at being roused in such an untimely fashion, and I wasn't too popular with any of my shipmates over this lapse! When we had settled the boat back on course I resumed the helm and was wide-eyed for the rest of my watch.

'... the boom slammed across with a thunderous reverberation that woke everyone.'

I don't think I would ever make a navigator. I simply did not understand the mechanics of how we could sail for five days in one direction and manage to find Bermuda exactly where it should be, although Stefan, who was a good sailor, tried to explain it to me. All I do know is that it was good to see land and to make harbour in still water with sunshine to warm us and no rain to soak us or salt to penetrate our clothes. Our first task was to clean ship, then we took everything to the laundry to have the salt washed out and after that enjoyed a good meal.

We spent only two days in port, but in between the chores and filling up with fresh water and diesel, we hired mopeds to explore the island; almost everyone on Bermuda gets about on a moped—the speed limit is 20mph, the maximum length for a car is 4½ metres, and however important or rich you are, the law allows only one car per household. Bombing around on a moped was good fun, even though I went over a bump and lost my camera.

We were looking forward to resuming the voyage, but once under way it wasn't long before we again found the rough seas and constant wetness unpleasant. For another five days we had to grin and bear it before making landfall at St Barts, one of the northern islands of the West Indies. Here we cleaned the boat and ourselves once more, and hired a car to look around the place.

From St Barts we island-hopped to St Lucia—which is not at all the same as going from island to island in the Mediterranean, because the Caribbean islands are far apart and the water is turbulent; there are not many very small craft to be seen in that part of the world. In this way we finally made it to St Lucia, where we took a mooring next to Mum and Mike's boat, which I had never seen before.

The rest of the crew all had something to occupy them: Richard Morgan had a job in the Caribbean for a while before returning home; Stefan had to look after Mum and Mike's boat; his Swedish friend was going to join another crew. I found myself on my own and at a loose end. At first it was enjoyable, after a month of sailing, to have a rest in the sun, swimming or sitting on the beach, but after a week I was bored. I hadn't enough money to spend on parascending and water-skiing, which I would have loved to have tried, although the owners of other boats did take me on a few trips. We would go to one of the bays around St Lucia, or to Martinique, the nearest island which is a French possession. There were a few sailing races

'My objective was to be selected for the British team in the European Junior Event in September.'

and I crewed in one or two. I stayed in St Lucia for a month and might have lingered, but boredom drove me to telephone home and say that I was returning.

The journey back was not the pleasantest I have made, either. I took the cheapest flight, which meant a trip to Barbados in a small biplane whose engine gave the impression that it might fail at any moment. When we eventually landed at Bridgetown, the capital, it was 10 o'clock on a Sunday morning. All the shops were closed, so there was no point in going into town and I couldn't afford to go sight-seeing in a taxi. My flight was not until 10pm, and there was nothing to do but sit in the airport for twelve hours and wait. And when it did take off, it was late: altogether a horrid end to my holiday.

CHRISTMAS 1982

It was by now two weeks to Christmas, which I spent on Exmoor with Mum and Mike; Mike still owned the Crown Hotel in Exford, which he opened for a week or so to accommodate our family and guests. We all wanted to go staghunting on Boxing Day, so Mum lent some of us her hunters. This meet is always held at the hotel, which meant serving mince pies, sausage rolls and glasses of port to the field—I remember we had a good day. After two months away I welcomed getting back to riding; although hunting when I was unfit was rather painful.

WILTSHIRE, SPRING 1983

In mid-January 1983 Mum and Mike went to the Caribbean to stay on their boat until the end of April; I had to find somewhere to stay, because I couldn't drive the lorry. As I had got on so well with Annabel Scrimgeour at the Pony Club Associates' camp the previous year, she agreed to have me with Piglet, Friday and Aloaf at her place at Lockeridge, near Marlborough, for the spring season, and very kindly said she would be able to drive me to the competitions and teach me. My objective was to be selected for the British team in the European Junior Event in September. Nineteen eighty-three would be my last year as a Junior—I had two good horses and with Annabel's help I should have a good chance. Before that, my aim was to be picked to ride at Windsor, which I had just missed the year before.

At home, I got the horses in and walked them for a month on the roads while they were woolly; at the beginning of February I clipped them and started to do a bit more work. I then attended a show jumping course given by Iris Kellet and John Hall; they come over from Ireland every year to give this course at the Catherstone Stud. Annabel was also on the course, and when it finished in the middle of February we returned to her place together. Her house was full, so I stayed with friends of hers in the village, the Ryans, who also had horses.

While I was there, looking after three horses on my own was quite hard work. I would start riding at eight every morning; by the time I had ridden one and led another for an hour and a half, and ridden the third for another hour and a half, then schooled each of them for half an hour it was gone one o'clock. The Scrimgeours are quite keen racing people, so we used to spend the afternoon watching the racing, when there was any, on television, and resume work in the stables at about four. They had quite a small yard of about ten boxes and there were other pupils as well as myself, but they did not have their own horses. I had a great time and learnt a lot.

When I was leading Piglet he would sometimes get loose and canter home, which was most alarming. Lockeridge is surrounded by country lanes but we had to cross one major road—luckily, each time he slipped the leading rein we were on the home side of it. There is excellent ground for cantering on the Marlborough Downs, with lots of hills; it is a really lovely place to work horses and keep them fit and a lot of racing yards have their gallops there.

I used to get my own breakfast at the Ryans before going to the yard, and come back at about 2pm when I usually made my own lunch. Having watched the racing I would do my horses, then go for a run: I felt that I should be fitter to keep my three going properly. Since then I have realised that it isn't necessary to do so much work to stay fit—I am probably growing lazier! Mrs Ryan would cook us a meal in the evening, put my washing in the machine and generally look after me as Mum would have done. When my birthday came round it was the first I had spent without Mum and I felt rather bereft, but the Ryans were lovely and gave me a dinner party.

Training was going well. I still found Aloaf big for me, but Annabel spent a lot of time helping and I felt that I was improving. We tried various bits because I found him so strong across country. I was invited to do some Junior's training with Gill Watson who lived near Oxford, so Annabel drove the lorry and I followed in her Subaru. Expecting to catch up with her in five minutes, I hadn't asked for detailed directions, and all I knew was that I had to go to the M4 at Newbury. When I reached the motorway I went onto it instead of under it, and found myself at Reading. I turned back and headed for Oxford; on the way I saw a signpost to Didcot, which was a place I knew, recalled other local names and at last found Aston Park. My lesson was due to start at 10am and I was twenty minutes late—Annabel had already tacked up my horse and put the other two in the stables, and I felt thoroughly embarrassed. It never happened again as Annabel gave me a road map for my birthday, which I still use.

'I began to appreciate the value of taking advice from several people and then figuring out for oneself what is best for the individual.'

This was the first time I had been on a course with Gill Watson; there were six other junior riders besides me, all with one or two horses. It lasted three days and we worked each horse both morning and afternoon, starting with flat work indoors, then jumping. At first I found it difficult to adapt to the way in which Gill was trying to help me, because it was different from my lessons under Annabel. I was too young to realise that even though Gill went about matters in a different way, the results were the same. To me, what Annabel said was gospel; I thought that Gill was trying to change my ways and resisted this, whereas she was in fact being helpful. I began to appreciate the value of taking advice from several people and then figuring out for oneself what is best for the individual horse.

We did a lot of jumping practice with Gill; this was highly enjoyable as Annabel's school was not really big enough, and was particularly good for Aloaf, always more difficult than the other two. Furthermore, the course was a marvellous opportunity to get to know the other junior riders—we were all living with various families and I stayed in the same house as Gill Young, who had ridden in the Juniors at Rotherfield the year before. She

had her own car, which was useful; some of the others had to walk quite a long way. Pupils usually lived in caravans or lorries, but it was too cold for that in February. We used to go to the pubs in the evening, where we became well acquainted with each other.

SPRING TRIALS 1983

As always, the season started in March at Crookham; I took Aloaf in the Novice which he won, despite having a fence down in the show jumping, and he was upgraded to Intermediate. Piglet went in the OI and was last in dressage, then knocked two fences down in the show jumping; although he went clear across country, he did a very slow round and nearly knocked my leg off on a tree from sheer excitement. Friday's first event was a Junior Novice trial at Tweseldown which she would have won, but as she was already Intermediate, we had to compete HC (hors concours, *ie* not in the competition).

'... I had no control because only one rein was effective. To continue could have been extremely dangerous ...'

I took Aloaf to Aldon for his last Novice, hoping to be placed again before he competed in an Intermediate. He did a good dressage and a clear show jumping, and started off sailing round the cross-country in fine style until I was approaching the coffin and asked him to turn right—he went straight on. I circled, feeling annoyed because he had not turned properly into it, and he popped over. I carried on, not foreseeing any further problems, but as I cantered him round a corner to a bounce fence and asked him to slow down, he didn't check at all and went straight into the first part of the bounce and jumped it as though it were an ordinary fence. Because he had not slowed, he landed so close to the second part that he could easily have fallen, but luckily he is very clever and saved us both by tucking up his forelegs quickly to get over the second rail.

Then I saw why he hadn't turned or checked when I asked him to: the leather cheek piece of the gag bit had broken and the head piece had slipped right round. The bit was held in his mouth by the nose band, but I had no control because only one rein was effective. To continue could have been extremely dangerous, so I decided to call it a day and went home.

A week later at Frensham Horse Trials in Surrey, things went better. I rode Friday in the Intermediate and Piglet in the Open Intermediate; they both did quite well in their dressage and gobbled up the cross-country with the result that Friday won her class and Piglet came third in his. And Annabel had a good ride on her Intermediate horse, Teddy, so it was a successful day for everyone.

This spring season of 1983 was going encouragingly. Aloaf made a good start in Intermediate classes, and he and Piglet were both placed in their Junior Open Intermediate trial and selected to do the Juniors at Windsor. As a competitor is not allowed to ride more than two horses at a three day event, Friday was picked to go to Kalmthout in Belgium where there was a Junior International competition; not a European Championship, but an important event just the same. So now they were all being prepared for three day events, and there was a lot more canter work to do at home.

Mum and Mike came home at the end of March from their sailing holiday in the Caribbean, but decided that as I was getting on so well at Annabel's it would be better for me to stay and compete with her help

than to return home. Another great advantage of being at Marlborough with horses to get fit was that the grassy downs were close by; it is much hillier than the countryside around King's Somborne.

My riding gradually improved under Annabel's influence. At the Pony Club Associates' camp the year before, and again now from the first day's training in her own centre, Annabel spent hours telling me to lighten the hand and use more leg; but it took me a long time to realise that the horses would not run away if I did this. In fact it seems that the more you give the rein, the less inclined they are to run away with you. For weeks Annabel kept reminding me to think forward, to give them freedom without dropping the contact, and for weeks I kept on expecting the horses to bolt. This was thoroughly repetitious for Annabel and must have been so tedious, but she is infinitely tactful and persevered until I found the courage and confidence to do what she said, and began to improve.

After a couple of Junior courses in the spring I was also making a lot of progress with Gill Watson, who was helping me a great deal with all three of the horses.

'For weeks Annabel kept reminding me to think forward, to give them freedom without dropping the contact …'

BRAMHAM 1983

That spring the weather was filthy. The Windsor three day event was cancelled because the ground was waterlogged, so the National Junior Championships were moved to Bramham the following week. I had taken all the horses home at the end of May, and Mum and Mike took me to Bramham with Aloaf and Piglet. It was very wet there, too, and on the morning of the briefing we were told that we would not be allowed to drive around the roads and tracks section, so we had to walk the whole fourteen kilometres. The next day they shortened it because so much of it was too wet, so we had tramped several miles to no purpose and were all pretty weary even before the event began. Nonetheless, both Piglet and Aloaf went well across country and Piglet was put on the short-list for the Junior Europeans.

From Bramham it was straight home to start getting Friday organised for Kalmthout three weeks later. Before going to Belgium I had another three-day course with Gill, together with Anne Loriston-Clarke as she was taking her mare, Wellingtonia, to Kalmthout as well. And I just had time to take Aloaf to Tweseldown to win his Novice regional final. I also took Friday in this event HC, and learned a sharp lesson that woke me up before the coming international. Because I wasn't competing, I just sat there at one easy fence, a single rail, and she stopped—it was typical of her not to bother to jump anything so trivial if I didn't actually ride her at it.

KALMTHOUT 1983

The day after Tweseldown, Anne Loriston-Clarke came to our house and we loaded the lorry for the Channel crossing, then Mum, Anne and I drove it to Folkestone where we were to meet the six other Juniors who were going; we also took Charlotte Ashby with her horse Papajo. We had thought there would be plenty of room with only three horses aboard a four-horse lorry, but when we had loaded hay, feed, tack, trunks and numerous other odds and ends into the one spare partition, the vehicle was packed to the roof even with most of the hay in the hay rack on top.

We spent a night in bunk beds at the race course and got up early to leave for Dover and the ferry. We were all worried about the horses having to travel in the lower hold, but we were allowed to see them whenever we wanted and they travelled well. It was hot down there and all they needed was a sweat rug, but we couldn't really tell how comfortable they were or how the heat was affecting them. The sea was calm, so at least we didn't have to worry about seasickness in either horses or riders.

I had been driving the lorry for quite a while, but Mum and Mike had decided that when we landed at Zeebrugge Annabel ought to drive, as I had never driven on the right. All of us competitors stayed at the same comfortable hotel, but the only transport we had from there to the show ground was a pickup truck we had brought to carry the feed and hay in, so for the first couple of days Gill or Annabel drove it while the rest of us packed into the back. But one evening the police stopped us and pointed out that only three passengers were allowed, which was a shame because traveiling like sardines and all together was quite fun. Kalmthout was also running a senior three day event in which Mark Phillips and Lizzy Purbrick were competing, which made it all the jollier with more competitors.

The course was on sandy terrain. The cross-country was quite wet and twisted in and out of the trees, different from anything at home and rather like a swamp, with attendant gnats and mosquitoes whose bites none of us escaped. Dressage on the sand arena was a new experience, too, and Friday didn't do very well, but she was the only one to go clear and inside the limit on the cross-country, so we finished fifth.

Kalmthout marked the end of the spring season, and when we returned the horses had their summer break. I had enjoyed meeting the foreign competitors and hoped to be competing abroad again in the near future. Friday and Piggy were short-listed for the Juniors, for which the final trials were at Dauntsey in August. After they had had their summer break I brought them back in and started getting them fit, and when Dauntsey finally came round, Friday won and Piglet was placed. This meant that Friday and I had indeed qualified for a place in the team and would do the Junior European three day event in Rome.

The next event was at Locko: Aloaf had qualified for the Novice Championships, and Piglet for the Open. Aloaf came third, but although Piglet had a clear round he was not placed. Aloaf also won the Pony Club Area Trials, in which I have always tried to do well.

THE AUTUMN SEASON: ROME 1983

Riding for your country is a great honour and challenge, and can bring enormous fun, too. It is a wonderful experience to travel abroad and meet new friends, to build up through training and competition a firm partnership with your horse and team-mates—and if anything can develop those qualities of loyalty, trust and courage, it is surely our international sport.

Six of us had been selected to go to Rome to form a team of four, and two individuals: Helen Brown, Jamie Search, Anne Loriston-Clarke, Susannah Macaire, Sarah Williams and I. We had quite a selection of horses: Helen's was a stallion, Anne and I had mares and the other three were geldings. After a few more Gill Watson courses during the summer I

'It is a wonderful experience to travel abroad and meet new friends, to build up through training and competition a firm partnership with your horse and team mates—and if anything can develop those qualities of loyalty, trust and courage, it is surely international sport.'

The dressage phase at the Junior Championships in Rome 1983—Friday finding more interesting things than my aids to concentrate on

'As we stepped out of the aeroplane at Rome airport the heat struck us like a hammer ...'

was beginning to get a better test out of Friday, and hoped the results would be seen in the coming week.

A huge racing lorry from Lambourn took four horses and Jamie Search's lorry took two. It was going to be a four-day journey for them by road, so the riders were to fly out later, which would be less tiring. We saw them off at three o'clock on a Tuesday morning, and we all met again at Heathrow early the next Sunday.

As we stepped out of the aeroplane at Rome airport the heat struck us like a hammer and we wondered at once how the horses were taking it. At home the weather was still cool—here it was twenty-five degrees already. Annabel, Gill and Mr Search met us and Mr Search drove us straight to the place where the event was being held. This was quite high in the mountains and as we climbed the air grew cooler, to our relief; but it was still a lot warmer than in England, despite the breeze. We were delighted to find that the horses were in air-conditioned stables and very comfortable. They had travelled well, so we left them for a while with easy minds while we settled into the hotel where the French team was also staying. Gill, Annabel and Bob were with us but all the supporters were in another one.

After unpacking we returned to the stables and led the horses out to grass for half an hour. The surroundings were beautiful and the facilities amazing. Besides the excellent stabling there were indoor and outdoor schools, lunging and jumping arenas and, of course, the glorious countryside in which to ride. At that altitude there was more rain than in the plains, so there was lots of grass and the ground was soft. We half-regretted missing the road journey which had been through some spectacular scenery, particularly amid the Swiss mountains. It hadn't been entirely a pleasure trip for the drivers and passengers, however. The formalities at each frontier crossing had been lengthy and tedious, and four and a half days in cramped conditions had been tiring; the three grooms therefore needed a rest, so they had the afternoon off while we groomed the horses.

There were twelve British staying at the same hotel, so we all had supper together before turning in for an early night. Unfortunately the next morning began with a mishap, for Jamie's horse had cut itself in its loose box and he would be unable to ride it for the next two days.

On Tuesday the event organisers arranged a sight-seeing tour of Rome, giving each team a minibus. Gill drove ours; we were the last in the convoy, and when we stopped for diesel we became separated from the rest. Totally lost, we strayed about the centre of the city without seeing any sign of them, so decided to do our own tour. When we reached St Peter's we bumped into the Dutch team and were reunited with the whole party. Having seen as many of Rome's abundance of marvels as could be crammed into a few hours, we went to the polo ground to swim, have supper and socialise with the other teams. We had dressed up for supper, but afterwards the Italians decided to throw everyone else into the pool—so we chucked them in as well, and everybody went home wet but all the better acquainted with one another.

Next morning the briefing for the roads and tracks and the steeplechase was held, and we walked round the whole cross-country course. Our first walk was as a team. It seemed colossal, with several long combinations of banks and steps, road crossings and coffins. The quick way over the difficult water complex was a bounce onto a footbridge and over rails into

water. We all opted to go the long way. The only competitors who took the short cut were the Italians, which made one wonder whether they had seen the course before. Fence three came as a shock to us: it was a brush parallel in a dip, landing on rising ground. It was a monstrous fence, and most of us took the long route. Right at the end there was a pretty demanding drop fence into a quarry; it consisted of a plain sleeper drop, and a bounce out over some slanting rails, to land many feet below with the ground falling rapidly away from you.

No Junior course could have been bigger—it incorporated several of the 1960 Olympic fences, and having set off in good spirits, by the end of the walk we were all rather silent. However, we had no time to brood. The vets' inspection was at 4pm and all the British horses passed. When the team was picked, Jamie's horse was left out because it had not been ridden for a couple of days, so the team was Helen, Sarah, Susannah and, me to run last. Next came the draw for those who were to do dressage the next day, and after all this we did some dressage practice with Gill. This went on so late that we had supper at the camp, as we called it, instead of the hotel. The only drink available was water, or wine in cartons and we ended up with a great water and wine fight. Meanwhile Mum, Mike and David had arrived to spend the rest of the week.

'No Junior course could have been bigger—it incorporated several of the 1960 Olympic fences ...'

On Thursday I watched all the Brits and some of the others doing their dressage, and worked Friday. I walked the course again and it looked a little less daunting. In the evening there was a reception at Rocca di Papa, the local town, which we all had to attend and where Gill was presented with a plaque, a memento for her rôle as chef d'équipe. Helen and I were so tired we fell asleep in the restaurant.

Next day it rained hard all morning. I rode Friday, and Caroline Reed, who was grooming for me, plaited and bathed her and got her ready for the dressage, which was held in the afternoon. Friday gave her normal performance, head in the air and looking about; but she actually did her halts without moving and we were quite pleased—but she still had a long way to go before she would be any good at dressage. After this discipline she was then wanted for dope testing. I couldn't understand why, for I always thought they would pick a horse that had put up a really smart show; and it should have been obvious that I had not given Friday anything to calm her, because her behaviour was far from that. I had to wait half an hour for her to produce a urine sample, and only then could we put her to bed. We all walked the course again that evening—in pouring rain, and then talked it over with Gill, planning the times for each section and our tactics.

ROME 1983: CROSS-COUNTRY DAY

On Saturday morning we loaded up everything we would need in the ten-minute halt box: spare bridles and saddles, shoes, sponges, buckets, veterinary equipment. Helped by Audrey Ann Lockett and Mrs Rook, we took all this gear to the course early to bag a corner before anyone else.

Going last on cross-country day, watching everyone else and seeing all that can go wrong, is always an ordeal, but the track did seem to be riding well. Susannah, the first of our team to run, did a good round on the comparatively inexperienced Latin Tempo, and so did Sarah, which was encouraging for the rest of us; Anne had a fall in the water, but completed

the course. By the time I had to bandage Friday and get her ready I was thoroughly anxious, but as always, as soon as we got started and I had something to occupy me, I steadied down.

We took Phase A in a relaxed mood, admiring the view as we trotted along, looking at the watch to check that we came to each marker at the right time. Then the steeplechase, which had been riding easily enough. The fences were all quite different, all permanent, and there was even a triple bar with white rails, and stone walls and open ditches. The hedges were privet and rooted in the ground, not the customary portable brush fences, and were more box-shaped, and the ditches were all on the take-off side. Two Irish horses fell because they mistook the hefty fences for banks—a familiar feature to all hunters or steeplechasers in Ireland—and leaped onto them instead of over, and crashed through. Friday went well, but I was trying too hard to finish at precisely the right time and took matters a trifle too slowly, incurring 4.8 time faults.

It was a humid day, so as soon as I had finished, I was given some ice to hold between Friday's ears while I walked her on Phase C. The roads and tracks went up a steep hill, which was punishing in that temperature.

Waiting in the ten-minute halt box before starting the cross-country, I learned from Gill how the course was riding—our team was in the lead and couldn't be beaten, so my score didn't matter. So with the pressure off and knowing that the others had done well, I expected no problems. This attitude was disastrous: too relaxed about what I was doing, I had a stop at the quarry drop because I was not riding determinedly enough—as a rule I attack a course with vigour, and had I been under pressure I would probably have gone clear. It taught me that essential lesson, which is never to just expect a horse to jump when you know that the jump is easy, but always to ride as though it were difficult. I was so angry with myself—poor Gill: after all the work she had put in, I had made a stupid mistake that was no fault of Friday's but all mine. I was in such a bad mood that I couldn't talk to anyone the whole evening. Poor Jamie was having a much worse time than I. He'd had a bad fall on the cross-country and, on finishing the course, wasn't feeling too good. He was taken to hospital and kept in overnight. Luckily he was discharged the next morning in time to ride in the show jumping. Helen had gone into the lead individually and the team was lying first, which made up for my lapse; and at least Friday was fit and well.

'… with the pressure off … I expected no problems. This attitude was disastrous …'

There was a party that night in the hotel, with a singing competition in which each team had to stand on the platform and sing a song traditional to its country. The Irish won. We were sent to bed at midnight to get a good sleep before another early start, but the party went on and kept us awake—Susannah and I sat on the balcony outside our room and felt we might just as well have stayed.

ROME: SHOW JUMPING DAY

When we walked the horses out next morning they all seemed in fine fettle and passed the vets' inspection. At 11am we had to go to Mass, an unusual experience, where we all prayed for the team to win the competition and Helen the individual. The show jumping course wasn't big, but still had to be jumped clear; this all the Brits managed to do, so our prayers

were answered with both the team and individual championships. The prize-giving was an impressive ceremony, especially as standing on the rostrum was something new for us all.

Bob hadn't had much veterinary work to do, but during the prize-giving I put some business his way because Latin Tempo bit Friday on the tip of her nose, which needed two or three stitches. Friday has been sensitive about her nose ever since, and doesn't like to be touched there by even so much as a light finger.

After all the formalities, the water fight that erupts after most championships broke out. All over the stable yard people were dousing each other with hoses and buckets until everyone was drenched. No official parties had been arranged for that evening, so all the teams got together at our hotel and staged an impromptu one. This time it did not matter how late we went to bed.

'All over the stable yard people were dousing each other with hoses and buckets until everyone was drenched.'

Monday morning is always an anticlimax after a three day event. We went to the stables to pack the lorries and walk the horses out, Friday with a swollen nose but otherwise in good shape. Saying goodbye to all our new friends was, as always, a little sad, but we set off to catch our lunchtime flight in high spirits nonetheless and the glow of victory.

Next morning, it was straight back into routine. The Young Rider Europeans were held at Burghley shortly after, so I went to help Gill with the British squad; they won the team gold and Karen Straker and Polly Schwert won individual silver and bronze: a great result for Gill and the selectors. Aloaf was finishing the season with an Intermediate class or two and Piglet was to end his by doing Wylye CCI which was always held at the end of September/beginning of October.

WYLYE CCI 1983

Wylye was my first senior international three day event, and Mummy, Mike, David and a friend, Helen, were helping. Piglet and I came half-way down in the dressage. We were fifth to go in the cross-country—it would be the biggest course I had ever done, and made all the more testing by the Wylye hills. I had to carry 2½ stone of lead and it took three of us to get the weight cloth onto poor Piggy; he had to carry this extra weight from the start of the roads and tracks to the finish of the cross-country, all of which took over an hour—but he is an amazing horse and didn't worry about it at all. The steeplechase was the worst part. I was tense, and Piggy was so full of himself that for the first time he frightened me by the way he took off. But after he had made a mistake at one fence he settled down.

When we went to the start of the cross-country course, although he had quietened somewhat after the steeplechase, he was full of beans again; it was drizzling, but the going was good. The time in the ten-minute box seemed to pass in a flash. I was nervous, and had only had time to go to the loo quickly, and run through the course in my head, which fence was where and how I should ride it. Then all of a sudden Piglet had been washed off, greased and we were on our way round a really big track. We were one of the first to go so nobody knew how the course was riding, but Piglet always attacks his courses; this year everybody was worried about the pigsty combination, where the quick way entailed two corners with two strides between, at a difficult angle. Piggy was going so well that I

David, Piggy and me waiting anxiously in the 1983 Wylye CCI Steeplechase start box

'I was so elated that I couldn't stop talking for half an hour, giving a fence-by-fence description of how each obstacle had jumped and how brilliantly Piglet had coped.'

decided we would go for it. I thought I had the angle and pace right, and he seemed to be concentrating, so I took it on and he was a star. He jumped it perfectly, one of only six horses that managed to do so.

That safely behind us, we went down to the water which was also difficult, and again Piglet found it no problem. In the bottom of the valley there was a massive jump called the Bow Parallel with an enormous ditch underneath it, which I thought the biggest fence I had ever seen. This had worried me, but Piglet took it in his stride; it turned out to be a real rider fence, looking much worse than it was. Piggy was just beginning to tire up the last hill, but stormed on to finish within the time and there were not many others that did so.

It is the most wonderful feeling when you have finished a course like that, had such a great ride and the horse is looking good. I was so elated that I couldn't stop talking for half an hour, giving a fence-by-fence description of how each obstacle had jumped and how brilliantly Piglet had coped. Thankfully I made the required 11st 11lb when I weighed out—what a tragedy it would have been if I hadn't, after all his brilliance and lugging that heavy load around for over an hour. He was washed down, walked round, settled and bandaged up so that he would be warm in the evening. As I had gone round so early, we had the rest of the day to watch everybody else and were delighted that Piggy stayed well up the order in seventh place.

The show jumping was causing me some anxiety. He has never been outstanding at it, mostly because he likes to go as fast as he does on a cross-country. He likes to feel his fences, so never clears them by very much; it was no surprise when he had two poles down. We finished ninth, which I was delighted about because at this, our first CCI, I had qualified for next year's Locko Open Championships and for Badminton. Looking forward to my first Badminton would brighten the autumn and winter.

THE WINTER MONTHS 1983

With the season over and Aloaf, Friday and Piglet all on holiday, I had only one novice horse and a few of Mum's ponies to ride. We occupied the spare time by scrubbing out and painting the stables and painting the jumps, and out of boredom I used to ride poor Alight morning and afternoon, which meant a great deal of work for her but I'm sure it did her a lot of good!

I didn't have a horse to take hunting that winter, so took up beagling in Dorset. The meets are at noon, a civilised time that allows you an hour longer in bed than when fox- or staghunting; nor is there a muddy horse to clean up, only oneself in the bath. Beagling certainly helped my fitness but I did rip a few pairs of trousers in the process, jumping fences. Hares run in circles, so in fact you need do no more than stand coolly on a hill and watch them—at first I tried to follow the same line as the beagles and therefore ran many unnecessary miles; eventually the light dawned, and I let the pack go belting round me while I stood still. But it's really more fun to run after hounds than to be clever and take it easy.

Looking back over the year, there had certainly been some exciting challenges. With all the horses sound and healthy, as far as we could see, there seemed no reason why 1984 shouldn't bring its share of success, too.

Arduous top-level three day eventing involves the careful preparation of every detail, but even then success lies to a certain extent in the lap of the gods—the horse may go lame or have an 'off' day, or the weather may be too bad and the event cancelled. However, if everything goes according to plan, if you finish a really big track and have had a great ride, and the horse is looking good, it is the most wonderful feeling. And if the horse is home-bred like Friday and Aloaf, the satisfaction is even greater. Quite apart from the actual competing, to have this partnership with your horse recognised and confirmed at international level really is a thrill. And I was lucky enough to have three horses at this level!

In the new year, 1984, I gave up the sports centre and took on a part-time job in Stockbridge, which is near home and meant I could get to bed earlier. I was not a particularly skilful waitress. I took great pains trying to do everything right, and in the worry of getting it right I used to get everything wrong. Either I would take a meal to the wrong table, serve from the wrong side or give the wrong knife or fork. On a couple of occasions when I got really flustered, I spilled food on somebody's lap—I just couldn't cope and it was deeply embarrassing. By March, I felt I was not getting enough sleep to do the horses justice, so I gave it up; and with it, my pocket money.

8 «» Flying the British Flag

Piglet, Friday and Aloaf had all come in and were about to start walking. The spring season got off to a good start, even though my preparations for Badminton were not what they should have been. Piglet ran very well in the OI at Crookham and at Brigstock Advanced, but the Frensham Advanced event was cancelled after the show jumping because the place was waterlogged; so he had only one Advanced run before he went to Badminton. Friday and Aloaf were going to Belton to do the Young Rider Advanced trials, which would be their first at that level.

'Arduous two-level three day eventing involves the careful preparation of every detail ...'

BELTON 1984

I was a little nervous before the Belton cross-country; but then, I always worried about Friday every time she moved up to a higher class and a bigger course, wondering if she could do it. She would try so hard, but I would have felt most remorseful if I had found I was forcing her to try to jump fences that were really too big for her. I felt the same about Aloaf and his first Advanced: I was not really sure if he was ready for it. But there was no need for me to have worried, as Friday went excellently and finished second. Aloaf and I had steering problems: we by-passed a bullfinch and I fell off him. Mike caught him—it is very odd that Mike always seems to be standing at the fences where I fall off. I worked out that it was my first fall in competition for about three years, and as it was two days before Bad-

minton, I thought this must be a lucky omen: I shouldn't be due for another fall for a long time yet. I went to Badminton therefore with a most confident attitude; furthermore, I had made all the right preparations for these two events, and had been to Gill several times on a special course with other young riders who were bound for Badminton.

I have already described Piglet's and my progress round Badminton (p. 12); suffice it to say again that Badminton's challenge will always be unique, and those silver horses awarded to the first twelve will always be valued above every other trophy.

BRAMHAM 1984

Piglet then went out, on his holiday, which left me plenty of time to concentrate on preparing Friday and Aloaf for the Young Rider National Championships at Bramham, for which both had been selected: their first Advanced three day event. They had done only two Advanced tracks and the Bramham cross-country course was a big one, but they were ready for it: and proved it beyond any doubt by both doing double clears. On Aloaf, however, I made a mess in the steeplechase. Having made the time easily on the first circuit, I imagined that my second circuit would automatically be a bit faster because it hadn't got the standing start, so I didn't push him. I got rather close to several fences, and he is a horse that jumps big; so when he doesn't stand back he takes longer, and I ended up by having eight time faults. On the cross-country I had nine time faults, which left him in tenth place overall. Friday finished second, only one point behind Tanya Longson on Pink Fizz. With that result, Piglet, Friday and Aloaf all made the short-list for the Young Rider European Championships to be held in September at Luhmühlen, Germany. Friday and Aloaf had their holiday now.

'Piglet, Friday and Aloaf all made the short-list for the Young Rider European Championships to be held in Luhmühlen, Germany.'

SUMMER 1984

At the beginning of June I got all three horses back into work. Richard Walker had warned me at Badminton that I should be careful about Piglet; he had gone so well there but might have frightened himself, and Richard suggested I should do a Novice quietly with him to make sure he had recovered his confidence, before another Advanced. I entered him HC for the Novice at Rogate. When it came to the cross-country, he was so disgusted by the tiny fences that we had a stop and I fell off at a small combination—it was *so* small he didn't know where to put his feet; then he galloped off in the opposite direction, and it took a long time to catch him and finish the course. So it hadn't been such a bright idea to do a Novice event after all, and it was lucky that I suffered only bruises because I had not taken a co-driver. As a rule either Mike or Mum or some other responsible person accompanies me in case I have an accident that prevents me from driving home.

BSJA SHOW JUMPING

In May I had registered the horses for the first time with the British Show Jumping Association (BSJA). I had never jumped them under rules, so

entered Friday in a Young Rider's class at the Larkhill show that month, and the others for the Foxhunter and the Newcomer classes. The Young Rider event followed the Foxhunter and when I walked the course the fences (once again) took me aback by their size. They were 4ft 3in on the first round, compared with 3ft 11in in Advanced horse trials, and Friday hadn't yet jumped anything of that height, but she gave a good performance and went clear. She is always a fast jumper, too, so in the jump off, in which I went first, I didn't really worry about how quickly she went—and she not only had another clear round but also won the class, which was a great shock to all the show jumpers among the Young Riders.

This was a Vauxhall competition, which is a big event in the Christmas show at Olympia; you get points for winning Vauxhall classes, which the keen show jumping fraternity all travel the country striving to do. At this one, the success of a rider unknown in the show jumping world, on a skewbald mare that had no great reputation either, rather annoyed the show jumping specialists.

'... the success of a rider unknown in the show jumping world, on a skewbald mare that had no great reputation either, rather annoyed the show jumping specialists.'

After that I thought Friday and I might qualify for the show jumping at Olympia, so did some more Vauxhalls. She was placed in a few, but I tended to go too fast and have a fence down. We got fairly close, but didn't quite qualify; but trying was fun.

AUTUMN TRIALS 1984

Friday did it again: at her first event in the autumn she stopped at the water. I was not sure whether or not it was my fault, because she always does this at the beginning of the autumn season. When we next went to Gill's we did a school at the water at Aston Park, after which she won her next event.

Friday had been picked as one of the six to take part in the European Championships at Luhmühlen, so we went to Molland horse trials for our last run before this and she won the Advanced. Being chosen for the Young Riders meant that Friday was debarred from the Open Championship at Locko, so I took only Aloaf and Piglet. Aloaf came fourth and Piglet eighth, so it looked as if Aloaf was now right on target to go to Burghley. Rather than ride two there, I thought I would take Piglet to the Dutch Championships at Boekelo at the end of October.

LUHMÜHLEN 1984: FRIDAY FOX

At last the time had come round to get started for the Luhmühlen Championships. Tanya Longson, who had been on the short-list for the Europeans after winning Bramham, had sadly broken her wrist in a fall and was therefore unable to go. So besides myself there would be Polly Schwert on Dylan, who had gone well at Badminton; Ginny Strawson, who was Young Rider champion two years before, on Sparrowhawk; Philippa Magill on Headly Gladiator, another good performer at Bramham; Jonquil Sainsbury on Hassan; and Mandy Orchard on Coeur de Lion. We had a Young Rider course all together with Gill, who was off to Poland for a week where the Junior European Championships were being held, and who would meet us at Luhmühlen. Lorna Clarke, with her horse Glentrool, was accompanying us to compete in the senior event, a CCI.

'... People stared at the odd sight of a row of girls sharing a magazine, and three horseboxes parked for no apparent reason.'

We had a twenty-four-hour ferry crossing from Harwich to Hamburg ahead of us. Polly Schwert was driving her lorry from Devon and had to pass my door, so picked me up. However, Friday never travels well in strange lorries, and we had not been long on our way when catastrophic noises behind us suggested we would be wise to stop. Friday had pushed so hard against the metal sheeting at the back of the lorry that she had broken it. We mended it as well as we could and pressed on, until the next mishap; this time it was Lorna's lorry that had stopped at the roadside. It was Polly driving, her groom—Lorna was flying out later—but someone had already gone to fetch help, so we waited to keep Polly company and find out what had gone wrong. Philippa Magill and Mandy Orchard, sharing a lorry, drove up shortly after and joined us. I remember it was a Friday, the day *Horse and Hound* used to come out, so we sat at the side of the road reading it, while closely packed traffic streamed past and people stared at this odd sight of a row of girls sharing a magazine, and three horseboxes parked for no apparent reason. Finally someone turned up from a garage and diagnosed clutch failure.

As Friday was travelling so badly, we decided that Polly and I had better carry on with her and Dylan so that we need not drive fast, while Philippa, Mandy and Polly waited with Lorna's horse. At the stables near Harwich we found Jamie Mackie, our chef d'équipe, in a bit of a flap because only Jonquil and Ginny had arrived; and their horsebox had returned home. We settled the horses in and waited for Mandy and Philippa. Hours passed. When eventually they appeared, we learned that two of their tyres had been punctured and had had to be repaired. Polly with Lorna's lorry didn't arrive till midnight. Three lorries were going to have to share all the horses between them: four in Lorna's, and two each in Polly Schwert's and Philippa's. It was as well that we had arranged to meet the night before and not at the docks on the morning of our departure, or we would never have made the ferry in time.

Before boarding the ferry we transferred Friday to Lorna's lorry, hoping she would travel better there. Knowing that she disliked facing forwards, we put her in the partition that faced backwards, but she was still restless and by the end of the voyage had rubbed her tail raw. She is a typical mare and can be horribly fussy.

After Belgium the year before, I was beginning to know how horses feel aboard ship—they don't eat much and they feel the heat down in the hold—and how to look after them. All the shipboard noises—iron doors slamming, the throb of the engines, the rush and hiss of the sea against the hull—disturb them and it takes a long while for them to settle down. Someone has to be with them at all times, and at least one person sleeps in each lorry. By the time we reached Luhmühlen the horses would have spent thirty-six hours in the lorry. Actually, travel by sea is easier in one respect on horses than by road, because there are no bends or sharp corners, and no steep gradients to upset their balance; though obviously if it is rough they have to find their sea legs like the rest of us.

The ship was super, with every facility, and the restaurant was set right for'ard, with a fine view. There were fifteen of us, six in the team, Lorna, Polly, the grooms and Chris Schofield, chairman of the Young Riders selectors. By lunch-time the sea had become very rough, and one by one the diners disappeared until only four of us were left; we were rather

enjoying the heavy weather and the dramatic lashing of spray against the windows. The higher you are above the water, the greater the movement, so the horses were, in that regard, better placed than.ourselves.

AT LUHMÜHLEN

It was calm when we docked on Sunday morning and we were quickly ashore and through Customs. At Luhmühlen the facilities were excellent. The only slight problem we had was persuading the horses to enter their boxes, for there was a step down which puzzled them. They had a good wander around, led in hand, to stretch their legs and we did no work with them that day. The poor grooms had been given tents to sleep in, on iron beds, and when it rained the beds cut through the canvas which leaked; so they moved into the lorries. The riders stayed in hotels; we and the Italians were in the same one, fifteen minutes' drive from the stables, so the event provided us with a minibus and a driver for our trips back and forth from the stables.

Gill arrived that night by air from Poland, where the Juniors had won a team silver and an individual silver. On Monday the horses were tired, so we just hacked them round and did a bit of flat work. There was an Olympic-size swimming pool down the road where we spent most of our spare time; the weather that week alternated between considerable heat and heavy rain storms. I knew many of the riders who, like me, had come up from Juniors the year before, and it was fun to be in familiar company. Irish, French, Danish, German and Dutch teams were competing as well as the Italians and ourselves; and for the first time, Russians and Poles.

'The poor grooms had been given tents to sleep in, on iron beds, and when it rained the beds cut through the canvas which leaked ...'

For the first two days we were confined to the training area, so it wasn't until Wednesday when we were briefed that we were at last able to see the course. The World Championships had been held here two years previously and some of the existing fences had been built for that occasion. The steeplechase was a figure of eight and quite difficult to memorise, with permanent fences as in Rome—one was open water, and the hedges were all privet on top of banks, but narrower than in Rome. For both the cross-country and the roads and tracks the going was sandy and partly wooded, but mostly flat.

The course was designed so that after the first five fences which were plain and big, there were several combinations and clusters of fences, with long gallops in between. There were two amazing water complexes; the sixth fence was water and its size gave us all something of a fright. We would have to go over a rail, take one stride, then into water, a short stride, then out over another rail across an island, over a boathouse into water again. It provoked a lot of discussion. Coming out of the water there was one stride to some big upright white rails, followed five strides on by a big open hedge with a ditch in front.

After a long gallop the next fence was another involved combination of steps up and down, followed by a coffin, a plain fence and a farmyard complex. At the end of the course there was another water complex with a jump over a log into the water and a footbridge that had to be jumped in the middle by cantering through the water—it was these water complexes that inspired Mike to build something similar on our course at King's Somborne. Finally there was a plain bar fence with a roof over it.

Half-way round the course-walk, Polly Schwert and I got well ahead of the others. At some events there is a tradition that, when walking a course after the briefing, one stops for a drink about three-quarters of the way round. Here we were offered schnapps which is notoriously strong, and after that the last five fences did not seem to present much of a problem. After the very last fence there was beer and soft drinks, and by the time we had all got back to the stables, nobody felt daunted by any of the fences at all! But the alcohol soon wore off, and then there was certainly a lot to think about on that course.

We had a quick swim to cool off and made ready for the vets' inspection, which all our horses passed. Next, the team was picked: Mandy Orchard to run first on Coeur de Lion, followed by Polly on Dylan, myself on Friday and Jonquil on Hassan. I had asked Gill not to send me last, as I wanted to be under a bit more pressure on account of what had happened at Rome. Ginny and Philippa were the individuals. We were still not allowed up to the show-ground until Thursday morning, which was a little unfair to the horses that had to do their dressage on that day—the dressage arena was next to the ten-minute halt box and the start and finish of the cross-country, with all its flags and stands, and they would not have had a chance to get used to it all. Luckily the atmosphere was calm.

Friday and me extending in the dressage at Luhmühlen Young Riders European Championships 1984

LUHMÜHLEN 1984: THE COMPETITION

It was more electric on the next day, when there were more people watching. Friday and I had a moment of awful uncertainty when we started our dressage: we had to canter in, and as we turned to do so we were facing one of the steeplechase fences, which made Friday prick her ears, wondering what was going on. She just managed to calm down before we entered the arena, where she did well. At the end of the two days' dressage the British team was in the lead with the Germans and French close behind. Mum and Mike came out again to give me their usual great support.

Friday evening is always a busy time, organising everything for the cross-country. First we had our discussion with Gill, to find out where we were each going to jump every fence, so that the fence spotters—friends and supporters, one at each complicated fence—knew where we should be coming from, and what line we should be taking, so they knew what sort of report we would want from them. They were given small diagrams of the fences on which they could actually draw the lines taken by other horses when they jumped through. Runners would bring these to us in the ten-minute box so that we would have as much information as possible about how the course was riding. This is standard procedure—it does not help the first couple to go, but is most useful to all who follow.

A high state of expectation built up as we decided who was going to spot and who was going to run …'

A high state of expectation built up as we decided who was going to spot and who was going to run, exchanged views about how we were going to tackle the obstacles and how the horses were feeling after their gallop and a practice jump, until we were all keyed up for the morrow. Mark Mingo had arrived as an extra helper and slept in the stables that night to make sure that all the horses slept well and did not come to any harm.

LUHMÜHLEN: CROSS-COUNTRY DAY

Early on Saturday morning some of us went for a final walk round the course, to see how the overnight rain had affected the going. There seemed to be an improvement, as rain hardens sand and the horses don't sink so deeply into it. The ten-minute halt box was a longish way from the stables, so we had to install all our necessary gear there during the morning. But there was still a lot of time left for that hollow-tummy feeling of anxiety! As the third team member to go, my wait would be a long one.

I watched the first few competitors on the steeplechase and saw them ride some of the cross-country before it was time to go and get Friday and myself ready. Philippa Magill on Headly Gladiator was the first of the Brits to go, riding as an individual. She had a good clear with only a couple of time faults. Mandy was running first for our team and had a fall at the water, where her horse hurt a knee; Polly had a clear round but incurred quite a lot of time faults—I didn't learn that, however, until I was in the ten-minute box, when Gill put me in the picture. The course was causing rather a lot of trouble and nobody had finished the cross-country inside the time, but Polly's good round gave us considerable confidence.

Before I set off again on Phase D, Jamie Mackie told me that we needed a clear, inside the time. This really upset Mum, who said I always went fast anyway—she was worried lest I hurt myself. I didn't take much notice: I just knew we had to go clear, and that was that. Friday ran wonderfully.

'… my watch had stopped … I didn't know what sort of time I was doing.'

We were stopped at the last water as there was a hold-up on the course—and my watch had stopped, too, so I didn't know what sort of time I was doing. But Friday seemed full of running, so when I was restarted I urged her on faster, for we were only about half a minute from home. In fact we were already well up on the clock, and finished with nearly half a minute to spare. Only one other rider finished inside the time.

Had my watch been working I would not have ridden such a hard finish, but Friday seemed as fit as a fiddle and altogether this result gave the team and Gill a good boost. Friday went back to the stables while I waited in the ten-minute box for Jonquil. She was given the same instructions: to go clear and as fast as she could. She rode a super round with only 0.4 of a time fault, and this put our team in the lead. Only the three best scores counted, of course. We all celebrated rather well that night, especially as Jonquil was leading individually, I was third and Philippa sixth. Ginny on Sparrowhawk had had one silly stop on the cross-country and a few time faults, but was not badly placed either.

Friday flies into the water for the second time in fifty yards and looks much happier about it than do!

LUHMÜHLEN: SHOW JUMPING DAY

The show jumping course was quite different from any British event course; it was more like Hickstead. There were natural banks and water ditches with rails over the top, and a lot of rails were used which made the fences look bigger than they were; and the arena was large, with lots of jumps. However, Friday is a very good show jumper, so I was not worried. As this discipline was run in reverse order, I was one of the last to go.

At one day events Friday always used to be rather full of herself and sometimes very bossy in the show jumping, yanking at me and wanting to get on with it. At Luhmühlen I worked her until she was taking the jump as I wanted her to, not carting me into it or messing about, and this was a mistake—although she jumped very well, she lacked sparkle and touched one rail, which rolled off. That was most unlike her, and it occurred to me, too late, that having just done the speed and endurance test of a three day event, she was probably tired, and I should have taken her into the ring feeling a lot fresher.

But for that one fence down, we would have won individually. Hassan had four fences down, so poor Jonquil dropped from first to seventh place, but this made no difference to the team result as Polly had jumped well: we were the winners. A clear round by Philippa moved her up into second and I finished third. Mandy borrowed one of the Irish horses for the prize-giving, as hers was lame. Back at the stables there was a party with plenty of champagne and all the supporters and helpers and the other teams joining in.

There was a party in the stableyard that evening, during which we decided it would be great to have a Union Jack. Mark Mingo, two of the Irish riders and I borrowed the Land Rover and went to the showground where we found that only the blue Mercedes flags had been left, about eight of them, stapled to the flagpoles. We couldn't climb these, so we felled a couple and thus could take the flags back with us: totally out of order, but that was how we felt at the time.

BURGHLEY 1984: ALOAF

The next day I had to rush off with Mum and Mike to catch a flight to England, as I was riding Aloaf at Burghley the following week—Annabel Scrimgeour had had him while I was away. Mary, my groom, stayed at home looking after Piglet who was going to Boekelo later in the autumn. After the usual rigmarole of the vet's inspection and the passport check, Aloaf had a leg stretch before I stabled him and we both had lunch. Then I rode him to the collecting ring and round the park to get him used to the area; we did a little flat work, I let him graze and, later, put him to bed.

Early on Wednesday we attended the briefing and walked the formidable cross-country course. Aloaf had gone so well at Locko, I thought this big track was within his scope, but he had never seen such large crowds and there were other novelties that would also excite him. All the top riders had returned from the Olympics and were to ride their second horses, so the whole competition was specially awesome—it quickly brought me back down to earth after our win the week before. Gill, who had come to help Mandy, myself and a few others, gave me a dressage lesson that afternoon. Andreas von Imhoff, a German young rider whom I had met in Rome and at Luhmühlen, was also over for the week—his horse was on holiday, but he wanted to practise his English so was staying with us for a couple of weeks; and Mum and Mike arrived with the caravan that evening—such extra support gave me confidence. I had some more dressage coaching that evening to prepare me for next morning's test.

On Thursday, after I had plaited Aloaf and generally made him ready, I rode him for a while under Gill's eye; then up to the working-in area twenty minutes before I was due in the ring, where Gill was most expert in getting me to calm down and concentrate on the right things so that I did not upset Aloaf. He finds crowds disconcerting, so I wondered what on earth would happen today and feared he would not concentrate. Sure enough, he started to go backwards and had to be led into the arena; but as soon as we got to the white boards he realised we were about to enter a dressage arena, put his head down and behaved happily because he knew what was expected of him. We were all pleased with the dressage test he produced, and at the end of this phase he was lying about twentieth. He was only eight years old and still rather green at Advanced level.

Burghley 1984—Aloaf concentrating while he reins back during his test

Anxious moments before the cross-country, with Mike and Jo ready to give assistance

BURGHLEY 1984: CROSS-COUNTRY DAY

I had a day and a half to walk the cross-country and steeplechase course again and get everything just right. By Saturday morning I was fully confident about where I would be going over all the fences, except the second last, the brandy glass. This fence was difficult: the central route was a bounce with two parallels, which seemed very big at the end of the course if a horse was tired; or there was a set of two angled rails to a corner which needed very accurate riding, but I thought it was a nice line. The alternative was to go into the brandy glass, turn and jump out over a rail, turn sharp left—trying to stay inside the penalty zone—and then jump a corner. When I looked at this fence again on Saturday morning I thought I would do the two angled rails to the corner.

Setting off on Phase A on Aloaf is the worst part. You have to weigh in so you can't take your horse away to quieten him, and Aloaf gets so worked up about starting that he is almost impossible to tack up. But once we did start, everything looked good and we completed the steeplechase inside the time. Lucinda Green had been before me and in the ten-minute box told me she had taken the two angles and the corner at the brandy glass, but that you needed a very accurate horse to do this: so Mum, Gill and I thought I had better go the long way round—if I had gone clear until that point, I would be furious if I had a run-out at the corner so near the finish. But I was still adamant about doing the two angles and the corner because I thought Aloaf was very accurate, and he had always jumped whatever I asked him to. He had never finished inside the time on either a one day or a three, but I also felt that as he was a good galloper and by now old enough to have learned to cover the ground a bit more, he could try and do so today.

He jumped superbly, meeting every fence in his stride and taking them boldly but carefully. At half-way we had time in hand but I kept on in the same rhythm. When I looked at my watch after jumping the lower trout hatchery, it had obviously stopped so I had no idea how much time was left.

39
AMB

Aloaf jumping with great care and confidence at Burghley 1984, where he finished fourth

I took the longer alternative at the fence before the brandy glass, a bounce of bullfinches, which I thought quite a test for a horse, and at the last moment I decided to go the long way at the brandy glass, too. But having planned to ride it the short way, I had not studied the alternative closely enough. Also, I was afraid that as my last-moment choice would take longer, I might lose too much time: so I jumped out of the brandy glass but not close enough to the flag—Aloaf turned fast, and was only a stride off the corner! I just kicked. He saw the fence and, with his enormous scope, jumped it. He really tried for me, and was thoroughly brave and honest—I could have ridden that fence a great deal better. We galloped home half a minute inside the time. He had never even noticed the crowds as he went round the course, he was concentrating so hard on what I was asking him to do. What a good boy he was.

This performance proved that he was a real three day event horse, much better than for one day events because of his long stride and big jump. It was thrilling to get a young horse like this really going—he has always been a big horse for me to ride, a man's horse, but utterly genuine and honest; and, because he was home-bred, it was all the more exciting.

I quickly told Gill how the course rode so that she could pass it on, then we settled Aloaf into his stable and went back to the ten-minute halt box to watch everybody else on closed-circuit television. Aloaf was in the lead, but Mandy was soon to go on Venture Busby: she had a wonderful ride and came in ahead of me, so we were first and second at this stage. Ultimately, we finished second and fifth, and Gill and the Young Riders' selectors were delighted that we had done so well on top of our success at

Luhmühlen—it was yet another night for celebration. In the show jumping on Sunday afternoon we again had a job to get Aloaf into the ring—then he did a clear round. Mandy had a fence down, which left her fifth overall and me in fourth place; Ginny Leng (née Holgate) won on Nightcap.

BOEKELO 1984: PIGLET

I had a four-hour drive home to get to Piglet, who was now the only one left in work; I was taking him to the three day event at Boekelo in October. Meanwhile he was to run at Gatcombe, Mark Phillips's home, in two weeks' time. The horse trials there had started in 1983, but this was my first visit. Piglet did an appalling dressage as usual and came last; but excelled at the cross-country, to give me great confidence about Holland.

'It was astonishing that the organisers managed to keep the event going in such wet weather.'

Tanya Longson had recovered from her broken wrist and brought her horse Noffy (Pink Fizz) in my lorry to Boekelo; the night ferry from Sheerness took only seven hours and we had a three-hour drive to the venue. We arrived late in the morning, ideal timing to get the horses settled in. They were all stabled in a big marquee divided into little stalls, and conditions were not pleasant because it became muggy and humid, and rain made this atmosphere worse. There were eighteen British competitors, and we all lived in a nearby hotel, with Charles Harrison as our chef d'équipe.

After the vet's inspection Piggy and I were picked to run first for the British team. Lucinda Green had Village Gossip, with Richard Walker on Accumulator and Mary Thompson on Divers Rock. The rain made the going deep in the dressage, which helped our test because it slowed Piggy down; he didn't do badly, for him, and finished half-way up the order. It was obviously the cross-country that was going to cause the trouble, especially as it would be difficult to get the time in the sodden conditions. It was astonishing that the organisers managed to keep the event going in such wet weather. They used machines to drain the land, but did have to cut out a few fences, which reduced the cross-country time from twelve and a half to ten minutes. As at all foreign events, hospitality was very good; Mum and Mike had come to support me yet again.

BOEKELO 1984: CROSS-COUNTRY DAY

On Friday evening Charles Harrison gave us all the customary talk about tactics at the fences, partly so the spotters would know which way we were coming. I was looking forward keenly to the cross-country: it is such bliss riding Piglet, who loves it so much. Next day I was quite high in the starting order, so there wasn't much time for butterflies; the weather was overcast and the going had become heavy, but Piglet went well on the roads and tracks and I managed to control him on the steeplechase. The sandy going was quite firm on both sections. At the ten-minute halt box there wasn't much information, though I knew that I had to attack the course but not go too fast or Piglet wouldn't finish strongly on that heavy going, although he is the only horse I have ridden that gallops over the wet instead of being bogged down.

The first fence was rather spooky: a brush with a ditch in front and 'Boekelo' in yellow flowers; but it meant that you had to attack right from

the start, which set the right attitude for the rest of the track. I had to take the next steadily, as the landing was soggy and threatened a fall if taken too fast. By the time we were over that and across the next field, Piglet was used to the wet going, kept ploughing through and jumped brilliantly. He never jumps any more than he has to, never gives you the feeling of over-jumping and only ever skims over the top, but he seldom touches anything. Three-quarters of the way round he was still pulling my arms out and steaming along. I was getting tired but knew that he had ample stamina and gave up trying to slow him down. He hurtled over the last few fences and was the only horse to finish inside the time all day. The vet who took his heart rate at the end of the course said he was superbly fit, which was a great relief.

I was so carried away by the excitement of Piglet's performance that I forgot to go to the ten-minute box to tell Charles Harrison how the course had ridden, for the benefit of the other British competitors, and it was not until someone came to remind me that I rushed off. It is most important to pass on tips such as where to find the best going and what to look out for, to help the other British riders.

BOEKELO: SHOW JUMPING

At the end of the cross-country Piglet was in second position and the team was in first. Tanya had had an outstanding ride on Pink Fizz and was fifth, Rodney Powell was ninth on Catkin. For me, the worst was to come, as Piglet's show jumping has always been nerve-racking and there were not many marks separating the leading horses. The fences here were solid and not too easy to knock down, which was just as well. I was not jumping until the afternoon, so had to sit and watch almost everyone else. Working in for the show jumping, Piggy was as crazy as ever. He doesn't know how to trot into a cross pole, but always canters sideways. We jumped a cross pole once, then put in a fairly big upright to give him something to think about. At any practice fence he goes sideways, shakes his head, then jumps so quickly that it is not surprising that he often does not clear them. The reason he is so fast across country is that he brushes over his fences; but of course in the show jumping they won't stay up if he does that. In the practice arena I jumped him over some fairly big parallels to try to make him jump a bit bigger.

He loves crowds and we made a jaunty entrance. It was my good luck that he felt like showing off and therefore gave all the show jumps an extra centimetre of height. He still rattled a few, but fortunately those heavy poles stayed put. The result was certainly gratifying: the team kept its first place, with Richard Walker third, Mary Thompson sixth, and I second. Karen Lende from America, on The Optimist, was the individual winner.

Traditionally, at Boekelo, the winning team gets a six- or seven-foot-long loaf of fruit bread; this is devoured afterwards in the stables, with champagne provided by the winners.

So the 1984 season ended with everybody in high spirits. All three of my horses had proved their fitness and ability in top-level competition, and what is more had beaten some of the best partnerships of the time, so I was particularly thrilled with the successes of that year. In performance they trusted me and did their best for me—how lucky I was!

Aloaf into water

Success in any competitive sport is tenuous, but especially in eventing because the horse is so vulnerable—success or failure can so often just hang on a bruise or a knocked leg, the highs can turn overnight to a low. One moment you feel euphoria because your horse is giving a brilliant performance, the next might bring acute frustration and fury if you make a silly mistake and fall or miss a placing. The spring of 1985 brought highs with Friday, and lows, too—a fall with Piglet; at Badminton a mistake and a fall for me. Yet Badminton and Bramham 1986 brought real highs . . .

9 ◊ Silver Horses, Whitbread Spurs

The winter of 1985 was long and rather boring, but made brighter by the good news that I had been awarded the Range Rover Scholarship for being the most promising Young Rider of 1984. The scholarship meant that two of my horses and I could be based at Gatcombe Park with Captain Mark Phillips. Mike and I went to Gatcombe to discuss it with Captain Phillips, but, although I would have loved to have spent some time at Gatcombe and benefited from all the help that was available there, I had three horses and it was impossible for Mark to have them all. We felt that as they were such good horses it was equally out of the question for me to leave the third one at home for so long. Hence I regretfully turned the scholarship down, and it went instead to Ros Bevan.

THE NEW YEAR 1985: SKIING

I managed to take a holiday in January, skiing with my stepbrother and about thirty others from the Lanz sports centre that he runs. We all stayed in a big chalet and had a glorious time, out on the slopes from dawn to dusk. In the evenings we went to a restaurant or nightclub, and the walk home uphill to where we lived at the top of the town was strenuous. I was already fit because I had been swimming every evening at the sports centre, and all this climbing made me even fitter. It was great to see David in such a relaxed mood, as he works so hard; and it was a wonderful two weeks away from the horses.

Mary Mears, my groom—she had first come to us as a working pupil—had been helping with Mum's hunters on Exmoor since we came back from Boekelo as all my horses were on holiday, and enjoyed it so much that she decided to stay there. Helena Phillips replaced her, a very good girl who had spent some time at the Holgates' event yard.

SPRING TRIALS 1985

Immediately on my return I had to start getting some of the horses fit. I welcomed the 1985 spring season, and planned to take Aloaf and Piglet to

Badminton, and Friday to Bramham for the Young Riders. A newcomer to the yard was Sunset, a skewbald mare, and Mum had also lent me her hunter, Archie, a little Welsh cob cross Thoroughbred.

Friday won her first event, and therefore got the new season off to a good start. However, our fortunes very soon reversed, because at Aloaf's second event, Brigstock, he was jumping a hedge with a ditch and stumbled, falling on his knees. He picked himself up and jumped the next fence to finish the course, but he didn't feel right; he had pulled a shoulder muscle, which prevented his competing for the rest of the spring.

Piglet remained in fine form. He had only one run, at Weston Park, before going to Badminton, but he is a horse that doesn't need much cross-country before a big event. I took him to several dressage shows, but it didn't seem to make much difference: he remained impossible at it.

Piggy trying hard to contain himself in the dressage, Badminton 1985

BADMINTON 1985

It was a great shame not to have had Aloaf at Badminton, for its terrain and fences would have suited him better than any other course. On the whole, conditions for the 1985 event were very good, but I remember that on Phase C, when I was coming back down the avenue on the roads and tracks, it was hailing and cold and during my ten-minute halt it sleeted and I shivered. The bad weather didn't worry Piglet, who set off on the cross-country with his usual enthusiasm.

At the quarry, I was expecting his jump in over the wall to be very big, as there was quite a drop beyond. But he surprised me by the clever way he landed short so that we didn't have a long drop; this gave me extra time before we went up the steps and out over the fence at the top, where there was another drop. And now, my tactics were wrong: for some reason I kicked up the steps, and because I don't usually do this, he took an enormous jump out and I fell off. He was so annoyed with me that he galloped off towards the next fence. I was cross with myself, too, as I got to my feet and rushed after him. According to the rules, I should have remounted at the place where I fell; I forgot about that, but it didn't seem to matter.

Reunited, Piglet stormed on, trying to make up for lost time, and jumped superbly round the rest of the course and finished with only eleven time faults besides the fall. In the show jumping, it was typical of Piglet that, when it didn't matter, he went clear. We finished twenty-sixth, but he had enjoyed his week and I had very much enjoyed riding him. It will be a long time before I ride another horse that is as special as he is across country.

BRAMHAM 1985

Friday had a highly successful spring, winning four events before Bramham and only missing the fifth because she had one show jump down. With all Gill's help the dressage was slowly improving and we went to Bramham feeling confident that she would do well, and were justified. Fourth after the dressage, she incurred some time faults in the cross-country but was nevertheless one of the fastest, and had a clear round in the show jumping. We finished second to Helen Ogden on Streetlighter, and to some extent this made up for my having fallen at Badminton.

At the Firbanks Drop—jumping off the end of the earth

The following week I took Sunset to a Novice two day event at Tweseldown, where she did quite well in the dressage and went clear in the show jumping. In the steeplechase came disaster: she made no attempt to jump the second fence but galloped straight through it, broke her off hind leg and, tragically, had to be put down. Such a thing had never happened to me before and I hope it never does again. Going home with an empty lorry was a horrible feeling.

AUTUMN TRIALS 1985

In the autumn, both Friday and Aloaf went well in the Young Riders final trial, and Friday was picked to go to Le Lion d'Angers in France for the European Championships, which were being held from 13–15 September. I was going to have my last go at the Pony Club Championships at Weston Park, riding Archie, Mum's hunter, as he had won the area trials and qualified for the Associates class at the championships. He was in the lead after the dressage, one of the first times I had been in this position, which made me think that at last I was going to win. But on the cross-country, having jumped up some steps, he hesitated at descending, backing a step or two three separate times, which meant he was eliminated. In fact I hadn't realised this and didn't notice when the officials told me, as I had by then got him down the steps; he finished the rest of the course clear. The refusal was typical of his naughtiness and I felt particularly cross with him because there were more difficult fences—coffins and water—where he normally stops, but this time took willingly. However, you can't help loving him; and we did win a cup for the best dressage.

The Pony Club championships had been held during the Rotherfield three day event where I was riding Piglet; I had asked for a Thursday dressage at Rotherfield so I could zoom up to Weston Park on Thursday night to ride there on Friday; then back to Rotherfield for the cross-country on Saturday. Piggy did his usual undistinguished dressage, but moved up to second place after getting only three time faults on the cross-country, which is difficult and hilly and suits him well. He had two fences down in the show jumping and we finally came fifth overall.

Piggy was feeling so well after Rotherfield that I decided to try and take him to Boekelo again. He had only done one one day event before Badminton and another at Gatcombe before Rotherfield, so I thought another three day event in a month's time would not hurt him. A couple of weeks after Rotherfield was the three day event at Le Lion d'Angers, and Friday and I had our final team training at Aston Park with Gill; after the last trot up, the six to go and the two reserves were selected. We were among the lucky ones, and my team-mates and their horses were Karen Straker on Running Bear, Vanessa Ashbourne on Hector James, Ros Bevan on Horton Venture, Claire Oseman on Another Fred and Anne Marie Taylor on Justyn Thyme. Jamie Mackie was to be our chef d'équipe again.

After lunch, a swarm of photographers took publicity pictures for the sponsors who were providing equipment for the team or contributing money towards training expenses. It was like having Christmas in the middle of the year, with marvellous presents of rugs, bandages, boots, coats and tracksuits.

LE LION D'ANGERS 1985

Mine was one of the three lorries we took to France. The three day event was held in a lovely setting, a château with a lake which is now the national stud. It houses scores of stallions, mostly Percherons, which take their name from the district of le Perche where they originated; they are greys and almost as big as carthorses—so Ros Bevan and I had to make sure we kept our two mares well away from these permanent equine residents!

The dressage, show jumping and steeplechase were all on the steeplechase course. We were a little disappointed with the cross-country when we walked it, for it looked fairly easy; it was quite twisty among the trees, but the fences were not very demanding, especially in comparison with those at Luhmühlen. Consequently, we guessed that a lot would depend on the dressage.

Our running order was going to be Ros first, followed by Claire, Anne Marie and myself last. The hazard that worried us most was not on the cross-country, but on the roads and tracks: an iron footbridge about twenty feet above the river that we had to cross. It was very narrow and planked with wooden slats so loose that they moved when we walked over them and would rattle under hooves, while the whole contraption swayed. A length of rope was tied along either side to give the impression of high rails. Karen Straker remarked that she would need a cognac when

Friday enjoying a bite of grass at Le Lion D'Angers, 1985

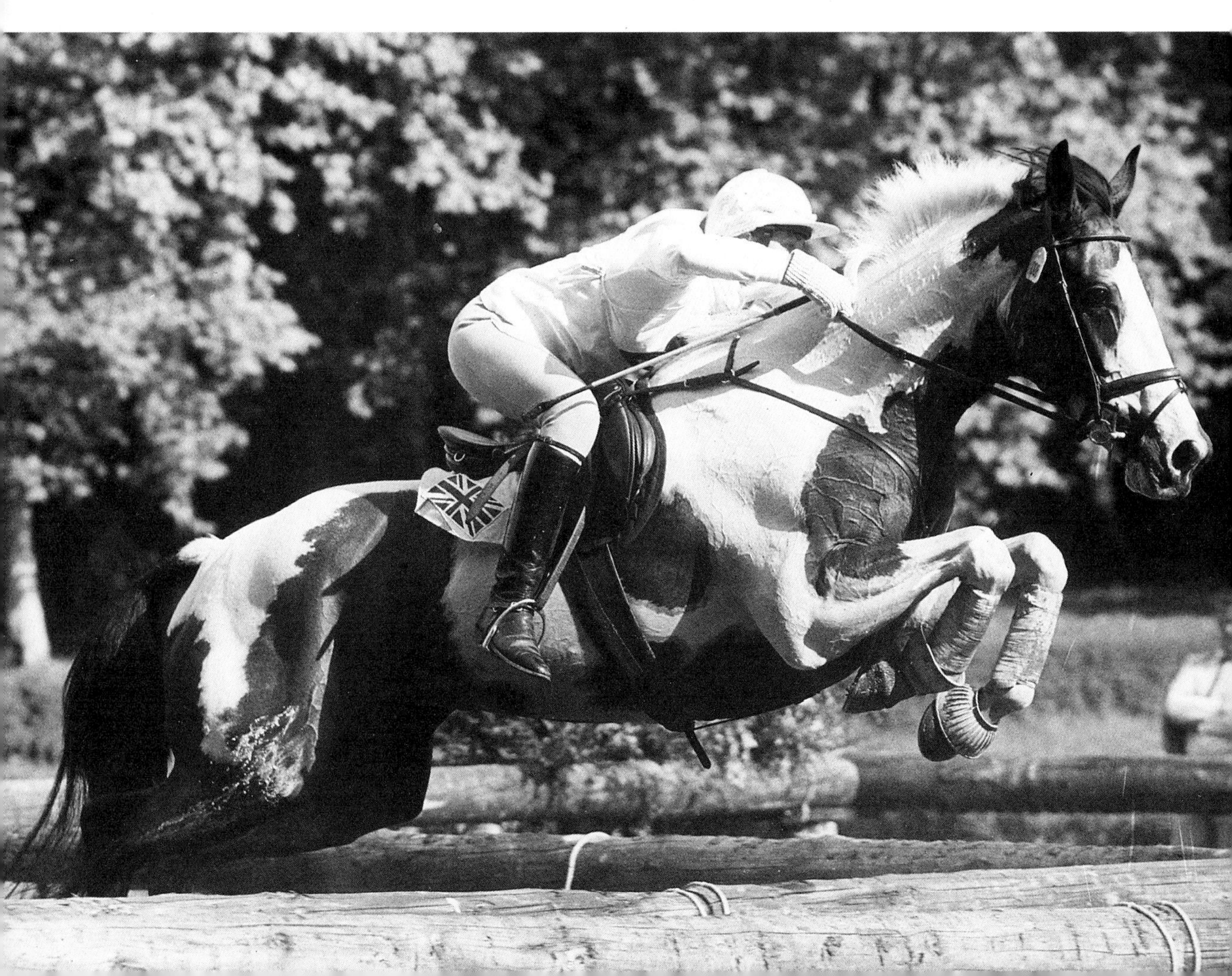

Friday jumping well across country at Le Lion D'Angers

she got to the other side! Fortunately we were allowed to practise on it, otherwise I doubt that some of us would have completed the roads and tracks. Swinging about above the river frightened us, but the horses were just as scared and didn't do anything silly, like taking a flying leap over the side.

All the horses behaved themselves in the dressage, and thanks to excellent tests by Claire and Anne Marie, we came out top. In the cross-country all six of us British girls had clear rounds and widened our lead. That night, Saturday, there was a big party and dancing in the château. Although I don't speak a word of Polish, I asked one of the Poles to dance. This he did with wild enthusiasm, spinning me all over the floor, weaving and twisting like a dervish while at least three records played themselves out, until I was exhausted and almost in shock; but at least we made some form of communication and enjoyed it immensely.

The show jumps on Monday were not very big, but quite airy, and it was important to go clear because the marks were so close together. Friday managed this well, to move up to fourth place, and so did Claire and Another Fred, to stay in the lead; but Anne Marie and Justyn Thyme had two down, which dropped them to seventh. Anyway, the team won, and Claire took the individual gold medal.

One ugly episode marred an otherwise triumphant week. We were staying at a hotel in a quiet village near the venue, and the cars belonging to Christopher Schofield, chairman of the the Young Riders selectors, and Audrey Ann Lockett, were usually parked outside—one night they were vandalised: the windscreens, rear windows and lights smashed. The Brussels football riot had happened not long before, so everyone suspected that the British number-plates had attracted this ill-will.

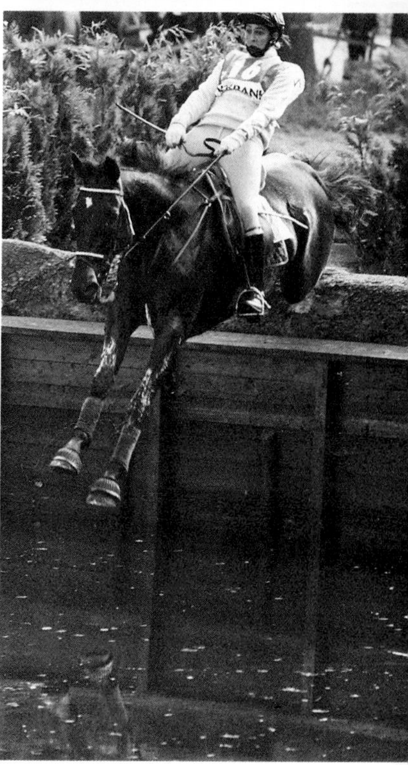

Hanging on as Piggy takes off a stride early into the water at Boekelo, and recovering well afterwards!

BOEKELO 1985

I had been chosen with Piglet to go to Boekelo again in October. Unfortunately the going was much better than the year before, so Piggy was only one of several horses that did the cross-country inside the time. Having done his moderate dressage but at least a clear round in the show jumping, he finished eleventh. With Helen Ogden on Streetlighter, Anne Marie Taylor on Jiminy Cricket and Lorna Clarke on Danville, we were riding for the British team, which finished second.

THE NEW YEAR 1986

At the beginning of 1986 I had only Piglet and Friday to compete on, because Aloaf was still on holiday, having pulled his shoulder and bruised a leg the year before. He wasn't going to start work until May. I had a newcomer—Donald—a grey, as well as two horses called Picasso and Harry who had just returned from a winter's hunting with Mum on Exmoor.

In February, Helena decided she wanted a different sort of job. Coincidentally, a school friend of mine, Angela Robley, had just returned from a visit to her parents who live in Kenya. Angela had ridden all her life and was seeking a job with horses: she came over for a couple of days to help me before Helena left, and when I offered her the vacancy, she accepted. Helena had lived in one of the farm cottages while I had been living in the main house, but I thought it would be more fun if Angie and I

86

shared the cottage, so on a chilly February day we moved in to fend for ourselves. We had a sitting room and kitchen, with two bedrooms and a bathroom upstairs. However, there was no central heating or double glazing and the roof was not well insulated. I shall never forget that first evening we spent in the cottage—it was Shrove Tuesday and we elected to make pancakes. As neither of us excelled at cooking, we were faced with something of a problem, and got the mixture wrong: it lasted for four days and we found ourselves eating pancakes for breakfast, lunch and tea—there were even pancake remains on the ceiling.

That same month sister Lucy went off round the world for a year, first to Hong Kong, then Australia and New Zealand. I would love to go on a trip like this, but with my commitment to the horses, I haven't time—it is something to look forward to doing one day. While Lucy went off to the sun, Angie and I froze in one of the coldest Februarys on record.

My twenty-first birthday fell on the Sunday we were to compete at Crookham, and we planned to have a champagne party there. I had only entered Piglet, and didn't regard our appearance as important—my main purpose was to take him into the dressage arena where he could buck and kick and get all that out of his system so (I hoped!) he would behave properly at the next event. But Crookham was cancelled on account of the freezing weather, which was a great disappointment as I had been looking forward to the party.

Angie and a great friend, James Humphrey, insisted on bringing me my birthday cake for breakfast in bed. I had intended to have a good lie-in, but Lucy had telephoned from Hong Kong at 4.45am to wish me a happy birthday, which was delightful. I went back to bed afterwards but my leisurely morning didn't last long and by 9am I was riding Piglet, giving him his canter work in preparation for Badminton; then Angie and I took out the other horses. I had some wonderful presents, my biggest being a Turbo Diesel Golf from Mike. Everyone on the road, *watch out*!

The following week at Aldon we came out for our first event and Friday won the Young Rider trial, just as she had the year before. I hoped this was a good augury for the rest of 1986.

Piglet had had good runs at Dynes Hall and Brockenhurst, which put him right on form for Badminton. Friday was also entered for Badminton, but I had decided I would run her only if the going was absolutely perfect; otherwise she would go to Bramham. In the meantime Angie and I had been up to Gill's a couple of times for tuition.

BADMINTON 1986

We were all set for Badminton. I drove the horses there, Angie brought the car, and Will Fair—a good friend who was helping with the lambing at home—brought the Land Rover and caravan. Having settled-in the horses, we went to help Will and Mark Aldridge put the caravan awning up; the field was a foot deep in mud and it was quite a windy day, so it was entertaining to see Mark and Will nearly lifted off the ground as the awning filled like a balloon while they struggled to secure it to the ground!

I don't know why it is that nearly every year our drive along the roads and tracks at Badminton becomes a race. Perhaps we behave like this because it is the first three day event of the season and everyone is eager to

'. . . we found ourselves eating pancakes for breakfast, lunch and tea—there were even pancake remains on the ceiling.'

'My twenty-first birthday fell on the Sunday we were to compete at Crookham, and we planned to have a champagne party there.'

Anxious moments before the vets' inspection, which caused no problem

make a start after the long winter break; or maybe it is because we know that when we walk the course we will all be a bit shocked by the size of the fences, so the feeling is to enjoy ourselves before we see them. This year was no exception. I got a lift in Rodney Powell's jeep, with several others. We made a quick start and were in front of everyone else while we all waited for Colonel Frank Weldon to appear and take the lead. Then David Green, who had ambitions of his own about who should win the race, made a grab for Rodney's ignition key and bent it—by the time we had got the jeep started we were left at the back.

Conditions on the cross-country were not good. I only had time to go half-way round before having to return for a dressage lesson on Friday, with Gill; there had been some rain and the ground wasn't too good underfoot, and it would obviously be heavy going for the horses unless the rain stopped and the sun came out.

This year we set off as we had done in 1984, straight out past the house to go towards the Luckington Lane fences first, then returning via the Lake. Fence four, which is normally a combination fence, comprised three separate sets of rails each in chevron shape with the point towards the approach: if you went the direct way, you would therefore jump the three points, with a bounce between the first two and then a stride to the last—this looked extremely difficult. However, the first walk is just to take in all the different possible routes, without worrying about exactly where you are going to jump the fence; most competitors will walk the course

Rodney and me 'walking' the Vicarage Corner at Badminton 1986—early confidence was later diminished as we continued around the course

another two or three times, depending on how they feel about the fences, or the conditions, or how they think their horse is going to jump each fence.

There was a new fence over the Vicarage Ditch, just a plain parallel with top rails that were big logs rather than poles, and no ground rail. It looked enormous, especially as we came downhill towards it. Next was the Vicarage V, followed by the Stockholm fence, which has been a feature for several alternate years: it consists of a log over a ditch at the bottom of a very steep slope, so that the horses almost slide down into it and then have to jump at the last second, with no alternative. The Lake fences had also had a facelift, and there was a new jetty in the middle: we would have to go over a big rail into the water, to the jetty which was a sort of Normandy bank—onto the jetty and bounce over a rail back into the water—and out over a boathouse. It looked frightfully complicated, but on the first walk one just looked at it, thought 'Help!' and worried later about how to jump it. My first ride was to be on Piggy, number 18; Friday came towards the end.

By the time I went in, the dressage arena was already looking like a bog. This helped a little, as Piggy had to work so hard that he couldn't run away with me as much as usual and didn't disgrace himself too badly. When Friday's turn came, I put her in a double bridle for the first time and she pleased us by staying calm and coping well with the mud.

However, I decided that it would not be fair to take her across country in those conditions. She is only half Thoroughbred and the time was two and a half minutes longer than she was accustomed to; in addition, she had never before carried the compulsory full weight (11 stone 11lb). Had the going been perfect, I would have tried her, but asking her to carry the full weight over the full distance in the mud would be unkind. So it was all up to Piglet.

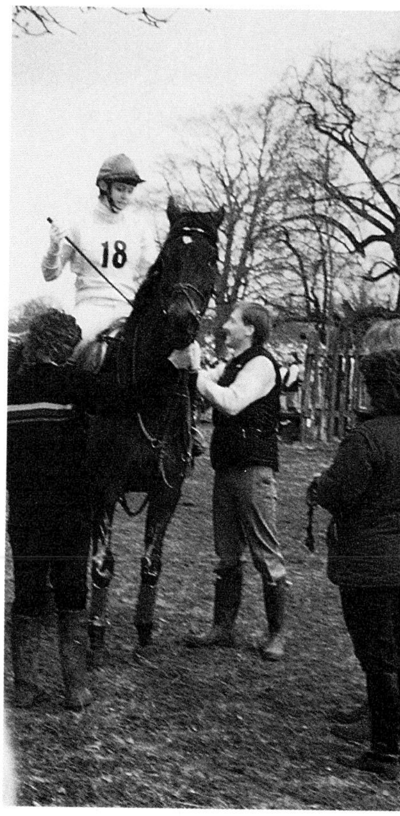

Mum, David, Gill and Angie all to hand in the ten-minute box before the cross-country phase

BADMINTON 1986: CROSS-COUNTRY DAY

All that week the weather had been showery with sunny spells. I was the fifth or sixth to start on the cross-country, so there was not much information available in the ten-minute box. Gill could only tell me that Ginny Leng, who had been the first to go, on Night Cap, had had a run-out at the last part of the combination in the Lake. Gill advised me to hang onto the offside rein and keep to the right over the first two parts, in the hope that when we landed over the second part the boathouse would be in front of us.

Piglet set off at his usual speed, flying along the first part of the course. At the fourth fence, the Chevrons, we went straight and he bounced it perfectly—one of only two horses to do so. Piggy skimmed over the mud as though the ground were dry, making no apparent effort, and jumped so big that he cleared each fence with room to spare. At the Stockholm he went brilliantly, sliding half-way down the slope and then hopping over the log. Coming up the hill towards the Lake, which was a long gallop and about half-way round, he was still tanking at me. My watch showed that we were on time to finish inside the time. I considered this a bit fast, in view of the going; but if I try to slow Piglet down, he fights and wears himself out: so I could only pray that he was fit enough and let him go at the pace he chose.

Pages 106–7: Piggy and me trying to find our way at the start of Phase A

START

TBREAD
PIONSHIPS
MINTON
PHASE·A
18

Coming down the hill into the Lake after the Whitbread Drays, I still thought we were going too fast; but it was the sort of speed he likes and when he comes to a fence he slows himself down in the last strides before he takes off. He jumped hugely over every part of the water complex: into the Lake, onto the jetty and over the rail; and with me hanging onto the right rein, he stayed to that side and pinged out over the boathouse like a rocket.

At that point the course turns away from the house towards the Normandy Bank, the first time it takes a direction away from the ten-minute box. Piggy wanted to gallop along one of the ropes instead of in the middle, for the same reason, I suppose, as when racehorses prefer to gallop on the rails rather than wide of them—because it is less tiring. Also, I think it may have been because of Friday. It was the first time Piglet had been to Badminton with company, and Friday being his lover he was perturbed at the thought of going away from her again. But I suspect that it was fatigue more than amorousness!

Nonetheless he galloped on, and after we had taken the Normandy Bank and the Ski Jump he attacked the Coffin with his usual zest, with his head up so that I couldn't even see the fence. If I do take a pull he just puts his head straight up even further, so it is easier not to take a pull and to let him come in a bit fast. We negotiated that one safely, then came the quarry. This year we had to jump onto a platform, drop off the other side of it, turn left and go up the quarry slope over the wall. It was the first time I had ever felt Piggy tired. He jumped onto the platform and almost stumbled off it. When he landed he was very tired and when I turned him at the bottom and looked up at the wall, I realised that he wasn't with me. I had to hit him, one of the few times I have ever had to do so. He found renewed energy and we were over the wall in a flash. From there on he galloped a little more slowly but at every fence he made a tremendous effort and didn't touch any of them. Coming to the last fence, the Whitbread Bar, a nasty one for a tired horse, I got him straight, gave him a few slaps on the shoulder and said 'Come on, Piggy, wake up! You've got to jump this one.' And he did, beautifully, to speed on to the finish. What a wonderful horse he was, to keep on trying all the way round. We finished a fraction outside the time to pick up only a few time faults.

When Piggy returned to his box, Friday was wondering why she wasn't being bandaged up and why she wasn't doing the cross-country. Piggy was telling her how brilliant he had been, and she was most upset at not being able to have a go herself. Poor Friday, she would have to wait for Bramham.

I went back to the ten-minute halt box to watch the closed-circuit television for the rest of the day. Nobody was getting near the time and the going was causing a lot of trouble. A lot of people were withdrawing: to jump fences of that size on such heavy going was extremely difficult. Later in the day the horses with the better dressage marks were started—they could all have beaten us—their riders were unlucky. Mark Todd had a silly

Piggy recognises this fence from last year when he only just made it. This time he puts in an extra big effort

Trying hard to give more than the customary ¼cm in the driving rain

Piggy gallops through the heavy going at Badminton 1986

stop at the Coffin on both his horses, Bruce Davidson also had one there, and Rodney Powell on Pomeroy went well but not quite as fast as Piggy. The last to start was Ian Stark on Sir Wattie, who attacked the mud as well as we had and just beat me. He had more time faults than I, but did a much better dressage.

On Sunday morning we took Piggy and Friday for a good trot round the park. We went to look at some of the fences we had jumped the day before and wondered how we had ever done it. The show jumping had been brought forward from the afternoon because it was so wet—the car parks had been shut because so many cars had had to be towed out the previous day. Spectators had to walk miles, having left their cars parked all along the nearby roads.

'It poured with rain and I couldn't see the fences because I had to keep putting my head down.'

I was the second last to jump. It poured with rain and I couldn't see the fences because I had to keep putting my head down. The show jumping ring had also become very muddy, but Piggy gave me a lovely ride until he

hit a fence. This worried me and I reminded him that he had to pick his feet up a bit more, after which he duly cleared the rest. Luckily that one fence down didn't cost me my place. Ian Stark also had one fence down, but that didn't alter his position either. So he won the Badminton Championship on Sir Wattie, Piggy and I came second and Rodney Powell was third on Pomeroy.

This was one of the most exciting times of my life. I won the Whitbread Spurs, the prize for the best cross-country round by a rider under twenty-five, which I had missed in 1984 by going too fast. This year we were outside the time, but Piggy had been the fastest of all the horses on that atrocious going, again proving what an exceptional cross-country horse he is.

Mum and Mike, Gill, Angie and I just couldn't quite believe what had happened. It was an amazing result and all my thanks go to them and dear Piggy.

SILVER HORSES, WHITBREAD SPURS

'This was one of the most exciting times of my life. I won the Whitbread Spurs, the prize for the best cross-country round by a rider under twenty-five ...'

BRAMHAM 1986

It was now Friday's turn to show Piggy how brilliant she could be: I was taking her to Bramham for the Young Rider National Championships, in which she had finished second for the last two years. She made a decent start with her dressage and was lying sixth, coming a little more relaxed than she used to, standing still for longer and working in a rounder outline. She was also beginning to stretch her neck out a little more, to make her short neck appear longer. It was a lovely cross-country course although quite hilly for her, but having been fit enough for Badminton a month earlier, she was really jumping out of her skin now, and raring to go.

She jet-propelled round the steeplechase and nearly pulled my arms out of their sockets on the roads and tracks, so I knew she was feeling on top form. In the start box we could hardly keep her still while we washed her off to cool her down. She loved every minute of the cross-country and must have been asking herself why she hadn't been allowed to do the same at Badminton, having been taken all the way there. She was still full of running when she finished, with only ten time faults, which put her in first place.

Her show jumping round the next day was immaculate: it ensured her first win in a three day event, and proved beyond any doubt her consistency after coming second in two successive years. And this was *my* first, too, in a three day! The prize was a lovely bronze Shaitan's head, the horse on which Gill Watson won Burghley in 1969, and a bursary from Range Rover.

Bramham was the last event for that spring 1986, and Friday was now able to go home and chat to Piggy and tell him that she had won her event; and I am sure they had a little argument while they were on their summer holiday, about which horse was the better. But as they loved each other it didn't really matter which of them was, and I was equally delighted with both.

Piglet and me, having finished second at Badminton in 1986

COMING OF AGE

The autumn of 1986 marked my complete graduation from Young Rider to senior competition, and this was a considerable step. The standard of riding and the quality of the horses at top level is rising all the time, and usually only a few marks separate the first six or so in a competition. The dressage phase is therefore more significant—a below-average dressage mark has less chance now of being redeemed by a good cross-country. Riders are increasingly turning to the Continent for training: the Continental approach to dressage has long been accepted as the one to emulate, and Germany in particular is thought of as the very centre of classical riding. For me, the latter half of 1986 contained two milestones: my coming of age, and with it the transition to senior competition; and the chance to train in Germany.

10 «» Coming of Age

On Friday 6 June, in the week after Bramham, we held my twenty-first birthday party. A huge marquee was put up at the side of the house, the French windows from the drawing room opening directly into it—it was an enormous room with a wooden floor that was perfect for dancing. This was to be our last party in the house: I had moved into the cottage, my sister was abroad, and Mum and Mike spent a lot of time on Exmoor, so it seemed pointless to keep on such a big place. Accordingly we had sold it, and it was to change hands on 20 June.

The marquee looked wonderful—Mum had arranged the flowers and decorations, and Mike had organised the barbecue buffet. The hostess, however—me—attended her ball with an enormous and conspicuous bruise on her shoulder, and this is how it came about: on the Sunday, an event rather like a fête on a grand scale was going to be held in Salisbury to raise money for the renovation of Salisbury Cathedral spire, the tallest in Britain. One of the competitions was a three-phase affair, with clay pigeon shooting, fly fishing and the riding of motorised mini-tricycles round a course between bollards. We had been invited to make up an eventers' team: Rodney Powell, Brynley Powell (no relation), Chris Hunnable and myself. Bryn and Chris both shot, but neither Rodney nor I had ever fired a gun, let alone a twelve-bore, so I had decided I ought to have a lesson beforehand. I was given a twenty-bore which is lighter and has less recoil, and managed fairly well. Rodney thought he should have a lesson too, so on the afternoon of my party day I had accompanied him. Although I am right-handed, I shot left-handed; and obviously didn't hold the gun properly into my shoulder because it was the recoil which gave me the big bruise that was so conspicuous when I put on my strapless ball dress, to everyone else's amusement.

We danced until 5.30am next morning and some of us were still chatting in the cottage at 7am. Angie did the horses and told me to take the day off; so all the horses had a day off, too.

THE SALISBURY CATHEDRAL APPEAL

On Sunday, as soon as we had done the horses, we went to Salisbury racecourse for the cathedral fund-raising. I had borrowed a twenty-bore, but only twelve-bore cartridges were provided so I had to change guns. There were three stands, and we had to fire ten shots from each. The clays were catapulted in pairs, two going away and two from the sides, and I found this almost impossibly difficult as in my lessons I had shot only single clays coming towards me. My arm hurt so much that I managed to shoot only twenty-eight of my thirty cartridges, and hit only one clay! Rodney didn't do much better, but Chris shot quite well and Bryn did best of all.

'In the midst of all this, Prince Charles arrived in a red helicopter …'

In the midst of all this, Prince Charles arrived in a red helicopter. I was shooting at the time. Everyone else stopped but I didn't realise who had landed and continued until I was told I had to desist because 'Charlie' was coming. 'Charlie who?' I wondered. The prince showed us all how to shoot clay pigeons: he fired two casual shots and scored with both.

The fishing entailed casting a fly into hoops from various distances. I had never fished before, but my grandfather is a keen angler and had lent me a rod so I had practised at home; I managed to score at three distances and won a bottle of champagne for being the best lady competitor! But the fun really started with the motor tricycle race: we had a brief practice which deluded us into thinking it would be easy, then went in pairs around two identical tracks, one clockwise and the other anti-clockwise, demolishing bollards as we careered along. All of us mishandled the gears by changing down too low at the corners, which resulted in a slow, jolting progress. The whole day was most entertaining, and what is more, it resulted in a very successful fund-raising effort for the cathedral.

ON FILM WITH FRIDAY

Meanwhile at home, Aloaf—now sometimes known as Lofty—was back in work and had been walking for six weeks; and Piggy was about to come in after his post-Badminton break. However, Friday hadn't had a very long holiday this time: Gill Watson was producing two eventing videos in June, one for cross-country and one for show jumping, and had asked me to bring Friday and Picasso, to be her film stars! We spent five days on this production, starting right from the beginning by showing a three-year-old being schooled over trotting poles. Picasso, who was five, played the part of a four-year-old doing grid-work. Later, Friday and I were filmed to show the training of older horses. For part of the cross-country sequence I wore a crash hat fitted with a camera, to give an impression of what it was like to be the rider, but every time we jumped a fence, Friday's ears bobbed up into the frame. My headgear was uncomfortably heavy and I had to concentrate hard to hold my head well up—if I let myself look down, the weight of the camera made me feel as though I was about to have my head pulled off. In fact this was good practice, because the rider is meant to look up when jumping. There were four fences, all of Novice standard, and we had to jump them several times—to Friday's great delight. After finishing the runs with the camera on my head, we jumped some more fences so we could be filmed from the side, which added to Friday's enjoyment of the whole experience.

'Gill Watson … had asked me to bring Friday and Picasso, to be her film stars!'

TEAM TRAINING

It was time to start serious work once more. Friday had a little more holiday before resuming her dressage training to get ready for Rotherfield, in Hampshire. She was on the shortlist again for the Young Rider Europeans, which were being held there: twelve Britons would be competing, four in the team and eight individuals.

In the meantime Piglet had been shortlisted for the Alternative World Championships in Poland in September. The World Championships proper had been held in Australia, where only five or six countries had taken part—the others could not afford to send teams to the other side of the world, hence this Polish competition. I was to be in the senior team, so was lucky that it was after Rotherfield; I couldn't have competed as a Young Rider at the latter if Poland had preceded it, because once you have ridden in a senior team you cannot revert to the Young Rider class.

Pat Burgess—inspired trainer

It was a great honour to be selected for this senior team, and I benefited from the additional team training. This had always been at Wylye, the home of Lord and Lady Hugh Russell, but they were selling their farm, so the Duke of Beaufort allowed the team to train at Badminton. It was wonderful to have the chance to work with such senior riders as Ginny Leng on Night Cap, Ian Stark on Sir Wattie, Captain Mark Phillips on Distinctive, and Jane Thelwall on King's Jester; younger members were Rodney Powell on Catkin of Rushall, and Madeleine Gurdon on The Done Thing (Dusty). We were trained by Ferdie Eilberg for dressage and Pat Burgess for jumping.

I have worked for a long time with Pat, who also used to train my mother. She is inspiring and enthusiastic, puts the horses through excellent grid-work and induces her pupils to work hard at training themselves to sit strong and deep in the saddle. I go through phases of having a very good, strong lower leg position, but there are other times when I am quite loose in the saddle and have to concentrate hard on getting myself back to being much stronger; with Pat's help it keeps coming back.

I had had lessons with Ferdie a few years before when he was based at Cholderton before Mark Todd moved there, and it was a great help to have lessons from an instructor with a fresh point of view. Extra lessons and the team training session for Poland comprised the run-up to Gatcombe, where Friday and Aloaf were running in the Young Riders final trial and Piggy was to run in the ordinary Advanced section.

GATCOMBE 1986

At Gatcombe I tried Friday in a double bridle again and she didn't like it—she kept backing off instead of going forward into the bridle, so didn't do a good dressage test. Nor did Lofty (Aloaf): half-way through his test—for which of course I was wearing top hat and tails—the hairpins came loose from my false bun because it was so heavy and it started bouncing about; by the time I came to the extended canter I had lost my topper, bun and hairnet. At my final halt when I nodded my head I had loose hair, which was highly embarrassing, but also quite amusing for everybody watching. Poor Lofty had to jump over my top hat in the second extended canter, which inevitably caused him to lose concentration!

Left: Wearing a camera on my helmet while making the video in June 1986

The Young Riders were the first to run across country. Mark Phillips had built a new fence, a double of corners on a bounce stride; there was an alternative over two other corners, but this took much longer. I was the first to go, on Aloaf. I had walked these corners carefully and had thought them jumpable but with the great risk of a run-out. However, when I came down the hill there were a lot of spectators there, waiting to see who would jump them—including Mark Phillips, wondering how they would jump—and I decided that, as Aloaf had been going flawlessly, I would go for it. So I came down the hill, turned, got my line and just rode to it; we were slightly far off, but he is such a big jumper that it didn't matter. He jumped in, was rather shocked at having to jump straightaway again, *and* over another corner, but is so honest that he didn't hesitate. So feeling very pleased and giving him lots of pats, we raced on round the course to finish with a lovely clear.

With Friday I chickened out—having done it once, I just wondered how often one could do it well; so I decided to play safe and go the longer way. We sailed along over the rest of the course until we came to the upright rail straight into the water; it was tricky, and I gave her a quick tap on take-off, not appreciating then what I have discovered since: that if she is hit on take-off, she panics and leaves a front leg. It happened now and we had a fall, the first I had ever had in water; but she finished the course well. I walked up the long hill back to the horseboxes dripping wet and not even holding Friday, who strolled along wondering why I had fallen off.

She must have trodden on my arm, as it became very painful; and must have got me with her road stud, for there was a great red mark—I partly lost the use of my right hand and couldn't clench my fist. I still had to ride Piglet, who had done a really good test and a clear round in the show jumping. I went to the start and tried the practice jump a few times, but couldn't pull at all with my right arm because it hurt too much. I decided to try and do the course but pull up if I found, after a few fences, that it was beyond me. However, once I got going and supercharged with adrenalin, I concentrated so hard that I forgot the pain. I met no problems, even bounced the corners, and it wasn't until I'd finished that I realised how much my arm hurt. But Piglet had gone so fast that he won his section, and Aloaf won the Young Riders, so I had a thoroughly successful day, despite my fall.

On the next day the horses had to trot up in front of the selectors and vets; this is always done after a final trial. Friday was slightly unlevel and had obviously pulled or bruised something, which was enough to make the officials decide to have another look at her later. It was only ten days before Rotherfield Young Rider Championships, but they put Friday on the list and not Aloaf, hoping that she would come right in time. She did, and was perfectly sound by the time we got to Rotherfield; Aloaf was therefore aimed at Burghley.

ROTHERFIELD YOUNG RIDER CHAMPIONSHIPS 1986

At Rotherfield there were teams from Sweden, Poland, Russia, Ireland, Italy, Germany and Britain, and a field of forty-six starters. In our team were Vanessa Ashbourne on Hector James, who went first, Julie-Anne Shield on Crimdon Lucky George, Judith Copland on Sweeney, and

Friday in her final trial run at Gatcombe in 1986

myself on Friday, to go last. We thought Friday did a passable test, but the judges evidently didn't agree as she finished in thirty-third place. The cross-country was quite stiff and posed a lot of problems for some people. Alex Ramus, competing as an individual for Britain on Spy Story, was third to start and did extremely well to finish inside the time; Vanessa, on Hector, also went well and had just a few time faults. Friday and I had everything to go for. If we went really well we could pull up to third place despite our ruinous dressage.

Friday was feeling on top form and went round as though she were Concorde trying to set a new record for crossing the Atlantic; she completed her clear round inside the time, which did take us up to third place. Vanessa was lying first, and Alex second. Fourth was a Russian, Ivan Suvorev, on Galun, also inside the time; and Sarah Slazenger for Ireland on Desi, who had been second to last after the dressage, lay fifth. Julie-Anne Shields was seventh—Sweeney had had a fall but had finished the course. So the British team, having been third after the dressage, was now leading by 80 marks from the Italians who were second, with the Germans 70 marks behind them.

Before the show jumping two Irish horses sadly failed the vet—Desi, and Virginia McGrath's Bushwhacker—which meant that the Irish team was unable to finish the team event; a sad occurrence in any team competition. Alex Ramus went clear with Spy Story; Friday knocked one down but kept her third place in the overall order. Vanessa, under heavy pressure, unfortunately had two jumps down and dropped to second.

The British team therefore won comfortably and took the individual gold, silver and bronze medals which was slightly embarrassing as we were the host nation. We were all happy that Ivan Suvorev held his fourth position.

BURGHLEY 1986

The following week came Burghley. I live quite near Rotherfield, so could go home and school Aloaf during the event. Piglet was also entered, but he was going to Bialy Bor in Poland for the Alternative World Championships, so I withdrew him. There were seventy-eight starters at Burghley, where Aloaf took thirtieth place in the dressage, which was a little disappointing; it put him a long way behind Ginny Leng on Murphy Himself, who was leading after the dressage on 42 while I was on 60.

The cross-country was tough, as it always is there; the fences are big and beautifully built, and the terrain is undulating. I had a very long wait as I was last to go; nor did I have much enthusiasm when I did start, because I had worked out that even if I went clear and inside the time, the highest place I could attain was tenth, which wasn't much of an incentive. Aloaf jumped impeccably. There was one glaringly difficult fence, three-quarters of the way round: Martings Walls, a stone wall ninety-degree corner where a lot of people had been taking the longer alternative. Several of those who had tried the corner had run into considerable trouble, but I

Friday and me across country in the Rotherfield Young Riders European Championships 1986

84

JAMES
84

felt that Aloaf was capable of clearing it and honest enough not to stop; and he did so without hesitation. He is very honest like that: you can place him at anything and he will try his hardest to do as you ask. I dawdled a bit, lacking the winning spirit, had 2.4 time faults and pulled up to thirteenth.

Next day we cleared the show jumps with ease. Ginny won Burghley for a record fourth time running, and Bruce Davidson from America was second on J.J. Babu; and Lofty and I did move up to tenth. Rodney Powell had two fences down with his great old horse Pomeroy—he was retiring Pom after the event, and Pom came thirteenth, which was a great result for a horse that had done so much; we had a big party for him after the prize-giving.

'On the cross-country, fence four was a remarkable construction, a miniature house in a garden ...'

BIALY BOR (POLAND) 1986

Poland now loomed ahead. We saw the horses off from Badminton in two lorries, then had a couple of days to wait before flying out. Rodney and I were presented with the senior flag to wear on our jackets because the event was considered a world championship; this was a great thrill.

Angie had left in July to change jobs, and Sammy Davis, a friend of mine, came as groom. In order for the Poles to pay for our flight we had to fly to Warsaw, then go by minibus to Bialy Bor, in the north. It would actually have been easier to fly to East Germany, from where the drive was shorter. The road from Warsaw to Bialy Bor was full of holes, but the drivers didn't seem to mind too much how fast they swerved round the potholes or bucketed over them, so it wasn't the sort of journey to catch up on any sleep; and it was a long one, some four and a half hours. It did make us appreciate how backward Polish farming is: horses pulling ploughs, and no combines or balers, just old-fashioned hay ricks.

Our hosts were so hospitable: they had done their best to put everybody in good accommodation, and the horse facilities were excellent—a cool indoor barn with big stables. The grooms and farriers had to live in small caravans near the stables. Lord Patrick Beresford was chef d'équipe, and Peter and Annie Scott-Dunn were our vets; they and all the riders stayed in a holiday camp a few miles away consisting of small concrete huts, each accommodating two, with a sitting room, bedroom and bathroom—Madeleine and I shared one, we all ate together in the main area. The Poles tried very touchingly hard to feed us well too, but we did find it hard to appreciate dishes we were simply not accustomed to.

Besides the British, there were German, American, Polish and Russian teams, and a total of twenty-nine horses. This was probably no smaller a field than for the actual World Championships in Gawler (Australia), where only five teams had competed. The Poles had been to enormous pains to stage an excellent event. On the cross-country, fence four was a remarkable construction, a miniature house in a garden—you had to jump in over a gate, take one stride onto its roof (of rubber matting), over the top of the roof, jump off the other side, then take one stride and out over another gate. It was quite big and we wondered how the horses would react.

The fences were excellently constructed. The course ran close to a lake at the side of a hill where the going was sandy, and twisted its way through a lot of bushes and trees, but there was a good run at most fences. One of

Rotherfield, and Friday's fourth Team Gold in succession. We also picked up Individual Bronze to end our time in Young Riders

the other combinations on the course consisted of two upright palisades on a stride. The second one dropped into a dip, then you had to go up the other side to another palisade in an area of heather, which made the going difficult for the horses.

Welcomed with such hospitality and having walked such a beautifully constructed course, our immediate feelings were that it was a shame there were so few competitors after all the thought the organisers had given to all aspects of the occasion—they really deserved a big competition. They had put just as much thought and effort into the dressage arena, which was all sand—after every fifth horse, a harrow was dragged over the surface. Around three sides there was a grandstand which enclosed some in situ trees: these protruded through the roof. The judges' boxes were impressively built wooden huts.

Mum and Mike had arrived. There are not many hotels outside of the cities in Poland, but they managed to rent a room and bathroom from one of the event organisers who lived on the site. Henrietta Knight, chairman of the senior selectors, also came out, and there were a few from the press, but otherwise there was only family support.

The sand in the dressage arena was fairly deep, which was an advantage for me because it made Piggy slow down a bit and he couldn't shuffle quite as much as usual; he was twenty-second after the dressage. Ginny was first to go and led throughout with Night Cap; this disproves the theory that those who go early into the arena cannot do well because the judges haven't got their eye in. Ian Stark on Sir Wattie was second and Karen Lende on The Optimist—who had won at Boekelo in 1984—was third.

Piggy tries hard in the deep sand at the phase he hates so much, as the judges watch from their amazing boxes! Bialy Bor, Poland,1986

Annie and Peter Scott-Dunn (our vets), Madeleine, Ian, Me, Jane Thelwall and Lord Patrick Beresford, our chef d'équipe, barbecuing in Poland, 1986

Piggy was the discounted horse for the team score, and thanks to Ginny, Ian and Madeleine the British team was leading after the dressage.

Ginny went first in the cross-country. For the steeplechase fences they used fir trees, put upright in a wooden frame with the tops cut off. Night Cap hit a fence in that section, for he came off the course with a great gash on one leg, which was bleeding. A pressure bandage was put on and he carried on round the roads and tracks to go on and finish the cross-country with only 0.4 of a time fault. Madeleine had a run-out at a fence where, coming through the trees, she had to turn quite short into a ditch and brush fence—Dusty rounded the corner and carried on down the track instead of turning for the fence. Piglet went almost too fast again at the beginning—he was tiring towards the end and banked the hayrack, but finished inside the time. So did Rodney and Ian; Jane Thelwall had a fall at the upright palisades but completed the course. There were fourteen clear rounds: Britain stayed in first place, with Poland second.

The show jumping ring was a handsome structure in the centre of the stable blocks, surrounded by a smart white railing. It was very big; a lot of the fences consisted mostly of poles with not many fillers, which made them look bigger than they were. The first horse in, a Russian, did a fast clear round that made us think it was an easy course, but in fact it proved so troublesome that there were only three clear rounds, one being by Jane Thelwall on King's Jester. I knew there wasn't much hope of Piggy going clear—we had two down and finished eighth. Ginny won the gold medal; David O'Connor, an American competing as an individual, had a clear round and won the silver. Ian got the bronze and Karen Lende came fourth.

BALLYMURPHY

When I got home I had the time to concentrate on my two five-year-old novices, Harry the little Thoroughbred, and Picasso the skewbald gelding. In October I went to the Horse of the Year Show again for the parade of medallists, and took Friday. While there I watched a class for dressage and show jumping sponsored by Spillers Horse Feeds, and took a fancy to a bay horse called Ballymurphy. Initially the Carruthers, the owners, were not keen to sell; however, he was an Irish horse and the Irish had been trying to buy him all summer, and eventually the Carruthers felt that if they were going to sell him, better that it should be to someone who would keep him in England. After the show, I went with Mum to Cheshire to try him, and he impressed us favourably—every time I jumped a fence he bucked in enjoyment. A seven-year-old, he had done some eventing that year and gone well. Mum liked him so much that she bought him for me, so after I had ridden Picasso at Weston Park, I also brought Ballymurphy home.

GERMANY, 1986

While I was at Rotherfield, Mum and Mike had talked to our friends the von Imhoffs about my going to Germany during the winter for dressage training. They put us in touch with someone very suitable to help me: Rosemary Springer. It was therefore arranged that I would go to her in October for about six weeks, taking Aloaf and Murphy (Ballymurphy), whom I had had for only six days.

Sammy Davis had gone to Florida to work with dressage horses and friends had been grooming for me all summer as I hadn't found anyone permanent; yet another friend, Mary Benson, came to Germany in the lorry with me. We had the choice between a short sea crossing and a long drive on the other side, or vice versa. The Sheerness to Hook of Holland route was shorter and cheaper, and at that time of year the sea could be rough so the longer sea voyage might have been hard on the horses. We crossed at night and I slept in the lorry; we went ashore at 7.30am, faced with a twelve-hour drive which was further delayed by two hours at the Dutch–German frontier. We arrived at Neumünster, north of Hamburg, after dark and Andreas, Mrs Springer's groom, helped us put the horses away.

We gave them a day's rest before I had my first lesson with Rosemary. She speaks very good English and is an amazing person: at sixty-five she still trains and teaches, plays tennis and skis. She also does clinics in Australia and America, so is used to Thoroughbreds and can cope with the event horse's temperament. I learned a lot, but it took me a month before I could even ride a halt properly!

Mary returned to England the day after we arrived, and I lived in a flat on my own. With only the horsebox for transport, I couldn't get about much, so spent most of my spare time over there reading or writing letters: neither of which I really enjoy. With only the two horses, I finished riding in the morning and after I had groomed them in the afternoon, had time on my hands. I used to help in the Springers' yard—if one of the boys had a day off, the other would have fourteen horses to attend to. It was always good to see my eventing friends, among them being Bettina Overish, who

Scuba diving, December 1986

knew Mrs Springer well; Frederic Otto, known as Chico, who also had lessons from Rosemary; Christian Struck and Karsen Varnaker. They sometimes even managed to wangle me a party invitation!

Mum and Mike came out after six weeks and were most impressed by my progress. Mrs Springer found Aloaf difficult because he was so big but the head lad, Joerg Dietrich, helped me a lot by riding him really well. Aloaf loved being a dressage horse, which he found very secure; he used to be worked daily in the indoor school, and after a while when I was warming him up with a canter he would buck with exuberance. He was lovely to ride and beginning to show a lot better cadence in the working trot and I was beginning to be able to ride the movements better, sitting properly for the half passes and the shoulder-ins, not letting them lapse in any way and keeping every step the same. Having good mirrors also helped, so that when told to sit up I could see my posture and correct it.

Unlike Aloaf, Murphy did not enjoy dressage at all and the more we did, the worse he became. Each time I asked him to canter he would buck, not because he was feeling happy, but the contrary. I felt depressed when Joerg said he felt Murphy was not going to be a good horse—Murphy moves very wide behind and according to Joerg had a weak back. I had had this horse for only seven weeks, had expected him to be a superstar, and was being told only that he didn't look too good.

For the three weeks before Christmas I was hoping to go on holiday to Australia; when I told Rosemary she was shocked, and even more so when she learned I intended to take my horses home and not school them after all the work we had done. She insisted I leave them with her for the three weeks, and that I come back after Christmas to tune myself in again; only then should I take them home—to which I agreed.

AUSTRALIA

Australia was a trip that David Green had organised during the summer; there were several event riders in the group—Rodney Powell, Chris Hunnable, Mary Thompson, Melanie Hawtree, Daniela Sieff—and we were going scuba diving on the Great Barrier Reef. During July some of us going out on the trip who hadn't dived before started a scuba diving course in Southampton, but were unable to finish the course and obtain our certificates because we weren't able to find the time to do the open dive in the sea. And having been to Germany for dressage training, I could not afford more than fifteen days in Australia, of which some time was spent travelling and nearly a week on a boat at the Swain Reefs. Chris Hunnable, who was coming for only three weeks, travelled with me. In such a huge country two weeks were not nearly enough to see as much as I would have liked, but I hope to return on a longer visit one day.

My sister Lucy was working in Sydney, so after our long flight there we stayed overnight with her. We went on to Brisbane by coach, our immediate destination being the Greens' house where we met everybody else. David's parents very kindly put us all up, first before we left for our week's scuba diving, and again on our return.

We dived twice a day at first, morning and afternoon, to finish our course and pass a test. We began in groups of four or five, but when we became more proficient we were allowed to go off in pairs. Rodney and I

went on a dive together, trying to navigate underwater by the compass he carried. This little expedition could very well have ended in disaster. We kept pausing while he tried to work out where we were and on one of these occasions he must have suggested we go back; I, however, thought he was telling me to go on, so involuntarily we parted company, and the next time I looked round he wasn't there. You need only swim in opposite directions for a few seconds, underwater, to lose sight of each other—I kept looking for him above and below the surface, popping up and diving alternately, until I was running out of air; then I gave up and started back to the boat. Nobody there had seen Rodney either. Presently we did manage to spot him, but some distance away so David went to fetch him in a small boat as I told them he must be short of air. It is dangerous to lose contact with one's partner and our misadventure could have ended tragically. The correct procedure is for both to go up to the surface where the visibility is better than beneath it, and stay there until you find each other.

Me in scuba gear, just before a night dive in Australia on the Great Barrier Reef

The water is not without without its dangerous species, and sea snakes were rather frightening. Apparently if you are bitten by one of these there is no point even trying to swim to the surface, because you will be dead before you get there. Once, when fourteen of us went out on a dive with Dale, our instructor, we had just reached the sea bed when somebody must have trodden on a sea snake and disgruntled it, because it started to follow him. Dale saw what had happened, so bravely put his foot in its way and lured it away from the inexperienced diver. He swam slowly to the surface with the snake balanced on one of his flippers and managed to get out of the water before it realised what he was doing. Stone fish are equally poisonous and are another horrible hazard. You cannot see them and if you tread on one it is fatal—just knowing they are there is a constant worry.

Everything else is just wonderful, the little fish and the coral, and I hope one day to go scuba diving again, on the Barrier Reef or elsewhere. We moved every day to a different reef, and also visited a couple of islands—Turtle Island was aptly named, because all the turtles come to lay their eggs there. It has lovely sandy beaches and palm trees, and is so small that you can walk round it in twenty minutes. Daniela Sieff, who did Rotherfield Young Riders with me, thought it would be fun to sleep on this island one night when the boat was anchored close inshore; so we were duly taken ashore with a sheet and cushion each, and left there. We walked round the island that evening, watching the turtles. Although they are cumbersome on land, they are amazingly fast in the water. I tried to chase one when we were scuba diving, intending to grab hold of it and be towed along, but they go so fast my mask would probably have been pulled off—I couldn't catch it, anyway.

We spent a few days at the Greens' again before Chris and I had to fly home. Melanie and Mary joined us and we finally arrived home on Christmas Eve. The Australian holiday was a wonderful experience, but two weeks were just not long enough—I shall have to go back sometime! However, funds were running out, and I was keen to return home and get the horses started in the new year. I was also looking forward to going over to Germany again, to see how Aloaf and Murphy were progressing. All in all, the prospects for the spring season 1987 seemed quite exciting!

It is difficult to see how horse trials riding can survive at any significant level without some form of sponsorship. By 1987 the enormously high cost of running my own event horses was becoming a serious problem. An event horse costs about £5,000 a year to keep in competition; quite apart from the actual cost of keeping the horses, there are always countless additional expenses to consider: entry fees, training and travelling expenses, grooms, clothing, to mention a few. Mike had so far generously supported me, but now that my enterprise was expanding he was becoming increasingly worried about the financial side. In the winter of 1986/7 I had a yard full of good horses, but with no immediate solution, the future for all of us suddenly seemed to be very much in the balance.

11 My Future Secure

When I returned from Australia, Mum and Mike were on Exmoor, so Christmas Day 1986 was spent doing the horses at Hoplands. A new resident was Niffikim, a twelve-year-old advanced horse I had been loaned; his owner, Dr Neil Lawson-Baker, wanted me to event him in the spring. He was a flea-bitten grey with a pink muzzle and two white socks, was sweet-natured and tried very hard. We had one problem with Niffy at first: when we put him in a field on his own, he would jump out and come back into the stables because he loved his friends so much and wouldn't be without them! He had come to us in October and had done no more than walk as he had had some time off with leg problems; now he was just ready for schooling. If his leg proved sound enough for three day, or even one day, events, I contemplated buying him.

'An event horse costs about £5,000 a year to keep; quite apart from the actual cost of keeping the horses, there are always countless additional expenses . . .'

I had Christmas lunch at my grandparents' with Daddy and all my cousins, and spent the evening there too. On Boxing Day we all went out with the New Forest Beagles, all the cousins, aunts and uncles. That evening I was invited to dinner by Tim Everett, who lives in the house we sold, now called Danesfield. Mum and Mike (when in Hampshire) live in the old farmhouse, which we had done up and have re-named Hoplands. I hadn't met Tim before but he is now a great friend.

On 2 January 1987 we had a shoot on the farm, with which I helped Mike; in the evening I caught a flight from Heathrow to Hamburg, to go and see Aloaf and Murphy. Mrs Springer was away skiing, so Joerg was to give me lessons—he did not speak as much English as Rosemary, but got the message across just as well. He had put a lot of work into Aloaf and Murphy during my absence and they had come on a lot. I stayed about ten days, to work myself back into routine and get used to the horses again. Then the weather closed in—the temperature fell as low as -25°C on some days and the countryside lay under deep snow. Mum and Mike had come to Germany and were going to make the return journey with me, but on the day for which we had booked the ferry it was snowing hard, and

deep drifts had made the minor roads impassable. All my horses at home were fit by now, and waiting to be schooled, so we therefore flew home and once more left Aloaf and Murphy with Mrs Springer for Joerg to carry on training. At the end of January I returned to Germany, spent another ten days training, and finally brought them home on 13 February 1987.

Finding a really good groom was a continuing problem. I had had two pupils, but they left at the end of March. I was recommended a very sound girl called Alex Evans, who had done the Chattis Hill course and had been working with eventers, and as I was rather desperate, Alex started working for me without an interview, on two weeks' trial. She stayed, and shared No. 2 cottage with me and we did the horses together; later on, Helen Hall started working for me too, as there was too much for just Alex and me to do once the season got under way.

SPONSORSHIP

The horses were costing a very large sum, and the financial burden was too much for Mike to bear alone. We decided that if I did not find a sponsor in 1987, I would have to think about selling my horses and giving up eventing, perhaps keeping horses at livery instead. David Mason, of MacConnal Mason Gallery (whose daughter Claire events), had already offered to sponsor me a few years before when I was a Young Rider, but at the time

Niffy at Stowell Park Advanced, 1987—sporting my new sponsor MacConnal Mason's colours

Mike had liked our horses to run under his own name, so we had turned down the offer. Obviously I could not approach David now, having refused him the first time; but it was my extraordinarily good fortune that, early in the season, he made another approach and offered to pay for the keep of a few of my horses. After discussion it was decided that all my event horses would run under the name of MacConnal Mason Gallery, who would pay for the keep of five of them.

This was a great relief, as I could carry on eventing and it would cost Mike considerably less than it had done. He most generously continues to meet some of the expenses and buys some of the horses; Mum also buys horses for me. Without their continuing help I would not be able to carry on eventing. Having a sponsor was quite a thrill. The lorry was resprayed in the livery of MacConnal Mason, who also provided rugs for the horses, and jumpers and coats for anyone involved in helping with them. All we had to hope for now were good results in the current year.

'Having a sponsor was quite a thrill ... All we had to hope for now were good results in the current year.'

Claire Mason was having dressage lessons from Pat Manning, so David Mason suggested that I attend them with her. Pat teaches in a slightly different way from most people. Instead of telling you directly what to do to improve your horse immediately, she gets you to tell her what you think is going wrong and what you ought to do to correct it—this forces you to think for yourself much more. It is easy to be told what to do and to find your horse improving, but when you have to try to analyse the faults and reason out how to cure them yourself, the exercise becomes much more difficult. The lessons take longer, but you remember what you have learned and if other, different problems crop up when you are practising on your own, you learn to resolve these on your own too.

SPRING TRIALS 1987

We had a major setback just before the first event: Piglet got some heat in a foreleg, and the vet prescribed six months off. This of course ruled him out of Badminton. So Aloaf and Friday were now aimed at Badminton, and I hoped Niffy would go to Bramham; also that Ballymurphy might qualify for the Windsor three day event. However, Badminton was cancelled on account of the wet going so Aloaf's aim had to be shifted to Bramham, and I applied to enter Friday in a new event at Stockholm. The 1990 World Equestrian Games are being held there, so this 1987 event at two-star level was really being organised as an exercise in preparation for the latter.

Murphy's first event was a Novice at Wylye. He had always been ridden across country in a Pelham, but this time I rode him in a snaffle to find out how strong he was and whether he really did need a more severe bit. He went very well but had a stop at a sunken road because he came in a little bit too fast, so I decided that I did need better brakes. At King's Somborne Horse Trials that year I rode Friday, Aloaf, Niffikim and Murphy (now, there is a rule which prevents me from competing on my home course). Murphy went well, and after a few more events we were on better terms, and he finished up the spring season by winning the Intermediate at Bicton. Anyway, after his clear round at King's Somborne I had felt he was ready for Windsor, an Intermediate standard three day event which came just after Bicton.

My sponsor David Mason, with Mark Todd

WINDSOR 1987

Helen (Hall) came to Windsor with me—this was the first competition to which I took my lorry after it had been repainted in the MacConnal Mason livery. For an Intermediate three day event, Windsor 1987 was quite demanding technically—there were some difficult combinations, and I wasn't sure what Murphy would think of it all. I needn't have worried! He is such an easy-going character that he thoroughly enjoyed himself, and was quite unperturbed by the spectators. Nor does he mind being stabled away from home; he settles down quickly and his appetite isn't affected one bit. He has such a friendly nature and expression that anyone who sees him looking over a stable door cannot resist the invitation to go and have a chat with him—everyone who has worked with me or looked after him can vouch for this!

He put up a good performance in the dressage, and was lying in fourth place. We met our first problem on Phase A: there was a hazard ditch, where there was a choice between jumping it or taking a longer route around it—it was a silly little ditch, and when I rode him at it he refused to jump it! On the steeplechase, Phase B, I just cruised along—he has a big stride but we still incurred five time faults. This didn't worry me, as he is a young horse and very talented. Nor did I hurry him on the cross-country, but we took all the quick routes and he went beautifully, all within his scope and stride, to finish with only eighteen time faults—this was not

really slow, for there were only three or four horses that were faster. And in the show jumping he had only one jump down; this meant that he was placed third overall. Considering Windsor was his first three day event, this was really very pleasing.

BRAMHAM 1987

Bramham brought yet another disaster, this time with Niffikim; it also brought a good performance from Aloaf which earned him the recognition he deserved. Badminton having been cancelled, there were two sections at Bramham which meant a huge number of entries.

'... suddenly one hind leg gave way completely—he was cantering along on three.'

Niffy was lying fifth after the dressage; he was rather stiff, but was accurate and calm, for which he gained good marks. He had won his first event and been placed in all his other events, Advanced and OIs, this spring. Our main worry now was whether his legs would stand up to all the galloping he had to do. On the steeplechase he did the first circuit beautifully but was a trifle behind time on the second, so after the open ditch I urged him on a little bit more. He went away from the leg really well, but suddenly one hind leg gave way completely—he was cantering along on three. I leapt off but couldn't understand what had gone wrong, except that it was crippling him. Spectators could not see this part of the steeplechase, so Mum, Mike and Alex were waiting at the start in ignorance of what had occurred. Niffy was led off the course, put in a trailer and taken back to the stableyard.

His tendons, which had always been the biggest worry, were all right, and nobody was able to diagnose anything else. We took him home and kept him in his stable for six weeks, then finally we could take him to Newmarket to be X-rayed. This revealed that he had broken his pelvis; there must already have been a hairline fracture there, in that such a major break resulted merely from galloping. At the place where I had had to pull him up there was a dip, which may have caused him to jar his leg and cause the break. This was a great sorrow; in only one spring season Niffy had shown himself to be a wonderful horse, with the will to go very successfully in eventing. Happily he is now sound again; Dr Lawson-Baker has him at his home and he did a little hunting in the winter of 1988–9.

Aloaf did a creditable test and was doing a good cross-country until we came to a double of corners where the stride between them was quite long. My line was all right, but I had not set him up correctly for it. In consequence he got in too deep to the first fence and jumped too high, so was much too far off the second corner. I pulled him out because I didn't want him to land in the middle of it. He had a clear show jumping round and we finally took eleventh place. Rodney Powell won on The Irishman, and Jane Thelwall won the other section on King's Jester.

This was my first year out of Young Riders, and I had been aiming for the Senior European Championships at Luhmühlen in September; but after the silly stop at the corners, I thought perhaps we should leave it for another year. When Bramham was over, however, the selection committee put me and Aloaf on the list. This surprised many people, but Aloaf had been consistent twice at Burghley, was an outstandingly good horse, and the stop had really been my mistake. I was exuberant, particularly as I would be eligible again for team training at Badminton.

TRAINING AT BADMINTON, JUNE 1987

It was Friday's turn first for training at Badminton, in preparation for the Stockholm three day; only seven British horses were going. Stockholm came in the middle of June, which left us only ten days after Bramham for training; Lord Patrick Beresford was again the chef d'équipe.

Senior team training differs from Young Rider or Junior training in that you are not compelled to have lessons. Ferdie Eilberg and Pat Burgess will give (respectively) dressage and jumping lessons if you want them. They cannot attend every day, so on some days perhaps neither will be there, but your own trainers can come to teach you if you wish. It was encouraging to see the Duke of Beaufort taking a great interest—he used to sit on the bank, watching the lessons and even taking part in some of the jumping. Jane Holderness-Rodham sometimes came if anyone wanted a cross-country school over the special practice fences that Colonel Frank Weldon had built: a coffin, a corner and a step up and rail of Intermediate height.

Those training can also take their young horses, and depending on how many riders are taking part, might be able to take three or even four horses. There couldn't be a better place than Badminton for such training, with a vast area to hack in around the park and surrounding farmland where there are wide grass verges around the fields. Two or three dressage arenas are laid out and there are always some show jumps set up. To accommodate us, the old servants' quarters had been renovated—they are next to the stable block, however, which doesn't make for an uninterrupted night's sleep or a late lie-in!

Anne-Marie Taylor had the misfortune to fall during training and suffer a mild concussion, so she was unable to go; nor could Ros Bevan, as Horton Point wasn't sound. This left only Ginny Leng with Master Craftsman (Crafty), Lucinda Green with Shannagh, John Evans with The Cordwainer, Mary Thompson with King Boris and myself with Friday Fox. Friday was highly honoured at being asked to travel in the Holgate lorry, driven by Ginny's mother, Heather Holgate; the other three went in Mary Thompson's. Alex came as my groom, and Mum and Mike joined us later. We were in for a twenty-four-hour ferry crossing to Gothenburg, followed by eight hours' drive to Stockholm. We were to spend the night in Gothenburg, but when we arrived we couldn't find the stables; eventually the police came to our aid and grandly escorted us there, as though we were royalty . . . or under arrest.

STOCKHOLM 1987

The Stockholm three day event was held in a park in the centre of the Swedish capital, but the grassy areas were more like rough open fields than the smooth lawns of a London park. The horses were stabled in an Army barracks which was surrounded by busy roads and the facilities for hacking were poor—there was a small wooded park, but to reach it we had to thread our way through city streets and traffic which the horses were not used to, and the place was not attractive when one did reach it. We had known it would not be possible to top off our horses' fitness after we arrived in Stockholm: we had had to make sure they were in peak condi-

tion before we left England. However, the hotel in which the organisers accommodated us was luxurious.

There was a big international entry, with Mark Todd on Charisma and Tinks Pottinger on Volunteer from New Zealand; and teams from the USA, Belgium, Poland, France and Sweden. There were also individual riders from Denmark and Holland, as well as John Watson from Ireland.

The cross-country course was very much up to two-star standard. The fences were not always of the maximum permitted height but they were technically tricky, the ground undulated and the track wound through some woodland. One fence involved coming out of a wood and up a ramp, with a big drop off the top—it simulated the roof of a house with turf on it. By the end of cross-country day it had become dangerous—the turf had got increasingly scuffed as horses were preparing to jump and when they found there was nothing to support their front feet, they pushed their feet back, found nothing there on which to purchase, and so jumped down very steeply. It was a very queasy feeling when your horse seemed to disappear from underneath you, jumping straight down instead of outwards.

There was also an interesting farmyard complex incorporating a cottage; one of the alternatives was to ride up over the steep roof, jumping a rail on the way to it, jump off the roof on the other side, take one stride and out over another rail.

Another fence—we called it The Pimple—consisted of a big circular palisade with a circular bank inside it, divided by a ditch. The direct route was to jump the palisade, bounce onto the bank, bounce over the ditch, land on the other half of the bank, jump off this and bounce over the palisade. The long way meant jumping the palisade, going along the length of the ditch and jumping out of the palisade. In fact this proved to be not much slower than the direct route.

On parts of the course we could see where the ground was being prepared for more fences, to be built for the World Championships in 1990.

The roads and tracks involved trotting through traffic and across parks where the public were picnicking, not expecting us at all—we had to hope that they would see us in time so as not to alarm either our horses, or themselves! Because there were so many roads, the horses could not wear studs on this phase and we were afraid they would be in danger of slipping and falling on the steeplechase. The latter was on sand laid on hard ground, which made the going difficult; furthermore, although it looked flat, when we galloped we realised that the ground under the sand was uneven, so that the depth of the sand varied. This made it hard work for the horses, and only two or three did the steeplechase inside the time. It was also difficult to do the cross-country within the time: not only was it twisty and undulating, but there were also quite a few combination fences.

I was selected for the team and to go first. The draw made me the second competitor to run, following the Japanese competitor, Hisachi Wakahara (whom we nicknamed Wacky) on Lord Waterford; Wacky is based in England, at Tomi Gretener's. After me, it was Mark Todd's turn on Charisma.

Friday and Alex at Stockholm 1987

Friday did herself great credit in the dressage. After years of practising, she was just beginning to lower her head, stretch her neck and relax enough to stay calm throughout. She did all her halts and a very good walk. Then in the steeplechase she lost a back shoe. The farrier wasn't immediately available and I would have lost too much time if I had waited for him to replace it, so I pressed on, trying to keep her on the sand and off the road, and she was reshod in the ten-minute box. We scored only 1.6 time faults on the 'chase.

Being second to Wacky on the cross-country meant I had no chance of assessing how the course was riding, for he merely cantered round; he told me he would wait for me at the Pimple fence where he was taking the long way round and he hoped that I would go the short way. This was meant as a joke. At Windsor there had been a similar fence consisting of a post and rails around a Pimple: while Nigel Taylor was going the direct route, Wacky had taken the long one and they had arrived at the top almost simultaneously. The implication was that this time he was going to wait in the ditch so that I would have to jump over *him* as well as the ditch. He must have had a better ride than his score suggested, for I didn't catch up with him: why not, I really can't imagine, because he had seventy-eight time faults.

Friday slipped on the ramp drop but stayed on her feet; she negotiated the Pimple bank fence with the palisades immaculately, which made everyone happier, particularly the course builder who had designed it. We finished inside the time, a feat achieved by only four others—one of whom was Mark Todd. The rest of the team had good rides.

Mark Todd was leading, Bruce Davidson on J.J. Babu—from America—was second after the cross-country, and also third on his other horse, Noah. Tinks Pottinger was fourth, Ginny fifth and Lucinda sixth. I was seventh, with a lot of good horses and riders below me in the order so far, so I was greatly pleased with Friday. The show jumping was also on sandy soil—deep going and hard work. Friday had a clear round, as did Shannagh and Crafty. Noah had a few down and Mark knocked down four.

The final order at the end of the three days gave victory to the British team. Bruce Davidson was first individual on J.J. Babu, Tinks second, Ginny third, Lucinda fourth, myself fifth and Toddy sixth. It had been a truly world-class line-up, and I was really delighted.

'In July we had the splendid and totally unexpected news that Friday, as well as Aloaf, had been put on the long list for the European Championships.'

The journey home wasn't as pleasant as the outward one. At the docks we were told that the horses could not be taken on board because of high winds, so we had to spend five tedious days in Gothenburg before they were allowed to make the sea crossing; Heather Holgate looked after Alex and me admirably. When at last the horses were permitted to travel we found the ferries were over-booked, so I returned to England in Tomi Gretener's lorry as my horses at home needed working, leaving Alex to follow with Friday.

In July we had the splendid and totally unexpected news that Friday, as well as Aloaf, had been put on the long list for the European Championships. These two now had a break, which turned out to be a long one for Friday: she banged a fetlock quite badly out in the field, so we decided to give her the autumn off and bring her out the following spring.

NIGHTWATCH

'... In July I acquired an addition to the yard, Nightwatch ... He is a bit of a worrier and very big, a man's horse really, very long behind the saddle with a very long stride.'

My team of horses for the autumn had therefore diminished to three: Aloaf, Murphy and little Harry. I apologised to David Mason for not having five horses, the number I was meant to have running under his name, and also for not having much in the way of novices, either. David was not at all worried, and moreover, had another suggestion: his daughter, Claire, had a horse in her yard which she did not get on with, and he wondered if I would like to see what I could do with him. So in July I acquired an addition to the yard, Nightwatch—Banny for short—a nine-year-old; he hadn't evented for a couple of years but had some points. He is a bit of a worrier and very big, a man's horse really, very long behind the saddle and with a very long stride. I find him rather difficult to hold together, but I took him just to see what he could do and to assess his capabilities.

For his first event I took him to Brightling, where he was to run HC, because he had not been entered early enough to be in this competition. He was in the lead after the dressage and clear in both the show jumping and the cross-country, and would have been second. That was a good start, but on the cross-country I felt that he was frightened of his fences—although he jumped them clear, four strides before each fence he would rush into it as if he was so frightened to jump that he had to use his speed to get over it. Because of this worried attitude we came unstuck at our next event, where he slipped into a fence and stopped. Apart from that, he went well. In his third event the same thing happened—he got into a stride that was rather deep to a fence and obviously thought he couldn't make it.

We kept on having this problem. At his next few events he did not improve much—every time he got a bit too close to a fence he would stop. He would also stop if he slipped, because it frightened him. He didn't mind ditches or water, and as long as I was right at a fence, he would jump it; but whenever he was wrong he panicked. I persevered with him and he went very well at Aston Park Novice event, where for him the fences were bigger but more straightforward; he seemed to cope better with these than with anything that was a bit tricky. We decided to enter him for a few Intermediates to see how he coped, but he kept having the odd silly stop at a fence when he was not quite right at it or if there was a ditch that he did not like.

We had been trying all summer to resolve his bit problem, seeking one that he liked. He was very difficult to stop or turn, and it was a considerable dilemma finding one that he liked to show jump in—he was quite frightened of the bit, and when he got worried he knocked the fences down. In his last Intermediate for the autumn I rode him in a Pelham which obviously didn't work, for he had three down. However, there were only two clear rounds in the whole of the Intermediate class, so this was actually not too bad. As the cross-country was to be his last run before his three day, he needed a bit of a pipe-opener, so I spun round the course and he went clear with not too many time faults—and finished second.

This was a good performance for him, he was ready for a one-star CCI abroad, which would be smaller than Osberton, the Intermediate three day event in England; I therefore applied for the one-star at Waregem, in Belgium, an event of Intermediate standard that was to be held at the end of September.

Murphy came out in July feeling very confident after his Windsor three day event. He won the Intermediate at Stowe horse trials, and we decided we would enter him for the Advanced at Dauntsey, the Advanced at Molland, and then go to Gatcombe.

GATCOMBE 1987

Gatcombe was the final trial for Luhmühlen; there was a four-day team training session at Badminton just before, at which, as usual, everybody was in high spirits. I had a lot of help there from Ferdie Eilberg with Aloaf's dressage—it needs so much strength to keep him together, and even a man finds him difficult on the flat. I believe it also helps to concentrate the lessons, such as two in four days instead of once a week. At the end of the four days Ferdie had helped Aloaf and me so much that when we went to Gatcombe, Aloaf was lying seventh, just behind the leaders, after the dressage in the big Championship class, and Murphy was in the lead in the Advanced section—I had just managed to get through to Murphy and Aloaf in that time.

The shortlisted riders had been asked to go slowly on the cross-country because the ground was rather hard and we didn't want to wreck any horses before Luhmühlen. I went fairly slowly on Aloaf, though kicked on enough for it to feel a good ride. It is difficult to ride slowly, because you don't feel that you are going across country, so I let him go at what I felt was a comfortable speed and he went well. After his stop at Bramham, I still did not think that I had much chance of being selected for Luhmühlen.

Murphy coming down the Gatcombe steps to complete his second Advanced event and finish fourth

Helen, Murphy and Teazle relaxing at Dauntsey 1987

CROFT ORIGINAL
28

'It was hard to credit that in first year of Senior competition I should go straight into the Senior squad ...'

I had had a few problems with Murphy's show jumping, which Pat Burgess had helped me iron out during the team training at Badminton—in trebles, particularly, he had been gaining so much ground that by the time he came out we were hitting the final element. We thought we had discovered why he was doing this, and all it needed was for me to sit up a bit more—if I leaned forward, he would go at the fence immediately, but if I sat up he waited for me and did not gain ground so much. Coming through a treble was still fairly difficult, as you are leaning forward over the first part and hardly have time to sit up properly after jumping it to make the horse slow down for the second and third parts. But a lot of work through schooling grids and around the course at Badminton in the training sessions had evidently paid off, for he did a superb show jumping round to go clear.

Now we had to wait and see what he would think of the cross-country, which I felt was a big test for him. Fence three, for example, is a stone wall drop into a wood, something you wouldn't find on a normal Advanced course, and it can take a young horse by surprise. However, Murphy didn't seem at all worried by that or any other part of the course—he is so scopey, and gave me a scintillating ride, making all the fences feel small yet being sensible at the combinations, where he really had to think. When we finished, all I could think of was that he was a grand horse for the future.

The next morning we had a trot-up for the shortlisted horses and Aloaf seemed pretty good. It is nerve-racking, waiting for the selectors to decide which six they are going to take and who will be the reserves; there were obvious definite choices, but it was pretty tough for the rest of us waiting, telling ourselves we had as good a chance as everybody else. In fact, although I felt that Aloaf had gone excellently at Gatcombe, I could not forget that we had made that mistake at Bramham—so I was incredulous when I was selected among the six. The selectors obviously believed that Aloaf and I could produce the goods on the day.

It was hard to credit that in my first year of senior competition I should go straight into the Senior squad!—I told myself that I had got in only because Rodney Powell had broken his pelvis just before Gatcombe and would not be fit to ride at Luhmühlen. The others in the squad were Ginny Leng on Night Cap, Mark Phillips on Cartier, Ian Stark on Sir Wattie, Jane Thelwall on King's Jester and Richard Walker on Accumulator; Lucinda Green was reserve on Shannagh. The four for the team would be chosen when we got to Luhmühlen.

'Team selection was a significant personal achievement, and Luhmühlen was to be the high spot of that Autumn of 1987 ...'

We were to have one more team training a week later, before leaving at the beginning of September. Yet on that very day, a major calamity hit the team: Mark Phillips found something wrong with his lorry when he started it to go home, and as he got out to see what it was, he slipped and fell and strained several tendons and ligaments. Luckily there was time for him to recover before Luhmühlen.

Team selection was a significant personal achievement, and Luhmühlen was to be the high spot of that autumn of 1987; it is a major competition, and a severe test even for seasoned senior competitors. In fact there was everything to look forward to, with Aloaf and Nightwatch going strong, and some good young horses waiting in the wings. And most important of all were my sponsors, without whose help and backing my eventing career might have been curtailed much earlier than I would have wished.

The British teams at this time were doing well—since becoming chef d'équipe Patrick Beresford had seen three consecutive team wins. As in any sport, success always encourages the winning spirit and has a wonderful effect on confidence and courage—you take a chance, make that extra effort. Riding for a team sharpens this determination to do well, and is altogether a very special experience; problems and pleasures discussed and shared mean that friendships and loyalties develop and strengthen very quickly. The feeling of companionship and team spirit at our training sessions and at Luhmühlen was very real, and I was so lucky to be a part of it.

> *'As in any sport, success always encourages the winning spirit and has a wonderful effect on confidence and courage ...'*

TRAINING AT BADMINTON, AUGUST 1987

When we resumed team training, the usual attention to the horses' fitness continued. We used to take them by lorry to gallop, either to Tim Foster's at Lambourn or to Jeremy Tree's on the Marlborough Downs. With Ferdie's and Pat's help Murphy's show jumping and his and Aloaf's dressage also improved.

12 ‹› The Winning Spirit

One evening we were guests at a big dinner party in the Duke and Duchess of Beaufort's large dining room; we had a great time exploring the house with the Duchess, who showed us all over it. I have always loved old houses—I suppose living in one when I was young fostered this. The attics and cellars are always the best places! To return Their Graces' hospitality we invited them to dine with us in the big hall which used to be the old kitchens. After dinner we each stood up and gave a vote of thanks: to the Duke and Duchess, the selectors, and to Ferdie and Pat for all the help they had given the team; to the sponsors, the suppliers of our equipment, and to everybody who had helped us at Badminton. For me, this was an excruciating experience—I found it terrifying to stand up and address an audience of thirty or more. As I was the youngest, I got away with saying the least, but it takes me only a few seconds to go bright red, which I certainly was by the time I sat down! However, it all added to the spirit and companionship of the whole training session.

Whilst we were at Badminton a 'sponsors' day' was held, when photographs were taken of us and all the equipment which had been supplied for us to take to Luhmühlen. One was of the whole team wearing 'Equorian' brand clothes: the girls in hats, blazers and skirts of grey Glenurquhart check; the men in caps and jackets of the same, with plain grey trousers. We were all in lively spirits, and before the picture was taken Mark Phillips had raised laughter when he appeared in one of our skirts and wearing his flat cap as a sporran.

It was bad luck on Richard Walker that his horse, Accumulator, was not completely sound on the last trot-up; Lucinda Green took his place, with

Shannagh. Such a last-minute disappointment when everything seems to be going smoothly is always discouraging; however, Mark Phillips was recovering quickly from his leg injury and was fit to compete.

The horses were to travel in two lorries: Cartier, Aloaf and Night Cap in the Holgates'; King's Jester, Shannagh and Sir Wattie in the Thelwalls'. However, when we began loading them we found that Cartier, who stands 18.2 hands and bears the humorously contrary stable name of Pixie, could not fit into the Holgates' lorry—theirs has a rug rack at the back and he was so tall that his back was touching it. With ten minutes to spare before departure time, we had to put this gigantic horse into the other lorry, but it was too late to change any of the equipment and all we could do was transfer some of his food and hay. After this small drama we drove towards Sheerness. Not far from there we had arranged to meet a vet, as all the horses had to be checked before we would be allowed to cross. We had to park the lorries in a field, as they would have blocked the narrow roads. This didn't sound like much of a problem, until Heather drove the Holgate lorry into the field and whilst turning round became stuck in the soft ground. Of course the lorry was extremely heavy with the equipment for three horses and six people on board. Luckily we had arrived in plenty of time, as it took two tractors to pull the lorry out of the mud. In the end it had to be parked on the road, but fortunately no large vehicles needed to pass while we were blocking the way. The vet, having seen all the horses, sent us on our way and we reached Sheerness in time to board ship for the seven-hour crossing to Flushing.

On arrival at Luhmühlen we had a few days to settle in for we had arrived on Saturday night as no lorries are allowed on the Autobahnen on Sundays. Ferdie Eilberg came to help with our flat work and Dot Willis, Ginny's trainer, was there to help with the jumping. We rode in the morning; the horses rested and were led out to grass in the afternoon, and we passed the time swimming and shopping. The stables were so far from the show ground that we had not had even a glimpse of the cross-country fences until the day we walked the course. Going round as a team, one has the advantage of discussing the fences with the others. Mark Phillips had a bit of a problem in getting round. Although he was fit to ride, he was still slightly lame, so was provided with a small machine that looked like a four-wheeled motorbike. He met considerable difficulties at many of the jumps because there were a lot of ditches that forced him to make long detours. However, he managed to meet us at most of the fences. As usual, the course consisted of numerous combination fences with long gallops between them.

Aloaf and me in the dressage at Luhmühlen 1987

THE LUHMÜHLEN COURSE 1987

There were two small fences to start, then we came out of a wood to number three, which gave us all something of a shock because of its size: a big parallel with a huge ditch under it. In fact, by the time we had finished walking the course, this fence was to appear comparatively insignificant. Fence four was another gaping hole in the ground with enormous rails behind it; then to five, which was a farmyard complex, a four-part combination: an upright to a giant table, then a corner to another upright. Although it seemed very big, we felt it would be all right if it was ridden

strongly and accurately; the alternative was a bit wiggly. After a big plain hedge was a coffin made of huge logs—the banks to the ditch were steep, and the straight way would ride fairly uncomfortably, but we decided that it was probably the route to take. The next fence was to prove crucial: very big, a solid green brush on to a road crossing and then one stride to a massive white parallel with a drop. On landing you had to turn sharp right and jump another set of rails.

The next combination, of steps up and down in a wood, looked fairly straightforward; then another long gallop to the first of the water complexes: a trakehner, a few strides to a bank where you went up a step, bounced over a log, then down the slope over a second log and straight into the water; through the water and out onto an island, where you met a trakehner-type fence over a water ditch. This straight route didn't look

'... we found that Cartier, who stands 18.2 hands and bears the humorous stable name of Pixie, could not fit into the Holgates' lorry ...'

too demanding, but we took a good look at the wiggly alternative, just in case.

At the second water complex, the quick way into the water was a garden seat bounce which none of us really liked—we thought the horses would bash their legs on the chair and it looked uncomfortable. We all thought we would take the alternative—a log into water, then straight on to bounce out over a hedge.

Then a long gallop up a hill into a wood, and down the other side. So far the course had been quite flat, but this was a real test of fitness because it was about three-quarters of the way round and the horses would be getting tired. The combination after the hill looked like a brush fence but was actually straw bales covered in brush. We were all worried about this one because if a horse tried to bank it, which looked possible because it was wide, it could put its feet deep into the hedge. In fact this hazard was put right before the start of the competition, the top of the hedge strengthened so that it could be banked safely.

The next combination was to provide problems for Jane Thelwall: three or four strides down a slope to an upright gate, through a road crossing, up the other side and over another fence. This was quite a long combination, and all on a slight turn to the left.

Another big parallel came next, then a long gallop to the last combination: an upright rail, down two steep steps, a few strides to a fence, round a corner and another fence. On a tired horse this upright rail before steps seemed difficult; you would really have to get your horse back, particularly after a long gallop.

This was a 13-minute course, the longest I had ever done. Badminton can sometimes be up to about 12½ minutes, but at a championship the minimum time for cross-country is 13 minutes. Most CCIs are about 10 minutes, which is what we are used to riding, so 13 sounds awfully long and you wonder how your horse is going to cope with the extra time.

I could not have had better advisers about how each fence ought to be jumped. We all discussed what we thought of the fences, and had plenty of time to think about them. A little while later I had the shock of my life: I was chosen to ride in the team, which I had really not expected at all. Lucinda was to go first on Shannagh, I second, Ginny third and Ian fourth. Now I just needed a bit more help from Ferdie before my dressage the next day.

'A little while later I had the shock of my life: I was chosen to ride in the team, which I had not really expected at all.'

Next morning we set off early from the hotel for the stables. I had packed the clothes I would need for the dressage the previous night, and was in no hurry because Lucinda's dressage was in the morning and mine was not until the afternoon. I did not, therefore, take my bag out of the car, which was to cause another drama.

Meanwhile I had to ride Aloaf; we had not been allowed up to the show ground until now, so I took him up there to let him see the flags, the trade stands and all the other sights. When we returned from this short hack, Helen began to plait him up and generally get him ready, and I was thinking about changing—when it suddenly dawned on me that my bags were still in the car: and Ginny and Ian had said they were going to drive round the roads and tracks that morning. In about 45 minutes I had to get back onto Aloaf, and the clothes I would need were missing!

I began to panic about getting to my dressage test on time. I could not go

looking for Ginny and Ian, as we had no other transport about at the time, and it would take too long. Then Lucinda, having done her test in the morning—and done well—kindly offered to lend me her clothes, so at least I would get to my dressage on time, which was a great relief; but it is unsettling to have to wear someone else's clothes on such an important occasion. I had dressed and was ready to make my way to the arena when the car turned up, and I just had time to make a hasty change into my own garments.

This drama had set my heart racing, so to calm down and avoid upsetting Aloaf, I took the long trek to the show ground, a matter of some twenty minutes. When I arrived there, Ferdie worked me in. There is a lovely patch of heather at Luhmühlen, which is pleasant to work in because it makes the horses use themselves well. Aloaf seemed to be in good form. I didn't think Mum and Mike had managed to arrive in time to watch my dressage, which was disappointing, but I concentrated my thoughts on the task in hand. Aloaf perked up when we went into the arena. There were a lot of people and things to look at, but he contained himself and produced quite a good test—at least, everyone seemed pleased except me; though I usually do come out of the arena recalling everything that went wrong, and always think I could have done better, while the rest of the team remember the good bits, and hopefully consider you have done well. Outside the arena I noticed that Mum and Mike had turned up in the nick of time and had watched part of my test from outside the fence; it was an added bonus to know that they had arrived to support me. Aloaf had not disgraced himself: we were in eighteenth position out of fifty-eight starters. It is the cross-country that is the important part, anyway.

'... Mum and Mike had turned up in the nick of time and watched part of my test ... it was an added bonus to know that they had arrived to support me.'

CROSS-COUNTRY DAY (LUHMÜHLEN 1987)

Cross-country day was rather wet and miserable, but at least it was not hot and would be more comfortable for the horses. Having walked the course so many times, I thought that I really did know which way I was going to ride each fence. Jane Thelwall, number four and riding as an individual, was the first British competitor to go. She had a really good ride until the second to last combination, the big hedge and gate. She got very close to the gate and hit it, which set her off her line—Jester kept jumping, but ran to the right, while the line for the combination curved to the left; he ended up by jumping a crowd barrier into some trees, scattering the crowd. Jane was knocked off by one of the trees and by the time she had remounted, had wasted a lot of time. She also earned 20 penalties for leaving the penalty zone.

Lucinda was next on Shannagh, who looked very good although he reared and leaped forward in the start box—Lucinda just missed hitting her head on the roof and being knocked off, but set off on time. They were going well until they came to the solid hedge to the white rails. Having walked the course, *we* knew the white rails were there, but they could not be seen from the approach side of the hedge, so came as a surprise to the horses. Shannagh had jumped the hedge in very big and did not understand that he was meant to have a stride between; he decided to bounce, but as it *was* one stride, he was too far off the parallel and landed right in

the middle of it. It was a terrible fall. They got up and carried on, but had a stop at the first water when going the straight way, which we had all decided to try. However, he and Lucinda finished the course.

I had had a good steeplechase around the permanent figure-of-eight course—the one I had ridden before—and Aloaf was fresh and ready to go; so I came off the roads and tracks not knowing about all the problems we were having. Because Lucinda had bounced the white parallel, it was suggested I should come in a bit more slowly to give the horse time to see the parallel as he jumped the hedge before it; and at the water fence, it was decided that the rest of the team should go the long way, to ensure that we did not make any mistakes. Now it was all up to Ginny, Ian and me to go clear. I had planned to go straight at the water jump, but now had quickly to think of the alternative—I knew exactly where it was, where the penalty zone was and that you had to zigzag about, but because Aloaf is so big, he is not very handy at doing alternatives, so I was going to have to kick on between fences—but remembering the penultimate fence, which was big for a tired horse. Then I was told about Jane's incident, and that I had to be careful there, too, and keep on line.

I was all set to go and went to the start box, but there was a delay, so I had to come back and wait a few minutes. It is always a horrible moment when this happens. You try not to get nervous, but your thoughts dwell disturbingly long on what is to come. At last I was able to start. Fences one and two were no problem and I came to three thinking that it presented no great difficulty either, in comparison with the rest of the course, which was much bigger. But Aloaf reacted exactly as we had when we first walked the course—he jumped it, but was obviously thinking: 'My word, this *is* a big ditch, *and* a big fence—and Rachel hasn't ridden me strongly at it at all!'

This was a sharp reminder to me of how important the first walk round a course is. It is essential to remember your first impression of a fence, because that is how your horse will regard it, too. We landed, and I told myself to get moving and was a bit more motivated as we went towards the next fence, riding much more strongly into it: we flew it, after which everything went beautifully all the way until the hedge and white parallel where I had been told to come in a little bit more slowly because Shannagh had bounced it. Accordingly, I slowed Aloaf down. He is easy to slow down, and I think I overdid it—he is a most careful jumper anyway, and even if I had gone fast he would have jumped the first part of this obstacle with great care, anticipating something on the other side. Too late I realised that we, too, were going to be a long way off the parallel; I had to get the stick out and really ride him on for that one stride. He put in an enormous stride, got as near as he could but had to make a huge effort to clear the back rail—because he had stood off so far, he touched it with his belly. I had the sensation of stopping short in the air, but luckily he was underneath me when I came down. I had lost my stirrups and was half-way round his neck, but we managed to turn right and jump the next fence. He was such a good boy to concentrate and get us out of trouble; I must have shocked him deeply by expecting him to stand off so far.

We negotiated the alternative at the first water, which took rather long because he is not handy, but he was good at the next water and went very well for the rest of the course. He was a trifle slow, but I think that was because of the alternatives I had felt obliged to take, and also because he

Through the water at Luhmühlen

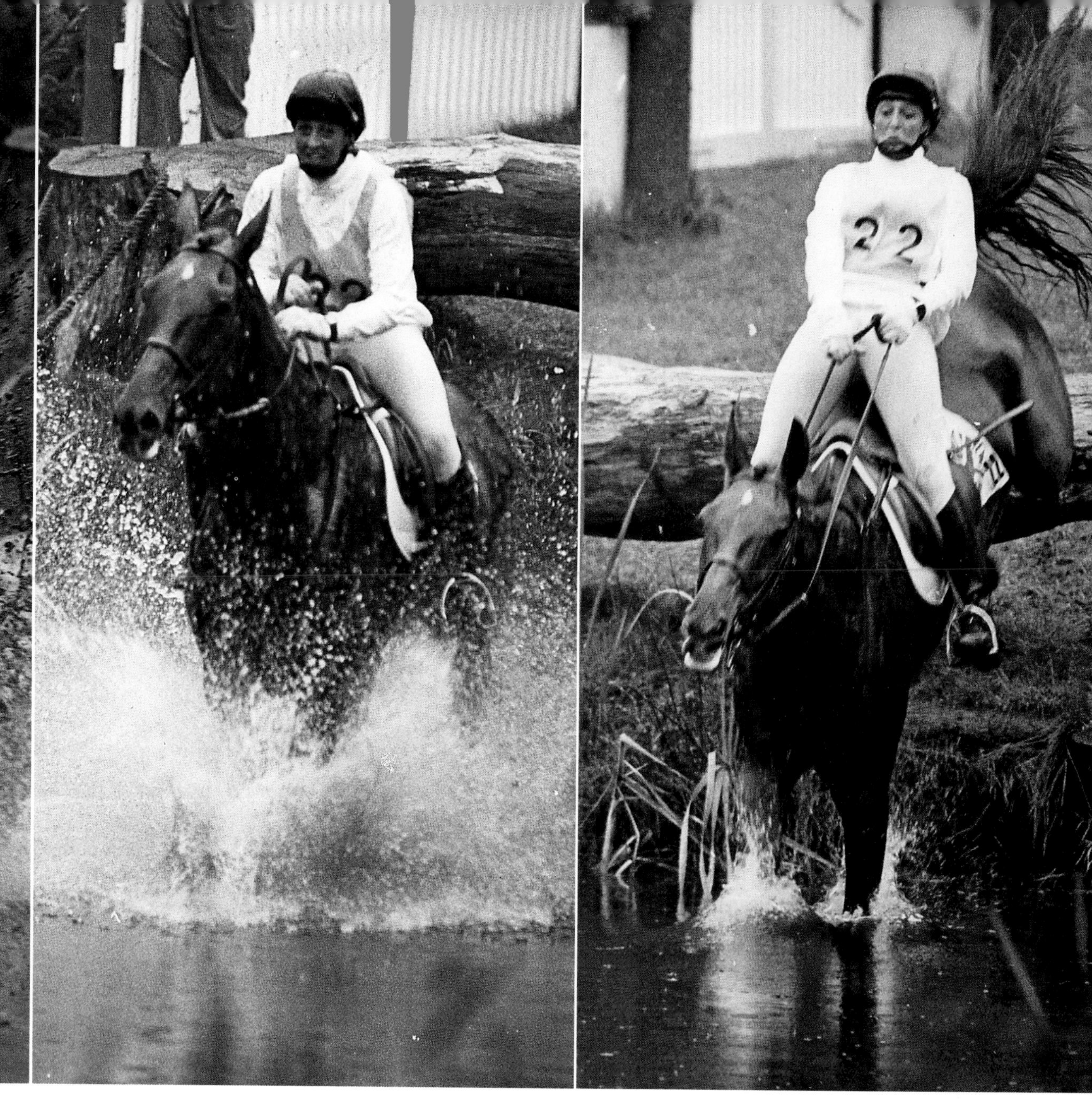

jumps carefully and so tends to waste a bit of time in the air over his fences. However, to my mind it is better to have a horse like that than one that is fast and not so careful. We finished with a clear round and a few time faults, but nobody was worried about the time—Lofty and I had got what the team wanted: a clear round. The team was still in with a chance if Ginny and Ian followed suit. They both did go clear, *and* inside the time, even though they took the long way at the water. After the cross-country, Ginny was first individually and Ian second, with me eighth; Mark did a lovely clear round on Cartier with a few time faults and pulled himself up to fourteenth.

Next morning Shannagh was feeling very sore after his tumble, so he was withdrawn; all the others passed the vet. I experienced another small drama before walking the show jumping course, for which you have to wear your show jumping gear: I had left my hat in someone's car, which

'We finished with a clear round and a few faults, but nobody was worried about the time—Lofty and I had got what the team wanted: a clear round.'

was locked; after a mild panic I borrowed a hat from one of the trade stands, just to walk the course in! At Luhmühlen the show jumping course is always very long, with lots of poles and big fences, quite a few of them unusual in the way of banks and permanent fixture walls with rails over the tops, and water troughs and other original features.

When the show jumping phase began, it was soon obvious that the course was causing some trouble. (There were thirty-four left in the competition at this stage.) Helen was outside, looking after a very laid-back Aloaf while I watched some of the early horses jump. I didn't want to jump him too much in case I tired him; after a few practice jumps he had seemed to be jumping well, so we left him at that. Jane and Mark had both had one fence down. When we went into the arena Aloaf seemed calm and relaxed, and jumped bigger and bigger as we went round, to finish with a brilliant clear. I was thrilled. All *he* wanted to do was leave the arena, as he hates crowds—he knew we had finished the course as soon as the clapping started, and could think only of getting out of there, as it was far too frightening. I was delighted with him. Now we just had to wait for Ginny's and Ian's turns.

I stayed with Aloaf and Helen, chatting about how outstanding he was, and didn't notice that the following four horses all made enough mistakes for me to move up in the order; only when someone actually pointed this out did I begin to get excited. Ian and Ginny had clear rounds; and Claus Erhorn, who was lying third, had one down but it didn't affect his position: the British team had won and Aloaf was fourth.

In the interval before the prize-giving, several heats were held of a race on fat cob-type horses, one of which Lucinda had been asked to ride. In the final, Lucinda had a bowler hat on and carried an umbrella, which helped urge on her fat little horse as it would hardly canter!—it was all very funny to watch. We were then all summoned to the press tent, and we were so jovial and chatting away so much that we nearly missed the presentations; Lucinda had to borrow a horse so that we could all line up mounted for our prizes. Immediately afterwards, we went to the British horse trials support group tent—Rosemary Barlow and all our other supporters had done invaluable work all week and were now holding a champagne reception for all the riders and helpers. To top it all, the weather was fine, a welcome change after the rain on the previous day.

So Patrick Beresford had nothing to complain about: this was the fourth consecutive team win since he had become chef d'équipe. We had had such a good time that I was reluctant to go home.

The team: Ginny, me, Lucinda and Ian

Left: Aloaf jumping to a brilliant clear round at Luhmühlen

HOME AGAIN

Burghley was held the following week. I didn't have anything to ride, but Mum, Mike and I took the caravan and went up to support our friends who were competing. On the Saturday I had to leave as I was to ride Nightwatch and my novice, Harry, at Taunton on Sunday. Both horses did well, so Banny was now all set to go to the one-star event at Waregem.

WAREGEM, BELGIUM 1987

The team which went to Waregem was small: Rodney Powell, Tanya Longson, Jane Starkey, Melanie Hawtree, Dawn Douglas and myself, with Mike Vacher as our chef. We were lucky to be in a hotel that overlooked the racecourse where the event was held, with the stables on the other side. The dressage and show jumping were to take place on the turf track, and all our working-in area was in the middle of the course. There was a trotting track as well, and every morning and afternoon the trotting horses came out for their exercise, which added variety to the occasion. It was surprising how frightened our horses were of them, and fortunate for us that this exercise was not allowed while the dressage was going on.

The Willis brothers, who build Badminton, had built the cross-country course, so the fences were beautifully made of lovely timber. This was the first time that a British team had been sent to the event, although it had been run for some years. When we walked round we were surprised to find that the fences were not particularly big, but our horses were fairly inexperienced and it was big enough to pose a serious challenge to them. The worst part was the steeplechase. The fences were a permanent feature for the race meetings, but were not the normal British chasing type—they were made of fully grown trees; and we had to do two circuits, each with

Left: Ian and me supporting Lucinda while she raced her cob!

four of them! The most worrying part of the competition would be getting over the first one—I would certainly have to ride at that, but once over, thought the rest should be simple enough.

Some of us had expressed doubts about our horses' performance over fences that were rather big for them, but Mike Vacher showed his confidence by putting me on the team with Rodney Powell, Tanya Longson and Jane Starkey. Banny tried hard in the dressage—even though he had never done a half pass before!—coped with all the flags and judges' boxes well, and did a calm and accurate test. After the dressage, however, the team was not lying in a good position, so there was catching up to be done on the cross-country. One fence that was causing a little concern was an inverted bounce of corners. Melanie was drawn number two and was the first to go for the Brits; she tried these corners and had a stop. Then Jane Starkey had a silly stop at a different fence, but Tanya did a very good clear round on her young horse, Time to Shine.

Then it was Banny's and my turn. We managed to get round the steeplechase although Banny did find the fences rather big; however, he was feeling very fit in the ten-minute box, so at the briefing I decided not to do the bounce of corners, as he had never jumped a fence like that, but to take the long way. This alternative worried me because he was difficult to steer and stop, and you had to jump two parts of the fence and then go round the back of it and jump two other parts; I was afraid I might not be able to turn well enough to prevent him leaving the penalty zone (as once you are in the penalty zone you must not leave it until you have jumped all the obstacles), and he stops if he sees a fence at the last instant.

Mum, Mike and me celebrating in the Horse Trials Support Group tent after the prize-giving at Luhmühlen

He goes fast across the ground, so we were well within the time and negotiated this fence that had bothered me. The one after it was a simple triple bar of moderate size, but after jumping it you had to turn sharply back on your tracks to go round the rest of the course. As I came to it I was on a long stride, and thought to myself that unless I shortened him a bit, we would be carried a long way after jumping before I could turn him—if I had a short stride in front of the fence I could hopefully turn him more quickly. Having kicked him all round the course without taking a pull at all, I intended to make him check just a little here, said 'Steady' . . . and he stopped dead. I was furious with myself for having this stop. I turned round, jumped it, and because he had been so fast he did not get many time faults. After his fairly good dressage, he was still up among the leaders.

'In the dressage, flowerpots were flying into the arena ...'

So now we were all relying on Rodney to do a good clear round on Private Benjamin (Nellie), his six-year-old mare, so that the team might just come up into the placings. And that was just what Rodney did. He swept round like a tornado to finish not far outside the time and put himself in first place, having been twenty-sixth after the dressage!

Banny had been tenth after the dressage and in ninth place after his stop; but the cross-country had caused so much trouble that, despite two of our own horses having had a stop, our team was first at the end of it. The show jumping round caused even more trouble, and Rodney had a couple down which lowered him to second place. Amazingly, after the problems we had been having with this discipline, Banny went clear and moved up to fifth. Tanya had only one down and came ninth; and the team won.

We had all had great support from our parents, and as Waregem was only a small event, everything was very relaxed—having only six riders created an air of pleasant intimacy, Alex and all the other grooms enjoyed it as well. We had even had time on Tuesday afternoon to go shopping in Brussels.

BOEKELO 1987

When we got home I concentrated on Murphy; all the other horses were on holiday. In October I took him to Boekelo where fourteen British riders were competing, with Charles Harrison as our chef. Helen came to groom for me and I gave a lift to an American girl, Jane Sleeper, and her two horses. As the previous year, we were all staying in holiday bungalows, five or six people in each; nearly all the teams were doing this now as it was much cheaper than a hotel.

There had been a great deal of rain, which made the going very bad. Britain during that time was being swept by Hurricane Gilbert, which caused widespread damage. Although the wind was not as strong in Holland, we had at one point to put the horses into horse boxes because the tented stabling looked as if it was about to take off. In the dressage, flowerpots were flying into the arena and the grandstand sheeting was flapping so much that it was a job to get the horses to concentrate. And by the time the last horses went into the arena it was so boggy that you could hardly keep them cantering down the centre line at the beginning and end of the test. Murphy coped really well and did a good test for the standard he had then reached, and we were particularly pleased at the way he overcame the many distractions created by the weather, because he is quite sensitive.

There is always a big entry at Boekelo and this year there were seventy horses and nine national teams. For the British team, those chosen were Mary Thompson on King Arthur to go first, David Green on Ayers Rock second, myself on Murphy third and Nigel Taylor on Formidable fourth.

Yet again we were not well placed after the dressage. The organisers were doing everything possible to get the ground right for the cross-country, including pumping water out to help it to dry; they made every effort to ensure that the competition could go ahead, although they had to make a lot of alterations. Fence three was completely rebuilt in a different place, which changed its character but at least meant that it was not taken out; fence eight, a hedge, had to be missed out altogether, and we had to take a different line through a field. There was a coffin-type water fence consisting of a parallel down into a river crossing, up the other side and another parallel; but the water was so deep they built a bridge over it! At twenty-four the two triangle fences had to be left out again, as they had the first time I came to Boekelo, and so did the following fence, a trakehner—we had to make a detour round some firm tracks in order to get to the next part of the course. It was amazing that the event ran at all and it was a great credit to the organisers that not only did it run, but that it also went well.

There were some interesting new fences. One was in the shape of a heart and built over a ditch, so it was a coffin-type fence. Another entailed a big jump onto a bank, quite a long bounce off over a hedge, and a big drop—we were not sure how the horses would cope with this one. Then the water offered three choices: either jumping a great big parallel over a ditch, across an island and then just jumping into the water and coming out; or jumping into the water, through it to a Normandy bank-type obstacle, and back into another lot of water; or (on the left-hand side) through the water, up a step over a rail, along and then jumping a parallel on dry land. There was certainly enough for both Murphy and me to think about.

There was also an S-shaped fence and in each loop of the S was a pond; so going straight through you could jump an upright into a pond and out of it over a fence in the middle, then in and out of the second pond and over a fence at the end. But we all decided to go slightly left to right across the diagonal which would miss out the two ponds.

Even with the bad conditions the course rode well, but the time was difficult to get. Murphy showed all his experience and coped with the mud so well that he came back with only six time faults, to put himself up into fourth position. David Green went up to third with a very fast cross-country round, and Mary and Nigel both went clear, so our team was in the lead. However, Murphy came back from the cross-country with a cut on his pastern—perhaps an overreach when he was galloping along a rather muddy track—which was bad enough to need stitches.

'This was the first time I had ever had a horse fail the vet's inspection.'

Next morning I got him out of his box and unbandaged him, and walked him for twenty minutes. He seemed quite stiff to start with and didn't really want to move his leg too much, but after his walk he loosened up. He seemed to be fine, so I trotted him and astonishingly he was level, which I had not expected. I showed him to Charles Harrison who was very pleased; and so we presented him at the vets' inspection—obviously if he had been lame we would not have done this. Everyone seemed to think he was fine and we all thought he trotted up sound—but he was not passed.

This was a bitter disappointment, and the team suffered by dropping a

place. It seemed so unfair to rule out a horse that had done so much work round the course—he only had a round of show jumping to do, which was nothing like as strenuous as the cross-country, and was then going on holiday for three months. His injury was really not bad enough to justify his elimination, but the vets thought the stitches enough reason to rule him out. This was the first time I had ever had a horse fail the vets' inspection.

Jean Teulère, from France, won the competition and Jane Sleeper, the American rider whom I had brought in my lorry, was second. The French team won and the British team finished second.

HUNTING AT HOME

In the winter of 1987/8 while the horses were on holiday I did not take a holiday myself—I had been away so much the year before in Germany and on the Barrier Reef that I thought it would be extravagant. So I spent the winter at home and passed the time hunting which I had not done for years, as all the horses are usually on holiday during the hunting season. This year, however, I had a new novice horse called Beaky; I had done a few events with him in October and thought that hunting would help him to think forward and make him a little bolder across country. I also felt that Banny would benefit from hunting, so decided to go out with the Portman in Dorset.

'On one very embarrassing occasion myself and many other members of the field were sent home by the Master . . .'

I enjoyed every minute of it, and both Banny and Beaky were lovely horses to hunt. I still didn't have much control over Banny, who would go flat out in a straight line—neither brakes nor steering were effective, so every time we went out I tried a different bit—but it didn't seem to make any difference. I didn't worry about it too much because I knew that when everyone else stopped, he would stop too! The Portman country is difficult because of the clay. The going is deep and the hedges are tall, and there is also a lot of barbed wire so it is as well to stick behind Richard Miller, the Field Master, as he knows where all the wire is. Often in a hedge line there might be only a section of wire taken down and if you were to go too far to his left or right you might find yourself in wire. My two horses certainly gained a lot of confidence from hunting, but we would have to wait until the eventing season got under way, to see if it did any good.

On one very embarrassing occasion myself and many other members of the field were sent home by the Master. I think being sent home is one of the worst things that can happen to you when out hunting; however, in this case it wasn't only a few of us but nearly the whole field—including some of the visitors from other hunts too! We had to go down some very boggy lanes to get to the field we needed to be in. When our hunt secretary, turned back I, like many others, thought she must know a way round the bad lanes and so duly followed her. She was quite unaware that she had half the field behind her, and when we all arrived in the field one down from Richard Miller and the rest of the followers the Master saw us and was furious. He was trying to send the fox out in our direction, and the land we were on was owned by someone who was against having any horses on it. I'm not really surprised he sent us all home!

That evening we all had a good laugh about it, as it had rained all day and the hunt had had a bad day—we hadn't missed anything. This sort of hunting gossip travels fast, as Mum and Mike heard about the Portman

field being sent home, the following night at a dinner party. Ever since, the episode has been a very funny in-joke, which is repeated somewhere during the Portman's Hunt Cabaret each year.

I was kept busy all winter with young horses that came to be broken in or schooled on; and in the middle of November Piglet came in because he had cut his face out in the field and needed to have it treated. We thought we might as well keep him in and start walking—as he had strained a tendon the previous spring, it seemed wise to walk him much longer than the month that I normally walk the horses. Friday, Aloaf and Murphy came in right at the end of December, after Christmas, to start their walking.

At the beginning of January I also started to break in Louis, a home-bred three-year-old colt by Welton Louis, one of Sam Barr's eventing stallions, and the first foal out of Spartangle, who had started eventing with Friday. Louis is the most lovely tempered horse. He is dark brown with no white

Tangle Louis, one of my home-bred horses for the future

on him at all; one disconcerting characteristic was that he was covered in warts—sarcoids—around his sheath, his chest and under his girth area. We had him tested and were relieved to learn that these were not cancerous or in any way a threat to his health; and he was very easy to break, so we rode him for as long as we could through the summer.

Looking back on such a successful 1987 made me realise how lucky I was: my top horses were proving tough and consistent, and with such generous sponsorship I could continue to compete with them at the level I wanted; and selection for the senior teams had certainly made all the hard work and effort worthwhile. It was just as well to enjoy success while it was in our grasp, too; much later, the wheel of fortune seemed to be less in our favour—mishaps and injury pointed up the vulnerability of horse and rider, and emphasised how very narrow is the margin between success and failure when you are competing at top level.

In horse trials as in any sport a constant necessity from one year to the next is good health and physical fitness. The horse's soundness and well-being is of paramount importance—if he is not physically tough enough, if he or his rider makes a mistake through fatigue or misjudgement, this now means more than merely disappointment: the costs are high, to miss even one event is expensive; sponsors will be let down; chances may be missed to qualify for more important competitions. And at the heart of this vicious spiral is the vulnerable horse and his equally vulnerable rider. Nineteen eighty-eight was Friday's last year in eventing: beyond all doubt she had proved herself equal to all these requirements, and was retired with honour and distinction. But although 1988 brought its share of success, it also brought bad luck and accident—particularly to poor Helen; emphasising once again how susceptible we are, rider and horse, how thin the line between success and failure.

At the beginning of 1988, however, the coming year looked full of promise. I was going to enter Piglet, Friday and Aloaf for Badminton and decide later which two I would ride. I also had Murphy, Banny and Beaky to ride in several other events. I had had to sell little Harry, which had saddened Alex as much as it had me; but he lacked the scope to develop into a Badminton horse so we had felt it was best to let him go, and try to find horses that had greater potential.

13 ◊ Friday Fox: Loyal Friend

After a highly successful year in 1987, David Mason had decided to continue the MacConnal Mason sponsorship for another two years, which was a great relief to Mike and me. My lorry had been giving trouble and for Boekelo in October I had had to borrow Claire Mason's because mine was being mended. I had had it for ten years, so we had decided it was time to replace it, and at the beginning of the winter had been to Lambourn and arranged to buy an HGV vehicle—this meant that I could have more living room and tack area.

It also meant that I had to pass a test so as to qualify to drive it. In January I had an assessment to determine how long a training I would need before taking the HGV driving test, and was told that about four days would suffice. Unfortunately the course was so booked up that I couldn't begin until March, which was right at the start of the spring season.

One week in March, therefore, I had HGV driving instruction from 9am to 5pm each day from Monday to Thursday, and took my test on the Friday morning. There was also a man pupil, and we drove all day with the instructor with stops only for lunch and tea. The lorry was not going well, but the instructor thought that the fault lay in our driving and not in the lorry. Eventually he drove it himself and agreed that there *was* something wrong; on examination it was found that the differential lock had been on all the time. Assuming this was the cause of the trouble, we carried on

Wearing a Britton jacket during a photo shoot for my sponsors Belstaff, with Hoplands cottages in the background

Changing hats for another of my sponsors, British Wool

'International Management Group ... had done a really good job and at the end of 1987 had found me two more sponsors ...'

driving but there was obviously still something wrong because changing gear was extremely difficult. This was reported to the course organiser and we expected it to be put right for the next morning.

However, when we started out on the following day we found that nothing whatsoever had been done; so we took it to the garage ourselves and found that the clutch had worn out—and so we were stuck without a lorry to drive the next day. We were based at Poole in Dorset and had to go all the way to Devizes in Wiltshire to fetch another one, which wasted a whole afternoon. We only had the following day on which to practise with this one, and as it was quite different I did not get the hang of it before my test; in the exam I could not change gear, and everything seemed to go wrong. This was a typical experience for me: exams and I do not mix—they make me panic, just as dressage tests used to until I learned to keep calm. I failed my first test, but luckily my own new lorry had not arrived so I had time in hand. Two weeks later I retook the test and passed.

We then decided that Helen, my head girl, ought to take the HGV test too, so that I would not have to do all the driving; besides, if I had a bad fall there would then be somebody to drive the horses home. Helen passed her test at the first attempt. In the middle of it a lorry came towards her so fast that she was forced against a hedge, and the lorry broke her wing mirror. I would have panicked, I think; Helen, however, suggested to the examiner that she should pull in at the next convenient place and stop, but when asked if she could carry on without a wing mirror she said she could. If that had happened on *my* test, I would probably have let go of the steering wheel and screamed!

Delivery of my lorry had first been promised for the beginning of the season, then postponed, but I was assured it would be in time for Badminton. Eventually it arrived at the end of May. International Management Group, whom I had joined in 1986, had done a really good job at the end of 1987 and found me two more sponsors: Bailey's Horse Feeds and Belstaff International. Bailey's were going to provide my horses with all their necessary feeds as long as these were within their range; this was a great help, and in fact the horses love the feed and have always eaten up very well. Belstaff International make waterproof coats and supplied my girls and me with them. This was most useful, for we seem to be constantly out in the wet, especially in the spring. Also, towards the end of 1987 Rupert Haddow, my agent from International Management Group, had arranged for me to go to Bradford to meet the managing director of the British Wool Marketing Board. The Board was already sponsoring one event rider, Ricenda Lord, and wanted to sponsor a second: I was delighted to be chosen, particularly as we have a sheep farm on Exmoor and also keep a lot of sheep at our farm in Hampshire.

MacConnal Mason Gallery were still sponsoring our King's Somborne horse trials, and now Belstaff, Bailey's and British Wool each sponsored a fence and donated prizes in kind. Mercedes were lending Claire Mason a G-Wagon and decided to lend me one as well; 'MacConnal Mason Gallery' is painted on each side.

Before the first event of 1988 I did some team chasing with Beaky and Banny, both of whom took to it well and gave me some highly enjoyable rides. Team chasing and hunting made them think more positively, and got them going far more freely and confidently, as they really enjoyed it.

CROOKHAM

As the start of the eventing season approached I had some dressage lessons from Pat Manning and help with my show jumping from Pat Burgess. We took the horses to Crookham first of all, and Beaky showed how much hunting had improved his performance by winning the Novice; while Banny gave further evidence of its benefit by winning the Intermediate and being upgraded to Advanced. I knew that Piglet and Friday would need one event before they would settle. I entered them both at Crookham in the Open Intermediate to let them enjoy being out for the first time. I hoped that at their more important second event they might have got rid of their bucks and therefore would concentrate a bit better. They confirmed my fears in their dressage tests but hurtled round the cross-country; they were far off the placings but it was good to know they were in such great form.

BELSTAFF AT SANDOWN

On 21 March I spent the whole day with Belstaff at the British Equestrian Trade Association fair at Sandown. It was interesting to see all the new products and to discuss them with knowledgeable people; and to help promote the Belstaff coats.

KING'S SOMBORNE 1988

In February and March we were busy preparing for the King's Somborne horse trials, as this year they were taking place in April, a lot earlier than usual. Badminton had hitherto always been held in April, but because in 1987 it had been cancelled on account of the bad weather, in future it was to be held in May in the hope of enjoying better conditions. So this was the first time that we were going to be a pre-Badminton event, which attracted a big entry and meant holding the trials over two days—in 1988 this happened to be Easter Sunday and Monday, so the number of spectators nearly doubled from the previous year. We were lucky again with the weather, which though cold was sunny.

'... this was probably Friday's last chance, as she was thirteen and almost certainly in her last year of eventing ...'

A new rule prevented me from competing but I thoroughly enjoyed helping to run the event; and I did in fact ride Piglet HC to give him some practice. As he is so bad at dressage there was not much point in taking him to a competition where I would have to pay an entry fee. Moreover, I had three other horses doing Advanced events and it would have been difficult to have fitted all four into the same one. Although Piglet's dressage was abysmal he gave me a superb ride across country and looked all set for Badminton.

When the time came to make up my mind about Badminton, Aloaf was my first choice and I had to weigh up Piglet's and Friday's merits before making a decision between them. Piglet had run at Badminton three times and Friday had not been there at all. Furthermore this was probably Friday's last chance, as she was thirteen and almost certainly in her last year of eventing: so I decided in her favour and applied for Piglet to go to a three day event in Germany later that spring.

Ferdie Eilberg had helped me enormously with Aloaf the previous year

at team training, so that by the beginning of April it had become clear that I really did need a man to give me a hand with him on the flat, so I started to go to Paul Fielder for lessons—Paul has been a friend of the family for years and at the time was based at the Catherston Stud with Jenny Loriston-Clarke, at Brockenhurst, which is not far from my home.

BADMINTON 1988

In May the weather at Badminton was much better than it had been the year before and on many previous occasions. I hoped that it would stay fine, as it would make the going ideal for Friday—I would never run her if the going was too deep, as it had been when I had brought her in 1986. This was also Aloaf's first Badminton: in 1985 he had missed it because he had pulled a muscle; in 1986 I had not brought him in in time to prepare for it; and of course in 1987 it was cancelled. So having competed there three times on the same horse, I would now approach the competition in an altered frame of mind with two newcomers.

As always, Gill Watson was there to help when I needed her. Before my dressage test on Friday she gave me some last-minute advice and tried to calm me and get Friday settled. Friday had improved during the last couple of years and would settle more readily than she used to, although she was still a little bit tense in places; she finished twenty-fifth. Aloaf was the last to go, so there were plenty of people watching, but he kept his concentration most of the time and came eighteenth—as he had at Luhmühlen the year before—which for him was pretty good.

Although I had decided not to run Piglet, I had entered all three horses and Piglet had been first on the list; Friday was therefore half-way down, so I had only twenty minutes between finishing the cross-country on Friday and having to start Phase A of the roads and tracks on Aloaf. However, I was not short of help: Helen and Alex were up for the week, plus Mum, Mike and my other usual supporters. The going was perfect by Saturday and I was looking forward keenly to my rides on both horses. We had clipped Friday a few days before so that she would not sweat too much.

Friday's steeplechase was highly satisfactory, and she gave me a great ride across country. This time the course set off over the barrels in front of the house to the log, and then the Pardubice. Fence four was the first combination, where the quick route was a double of inverted corners on one stride—Friday jumped it neatly. The fences up to the Vicarage V were nearly the same as the year before but just in the other direction, with a big parallel over the ditch at fence twelve. The Vicarage Ditch had been changed to a big open water with an upright behind it, and it really *was* a big ditch: but we met it on a good stride and soared over. Then the Stockholm fence, where you slide down the slope and over the log at the bottom: Friday popped over, then on to the Irish bank.

She jumped well out over the Horsens Bridge, and then after the Whitbread Drays came the Lake: there was a bounce of logs into the water, and the quick way out was up a step and a bounce over a rail; I had decided to go straight on, however, and just jump a hedge and rail out of

Aloaf bounds over the bounce and into the lake at Badminton

83
LAKE

the lake. We then had to gallop away from the house towards the Normandy bank where she put in an enormous effort; this was followed by the ski jump where there was an upright rail at the bottom which she took neatly and carefully; then on to the coffin, and the bullfinch.

The quarry was the same as two years before, with the platform and then the wall going out. Friday was just beginning to tire: this was a 12½-minute course and she had done only 10-minute courses hitherto but she battled on over all the remaining enormous fences to finish strongly with only a few time faults—she had jumped with brilliance and I had had a stirring ride, and this gave me great confidence for Aloaf's round.

We dashed off to the stables where Aloaf was waiting for me in the top yard, which saved some time. This allowed me ten minutes to sit down, relax, change numbers and think about riding my second horse. Aloaf also gave me a stupendous ride across country, and would have had a wonderful clear if I hadn't made a mistake at the Normandy bank. I saw a long stride into it, and knew we had to bounce the rail on the top so accordingly rode him strongly; but Aloaf backed off and, presumably wondering why I was kicking him, began to slow down—he has always been a careful jumper, and likes to size up the problem himself. Had I just sat there he would have put an extra stride in and bounced it well; but I overrode him so he became worried and stood off, and then tried to put a stride in on the bank when there was not room—he hit the rail quite hard, although he didn't fall. Because of the drop, by the time he landed he had his legs sorted out and landed quite well. But when he had hit the fence I had been catapulted into the air—even though I was not far out of the saddle, I knew I had gone before I hit the ground! I mounted again and we carried on, and he jumped the rest of the course very well.

In falling, however, I had twisted my ankle badly and by the time I had finished the course it had swollen painfully; ice and a bandage didn't noticeably reduce the pain or the swelling. Next morning I couldn't walk on that foot, so Mum agreed to trot up my horses—which embarrassed her, but she did it perfectly. Both horses were feeling fit and well after their rounds the day before and Friday had gone right up the order to seventh

Safely out of the lake with a huge leap

Course run-down with Gill after the cross-country

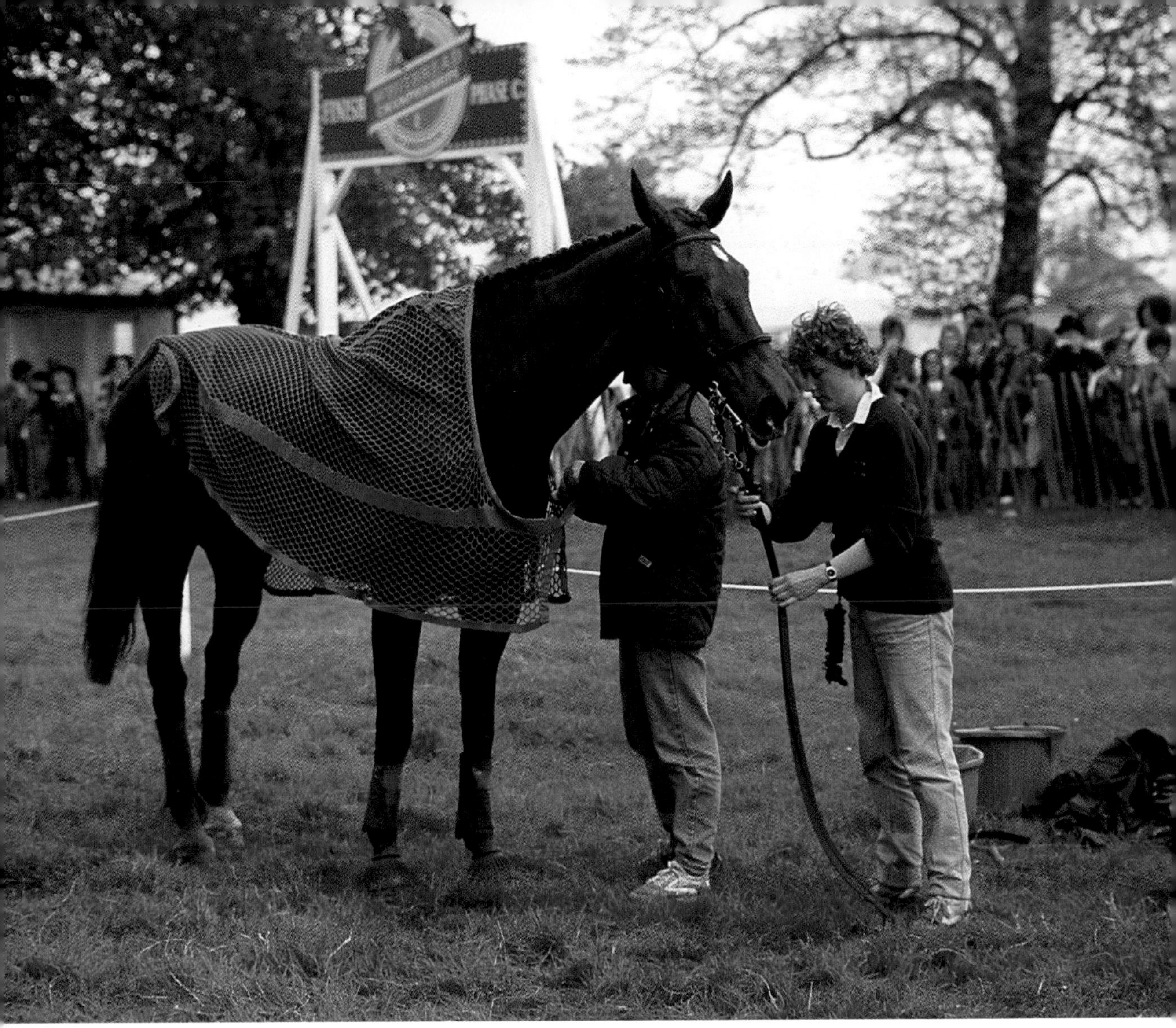

Helen, Alex and Lofty after the cross-country at Badminton 1988

place. Ian Stark was in first and second on Sir Wattie and Glenburnie, with Ginny and Master Craftsman third.

Gill Watson was marvellous—she had been a great help in the ten-minute box during the cross-country and was again at hand on show jumping day to give me a practice jump. Friday had one show jump down, but it did not alter her position in the order; and Aloaf did a clear round. Badminton 1988 was the high point in Friday's eventing career, and this was a wonderful result for her. Mum had been saying for years that I could do anything on Friday except Badminton, yet I knew all along that she could do it. She could certainly jump the fences; the problem was the distance—being only half-thoroughbred she hasn't the stamina of a thoroughbred, and a ten-minute course always suited her much better. But she had proved to everybody that she was a real jumper, and that is what a horse needs to be to get round Badminton.

It was very unfortunate about Aloaf because he is really a great jumper too, and had jumped very well round the course—the only mistake we made was down to me. So Ian won Badminton again on Sir Wattie but this time was also second on Glenburnie, quite a feat.

Friday and Aloaf now took a well-deserved rest. Murphy was getting

Friday and Aloaf in the parade

ready for Punchestown which was the following weekend, and there was not much time to spare. Banny and Beaky were entered for the Intermediate at Tidworth on the Wednesday and I was due to fly to Ireland on the Thursday. Helen was going to travel with Murphy; they had to go by air from Stansted because the ferries were strikebound.

PUNCHESTOWN, IRELAND 1988

My ankle was causing me a considerable degree of trouble and pain; I had a lot of treatment for it on the Monday and Tuesday, but was obliged to withdraw from Tidworth and so on Wednesday flew with Claire Mason to Punchestown, where we were sharing a caravan. The event is held on the racecourse and most people stay in caravans there or local hotels. The steeplechase is on the main course and therefore has lovely big fences—you go about three-quarters of the way round the official course, so it is just one long gallop with no figures-of-eight or circles. The cross-country track runs around the inside and outside of the steeplechase, and you can see most of the course from the ten-minute box. There were eleven British riders; I was unfortunate in the draw and found myself fourth to go out of fifty-five starters, but with the help of Gill Watson's calming influence before I went into the dressage ring Murphy did the best test of which he was capable—at the end of two days' dressage we were in fourth place. Karen Straker was in the lead on Corriwack, Katie Meacham was second on Ten Below and Mary Thompson third on Silverstone.

'Murphy seemed half asleep when I set off on the cross-country, so I woke him up a bit and he then went like a rocket …'

My ankle was still excruciatingly painful, but Susan Short had been most helpful; Susan was an Irish rider I had met when we were competing in the Juniors in Rome. She found me a physiotherapist who strapped my leg up for the dressage and was going to do so again for the cross-country. Luckily I didn't have to ride at all on the Friday, and the day's rest was welcome. The organisers had also been extremely kind. I walked the steeplechase when everyone else did for the first time, but kept twisting my ankle on the grass: so after that, each time I wanted to have another look at the course, I was driven round and merely walked the fences. Had I tried to walk round the whole course three times I would never have been able to ride properly.

Mum and Mike were holidaying on a barge in France and were very upset that they couldn't come to Punchestown. However, as Claire Mason was also competing, her parents, David and Vicky, had come to support us.

Murphy was in excellent form on Saturday morning and went round the steeplechase fast and with ease; we came in from Phase C fresh and full of running. Helen washed him down while I talked to Mike Vacher and Charles Harrison, who were our chefs. In fact there wasn't much to discuss, as I was the first British competitor on the course; all I could do was to go where I had planned. Murphy seemed half asleep when I set off on the cross-country, so I woke him up a bit and he then went like a rocket; we took all the quick ways, which gave a lot of confidence to the other Britons, and finished well within the time. Corriwack and Ten Below with Karen and Katie both went inside the time across country, so we were placed first, second and third at the end of the day.

Murphy looked wonderful next morning when Helen trotted him up

for the vets, (I was still unable to run) and was still feeling full of beans when we went into the show jumping arena. About three-quarters of the way round he started to get rather too strong and when I tried to correct him he rather took the fences on, so had a couple of them down. Consequently he dropped one place to finish fourth, with Karen and Katie first and second and John Watson third.

We didn't have much time to celebrate before flying back to England. I had to leave Helen in charge of Murphy's return journey as I was taking Banny to Breda, in Holland, the following week. Alex was coming with me and had had to leave on the Sunday in Heather Holgate's lorry while I was still in Punchestown. One frustrating mishap on my trip home was that I lost my top hat; I had sent some saddles to Punchestown and others direct to Breda, but my riding boots and a lot of other gear had to accompany me from one event to the other. My top hat didn't appear on the luggage carousel at London Airport and when I telephoned there from home I was told that it had still not been found, so I had to set off for Holland without it. Nigel Taylor, David Green and I met Ginny and Ian at the docks. We had not been able to leave Punchestown until Monday night, so it was now Tuesday; we were taking a night ferry to Holland and did not catch up with the horses until late on Wednesday morning.

BREDA, HOLLAND 1988

As at Punchestown, the briefing for Breda three day event was on Thursday and the show jumping on Monday. Seven British riders had travelled over to compete, but unfortunately Melanie Hawtree's Assertive was spun at the first vetting, leaving only six of us to ride. Ian Stark was riding Ginny Leng's Ballyhack as Ginny had had a bad fall at Badminton and had twisted her ankle so badly that she was not able to ride. Anne-Marie Taylor had Tombo; Nigel Taylor, Last Orders; Sarah Kellard, Hello Henry; and Mary Thompson, King Max.

Mike Vacher was our chef and showed his faith in Branny again by selecting him for the team, which comprised Sarah, Anne-Marie, Ian and me. Anne-Marie, who was first to go, drew number three; Mike's own horse, The Pope, was also running, ridden by Sergeant Richard Burns.

'The biggest problem I had on the roads and tracks was getting across the motorway bridges . . . We also had to go along the other side of the ditch that bordered the motorway, which was quite hair-raising.'

Breda is a one-star event, but over the years its standard has varied from being too big to too small for its status; this year, however, Mike Tucker was the technical delegate and had made a very good job of the course, to produce a really good one-star event. We had a delightful week and stayed in an excellent hotel with a swimming pool. Mum and Mike hadn't arrived, but Heather again looked after Alex and me wonderfully well.

Banny, in a double bridle for the dressage and looking impeccable, just managed to contain himself. It was difficult to get near the arena to work in, so there was a practice arena. To reach the one where the dressage test was actually held we had to go through a wood which led straight into the arena itself, so we were suddenly surrounded by flags and people. Banny looked around for a while but settled down after he had been round the arena once and produced a good test, for him, to take joint seventh place. Mary did a super test on King Max and was in the lead with Sarah and Ian not far behind: so to our astonishment the team was already in the lead before the cross-country.

The cross-country course was nearby and as we had no cars we cycled there, which provided an entertaining change. On Sunday morning Anne-Marie set off on the cross-country to show us the way. The steeplechase was quite a difficult figure-of-eight, with sharp turns and rather big portable fences. To my delight Mum and Mike arrived at midday, straight from their barge in France, in time to see Banny go.

The biggest problem I had on the roads and tracks was getting across the motorway bridges—Banny was terrified of them. We also had to go along just the other side of the ditch that bordered the motorway, which was quite hair-raising. Earlier in the week Alex had been bucked off by Banny when he had spooked, though neither of them had come to any harm, and I had one ticklish moment when he suddenly decided that he was too terrified to start the steeplechase. Persuading him to get going wasn't easy, but once he was through the start box and galloping round the fences he was fine. I was the last to go of the British riders. In the cross-country Anne-Marie had had the misfortune of a run-out when attempting the straight route at an arrowhead where I had decided to go the long way. Mary had gone clear and inside the time on King Max and was still in the lead; Sarah and Nigel had both gone clear but had incurred rather a lot of time faults, while Ian was also clear with only a few time faults; Richard Burns was inside the time.

Finally it was my turn. We negotiated the first two fences well enough and as we continued round the course I was surprised to find how much Banny had improved. The winter's hunting had obviously helped his courage and he was much more confident, and was plainly trying hard. We had one nasty moment at the second fence from the end when we missed a stride; the last fence we mistimed completely, and that was by the ten-minute box with everybody in there watching! How Banny stood up on the other side I don't know: but we had done a clear round and were inside the time. This took us into second place, with Mary leading and Ian third.

Mary, Ian and I were the last three to go in the show jumping, and preparing for it provided us with some comedy. In the arena the ground was hard and grassy, but the practice jumps were on deepish sand; Ballyhack was a wonderful jumper, but Banny and King Max kept knocking the fences down—whatever Mary and I did, we could not get them to pick up.

Ian went in before us on Ballyhack and jumped a beautiful round except for the open water with rustic rails over the top; Ballyhack was still rather green and evidently didn't like the look of the water, and had a rail down. When I took Banny in, I was sure we were going to suffer the embarrassment of having every single fence down. However, rising like a helicopter over some and slithering over others, he managed to lift himself over them all; it was a bit of a miracle, but somehow we went clear—I put it down to luck, because although he did try he is not very talented and doesn't have a good shape over fences. Then Mary came in with King Max and she also managed to go clear: no one watching those two horses in the collecting ring would ever have believed that they could complete a faultless round. At the end of it all, Max came first with Banny second and our team won.

I still felt Banny was not ready to go up to a two-star event. Through his hunting he had just become brave enough to compete at one-star level; but if I pushed him a bit further and he found it a little bit too big, or if he

'... I was sure we were going to suffer the embarrassment of having every single fence down. However, rising like a helicopter and slithering over others, he managed to lift himself over them all ...'

had a stop or a fall, I felt that was all it would need to put him off jumping ever again. So I thought it best to keep him at Intermediate level until he gained greater confidence.

SUMMER HOLIDAYS 1988

Aloaf and Murphy had both been put on the long list for the Olympics. The final trial was to be held in July, so they did not get much of a holiday before having to come up and start work again. I had a wonderful break, though: at the end of June I was very lucky to be invited on a week's delectable holiday with Claire Mason, whose parents own a boat in the Mediterranean. Claire, Rodney Powell, Louise Barton and Claire's cousin James Shepherd, flew to Nice and went on to San Remo, a few miles the other side of the Italian frontier, where the boat was waiting to set sail for Corsica. I don't know how Derek, the skipper, coped for a whole week with such a mad crowd aboard. We had a rapturous and relaxing time, enjoying the change of scenery, sunbathing and water-skiing; if we had any energy left in the evenings we would go dancing. The trouble with a good holiday is that when you get home you feel you need a few days off to recover. But we had little time to spare: we returned on a Friday night and on Saturday Louise and I were both competing in a dressage competition at Tweseldown; which I must admit we took in rather a casual fashion.

A fortnight later Rosemary Barlow held a ball at her house to raise money for the Olympics. I really don't know if any event riders were missing, there were so many people present, and many good friends among them—it was great fun to get together in the middle of the summer break, before the autumn season. It was a stupendous party; and I shall never forget stopping at a motorway services on the way home at about 4am and everybody staring because we were all in evening dress!

Two days later we held my sister Lucy's twenty-first birthday party, another big night at home. It was a joint celebration with a friend of mine, James Humphreys, held in a marquee on the lawn. Everyone enjoyed it so much that Mike, my stepfather, wondered what we could celebrate next year as we had run out of twenty-first birthdays. I thought we would have to give a Piglet or Friday retirement party as an excuse to entertain our family and friends again on the lawn.

THE SCOTTISH CIRCUIT

Friday, Murphy and Aloaf were now nearly fit for the first autumn events and I was going to take them on the Scottish circuit: our first one was to be at Witton Castle, in County Durham, a seven-hour drive; Alex came with me while Helen stayed at home to look after the yard. It was my first trip to Witton, and was not a memorable occasion. Aloaf was not quite fit enough to go cross-country, so did only the dressage; Friday was so naughty in the dressage that I went slowly across country; and Murphy was being abominably bossy on the cross-country course—after his good spring season he was beginning to think that he was the bee's knees and utterly brilliant. Consequently he was not really listening to what I had to

Murphy and me at Belton 1988

'It was a journey that made us feel more than a little vulnerable as we slowly passed capsized caravans and lorries until at last we came to the M6.'

say, so tripped up the steps coming out of the water, and when I finished the course we found that he had cut his knee. It was swelling quickly and had to be treated at once by the vet.

On leaving Witton we spent the night with Karen Straker, who lives not far away; Alex and I hacked the horses out with her in the morning before resuming our long trek north. We drove in company with Brynley Powell who was staying nearby, but when we got to the A66 to cross the Pennines all the lorries were being stopped because the wind had grown so strong that there was a danger of being overturned. This had already happened to one lorry, so we were told to stop at the side of the road so ours could be checked to make sure it was heavy enough and not too high to be at risk; we had to make sure that the hay was securely strapped onto the roof racks, too, and even this was precarious because the lorries were swaying even though stationary. It was a journey that made us feel more than a little vulnerable as we slowly passed capsized caravans and lorries until at last we came to the M6. We were staying with Stewart and Vivienne Christie on the outskirts of Glasgow. They were extremely kind to put us up, for Claire Mason, Bryn, Mandy Jeakins and Duncan Douglas were also staying there. The stableyard was full of other people's event horses and some five horseboxes.

The following day was Tuesday and we had dressage at Rowallen Castle. The cross-country was on the Wednesday but Aloaf was still not quite fit enough for it, and as Murphy's knee was not very good, he did only the dressage. I ran Friday but we had a difficult river crossing down a steep slope on one side and up on the other side. She was trying to go so fast on the climb that she fell on her knees and did not get up well, so I didn't continue.

The next day we had no event to occupy us, so went to look at some horses: I bought a bay ⅞ Thoroughbred who I have called Glentroy (Troy), and Claire bought a five-year-old named Woody.

My fortunes improved a trifle at Eglinton, where Aloaf and Friday took the first and third places respectively in the Advanced class; Murphy was still not running on account of his knee. Mum and Mike had not made the trip to Scotland but David Mason came to Eglinton after playing golf at Gleneagles with his brother.

On the Sunday after Eglinton we were able to make our trip home. We left early and on the way picked up Troy, who had been passed by the vet—I had only three horses in the lorry, so could fit him in. The journey took us nine hours and Alex and I shared the driving; we felt really at ease in the new vehicle, however, which was unlikely to break down and gave the horses such a comfortable ride.

DISASTER AT HOME

While we were away there had been a major disaster: Tangle Louis, the four-year-old stallion we had bred, had bucked Helen off in the field and she was in hospital with a broken back. We were appalled; and it is frightening to think how easily this sort of thing can happen. Help for Helen had been immediately to hand as Debbie, a groom of my mother's, had come to help while I was away; she had just returned from riding another horse out, so was able to go quickly to Helen's aid and get her to hospital. As soon as we arrived home Alex and I went to visit Helen, but knowing there was nothing we could do added a sense of helplessness to our distress. We tried to cheer Helen up, but without much success: if I had been in her situation, I don't think anything would have cheered me up, either. Fortunately, she has suffered no permanent damage to her back.

There was added confusion at home as a new student, Claire Shannon, was starting work the day after Helen had her fall; Claire was on a three-year course at Warwickshire College, of which the middle year is a practical one. Alex and I were about to go straight off to Badminton with Murphy, Friday and Aloaf for team training, before the final trial for Olympic selection at Holker Hall, in Cumbria. Debbie held the fort for us and Claire fitted in very well. In truth, it did seem tedious to have to go all the way back to Cumbria so soon after we had been there, but of course being selected for team training was a great honour.

Teazle and Tosh (Claire Mason's dog) joining in on the Pimm's party at Holker Hall

OLYMPIC SELECTION

Murphy's knee had not yet fully recovered, so he was again withdrawn after the dressage. At the end of the trial Friday was fourth and Aloaf, after a slow cross-country, tenth. On Monday morning, after a trot-up in front of the selection committee at Cartmel racecourse where we were stabled, there was a meeting to select the five horses and riders for the Olympics; only four horses run, not six as in the European and World Championships. I think of *all* such uncertainties, waiting to know whether you have been chosen for the Olympic team imposes the greatest suspense. Ginny and Ian were obvious selections, but when the final decision was at last announced, Karen Straker, Mark Phillips and Lorna Clarke were the other three; Rodney and I were reserves.

This was a great disappointment, and being a mere reserve was at first hard to take. Riding in the Olympics is the pinnacle of achievement, and of course any rider puts all his hopes on being selected for the team. I understood why I had missed team selection: it would obviously be very hot in Seoul, and as Aloaf is not a Thoroughbred, he would not have stood up to it as well as a horse that was; the selectors would have been particularly looking for this physical resilience, so it was in fact a considerable compliment to have been chosen even as a reserve. The drawbacks to being reserve were firstly that we had to have all the horrible injections that were necessary for entry to Korea, without having the distinction and fun of actually going there; and our horses had to go into quarantine for a month and therefore could not compete in any events during that period. But we were luckier than the fifth rider, who had to go all the way to Korea yet not actually ride in the Games. At least as a reserve at home we had Burghley to aim for.

GATCOMBE 1988

I took Murphy, Friday and Aloaf to Gatcombe and they all ran in the Championship class. Friday gave a superb account of herself: she raced round the cross-country, bouncing the corners and flying the corral fence—this is a palisade built on top of a steep bank, so you approach it up a slope; there is a drop on the other side and you get the feeling that you

Pages 170–1: Gatcombe 1988—course builder's problem. Mark Phillips passes me my stick and I leave him to go and complete the course, while he has to find a way of rebuilding it!

201

'Mark Phillips was left standing looking at his fence that I had totally ruined ...'

are flying as you take off, because there is a moment when the horse is almost suspended before it drops and lands. Friday must have jumped higher and longer than any other horse. She went immaculately over the downhill bounce, the water and the coffin, and stormed home with a reasonable time. Mum and Alex were there to congratulate her and take her up the hill to the lorry.

I changed quickly and then set off on the cross-country with Murphy. He was giving me an exquisite ride, still jumping very boldly and imparting that wonderful feeling of being on a horse that has a marvellous amount of scope. When I came down to the double corners I was not quite sure whether I was going to do the bounce, on him, but he was going so well that I decided to give it a try: we came into it on the right line and Murphy just kept coming—but he jumped so big over the first corner that he had no chance of being able to take off for the second, and we had a crashing fall that completely demolished the back rail of the second corner. It must have been awful to watch, and from the photographs and TV recording I saw it did indeed look appalling; but I rolled over, got up and was uninjured—and Murphy also got to his feet, and trotted away up the hill. There was therefore no obvious reason why I should not carry on, so when I got him back I remounted. Mark Phillips was left standing looking at his fence that I had totally ruined, passed me my stick and we continued on our way. Murphy went round the rest of the course as if nothing had happened and gave me a super ride; although it was no wonder that he was a little stiff the next day. I did not run Aloaf across country as the selectors had asked me not to, and on the following day he had to go into quarantine at Badminton.

Friday Fox was seventh at Gatcombe, in a very competitive championship field, and her performance was really top class. But now we decided that this triumphant result should be the occasion for her to bow out of her eventing career. With Aloaf and Murphy bound for Burghley, only two-star events were left for Friday; her seventh place at Badminton had been the high spot of her career and it seemed a shame to enter her for anything of a lower standing. Throughout her career she had been a consistent and excellent jumper, and had always given her utmost at each performance. She was the horse which had really launched me in my career; she had taught me such a lot over the years and right from the beginning had carried me safely over all sorts of courses, from show jumping at the Horse Of The Year Show to championship classes in horse trials. Friend, companion, mentor: at the age of thirteen and with innumerable successes under her belt, she had done enough. So we decided she should retire, and the following spring sent her to Gordon Giddings's stud near Warminster, and put her in foal to the thoroughbred Nader.

Confidence seems inevitably to go hand in hand with success, or vice versa: a punter is always advised to back the winning jockey—simply being successful boosts that jockey's confidence and inspires him to take that extra gamble which often means the difference between first and second place. But physical injury can erode that confidence in a matter of days; and as much as success breeds success, so misfortune seems to attract misfortune. Any horse trials rider must expect patches of ill-luck, and I certainly seemed to get my fair share in the 1989 season. But despite all the adversities which came my way, I knew that my dedication to horse trials, and to the horses that make it all possible, was unshaken; and that the confidence temporarily undermined was bound to return.

'I knew that my dedication to horse trials, and to the horses that make it all possible, was unshaken ...'

14 ◊ The Wheel of Fortune

The team training for the Olympics was at Badminton as usual; I took Aloaf, Murphy and Banny and Alex came with me—Claire joined us later with Troy, the four-year-old, as there were plenty of stables. During that time Karen Straker and I went to Locko Park, where she was to ride Fosseway Surprise and I was riding Banny in the Intermediate Championship.

LOCKO PARK 1988

When we walked the course at Locko the size of the fences surprised me. They looked as big as if they were of Advanced standard, but Banny had done only Intermediate classes. However, since we had come all the way, I thought we might as well give it a try.

I set off on the cross-country in the knowledge that Banny had at least done a good dressage. He jumped everything until we came to a white garden fence with fountains and lots of flowers: a strange type of obstacle, which made him nervous and spooky. The quick way was over two narrow rails on one longish stride: I managed to get him over the first part but he went straight past the second and there was nothing I could do—my steering is not very good on him! However, we carried on, even though some of the jumps were extremely difficult. One was an upright rail down into a quarry, followed by a log half-way down the slope, which I really didn't think he would have coped with. But he edged his way closer and, trusting in me, took off slowly and carefully to take it all neatly. His spooking at the white garden fence was his only mistake, so his performance gave me a pleasant surprise; my only worry was that he might have frightened himself, because the course was by far the biggest he had done and he is not a brave horse.

By the end of a month's team training Murphy's and Aloaf's dressage had really come on; I had also had some show jumping lessons with Troy and Banny. At the end of team training we had an open day when the public could watch a day's training, with Ferdie and Pat giving their usual

lessons. This was particularly good for the horses that had been in quarantine, as they had not been to a competition for nearly a month and it helped them get used to seeing people around again.

I was able to give Murphy one more run before Burghley, at Rotherfield in the Advanced, but Aloaf could not go because he was still in quarantine. Murphy gave me quite a good ride in the cross-country; although a little bold but we did not have any major problems. Alex won the prize for grooming the best-turned-out horse, which she well deserved. We then went back to Badminton for a few more days before being allowed home on 4 September, as all the horses that were due to go to the Olympics were sound. So instead of Korea, Rodney and I were going to Burghley, which was by now nearly upon us.

BURGHLEY 1988

Murphy was my first ride at Burghley, and after all the help he had been given during team training he again did a lovely test, better than at Punchestown, as he now seemed to be more established; he was placed sixteenth. With Gill as usual calming me down before I went back into the arena, Aloaf also did his best test yet, to come sixth: in fact only five marks separated my two horses.

'. . . I went right out of the saddle but unfortunately missed it on the way down and landed standing in the water next to him . . .'

The cross-country looked very demanding. Fence four had been built in the main show jumping arena and consisted of a bounce of parallels followed by one stride to another parallel, then a few more strides to a cognac glass. Both Aloaf and Murphy jumped this complex well but it gave them a bit of a fright because it was so technically difficult, and I wondered how they felt afterwards. Next there was a big drop with a landing that was not easy, but which once more both took safely. At the Lower Trout Hatchery, a big log into the water, Murphy jumped in so big that I went right out of the saddle but unfortunately missed it on the way down and landed standing in the water next to him; but we were fine and carried on. However, I think he *had* frightened himself at fence four, and with this second episode he became increasingly worried and started jumping bigger rather than stopping. The second water fence comprised an upright palisade drop followed by one stride into the water, then through the water and a jump over a weir into water the other side. It seemed to be riding on either two long strides or three short ones—Murphy came in really deep and jumped it so carefully that I thought there was room for three strides, but he got to two and a half and hit the rail, to dump us in the water yet again! I was soaked and poor Murphy was not too happy, so we retired. 'Never mind,' I thought, 'perhaps things will go well with Aloaf.'

My boots were saturated, so Ros Bevan very kindly lent me hers as she had already been round the course and had a good ride on Horton Point. As I told her, it was unlikely that I would fall off twice at the water jump, so her boots should come back dry.

Aloaf was on top form and giving me a superb ride across country. He went through the sunken circle and the dairy farm and all the other difficult fences and at the second water I did exactly as I had with Murphy: I got him very deep to the palisade, so again he jumped very carefully and landed quite short and, as before, I thought we would take three strides here. He took two and a half, hit the rail, went over and we were under water before we knew it! I decided that *this* time I was going to get up and press on: I couldn't have two horses retiring on the cross-country! Aloaf finished the course in good style and our fall was really my fault: I should have just kicked.

I thought for a long time about my falls, and came to the conclusion that I had been so psyched-up for the Olympics that I had failed to work up the same intensity of enthusiasm about Burghley. With big competitions such as the latter, one really has to have one's whole heart in it to have any hope of success. My thoughts were too much on Seoul when they should have been on Burghley, so things just didn't go right for me.

'My thoughts were too much on Seoul when they should have been on Burghley ...'

WAREGEM 1988

Before I got dragged too much into the doldrums I was home and already thinking about going to Waregem again with Banny. Once again we were quite a small party: there were eight British riders, and also Vaughan Jeffris from New Zealand who had been based at Gatcombe over the summer and was riding two horses. I drove my lorry to Belgium and took Suzanne van Heyningen with her horse Major Tom, and Tessa Lambert with her horse Grenville.

Mike Vacher was again our chef d'équipe, as the previous year, and had luckily obtained rooms for us in the same hotel, overlooking the racecourse. Since we were there last, most of the hotel had been turned into offices, and there was only one floor left for accommodation; so all the other teams had to stay much further away. The Willis brothers had again built a very good course but had changed its direction; it was not quite as big as at Breda and certainly not as big as for the Intermediate Championships at Locko Park, so I felt that Banny should not find it too difficult.

On the Tuesday before the event we didn't have much to do but ride our horses, and made up our minds that as we had already been to Brussels the year before, we would go to Paris this time. We had not realised how far it was. The organisers lent us two Polos and eight of us set off. We got lost on the way back, because in France there are no signposts indicating the way to Brussels—just as there are no pointers to Paris in Belgium. We were in a hurry to get back, too, because it was cross-country day at the Olympics and we wanted to watch the event on the television in our rooms. There were about twenty-four channels, so all night long we switched from one to another, picking up transmissions from Germany and England. We saw nearly everything, but were really not in a fit state to ride next morning because we were so tired!

The first day of dressage was quiet, but on the second day when I had to do my test it was rainy, and the wind was making the flags flap so hard that Banny found it difficult to concentrate so his test was not as good as it might have been; but he finished not far behind the leader. He made up for his lack of concentration in the dressage by sizzling round the cross-country full of confidence, and was the only horse to finish within the time—he is so fast. This brought him up to second place. Eddy Stibbe for Holland was in the lead on Kilmacthomas, an English horse that he had bought for Sally Corscaden only a few months earlier; and Lisa Evans (the next best British rider) was lying fourth on Royal Masquerade.

Banny was feeling fit and well on Sunday morning when he trotted up

for the vets. He managed to climb round the show jumps in his normal way, and this put all the pressure on Eddy Stibbe, with Kilmacthomas—who had one jump down, so Banny had won! Alex and I were enormously elated by my useless old Banny, who had tried his very best, and actually won a three day event; but I still felt that he was not ready as yet to do Advanced classes—this level of eventing for the time being seemed definitely what he was best at, and most happy to do. Lisa Evans on Royal Masquerade also went clear, to finish only one point behind me in second place, and the British team won. Even if the autumn season had not gone brilliantly for me, it had finished on a good note and we hoped that next year everything would come right again.

KENYA 1988

'There were some breathtaking views of the Rift Valley from a height of 11,000ft, where it was pleasantly cool, and giraffe, zebra and Thompson's gazelle could be seen just off the road ...'

When we got home nearly all the horses were on holiday and there were just a few novices in. Piglet came up at the beginning of October to get fit for hunting, and I spent most of November and December hunting him and the novices. I was also bringing on Troy, Louis and some of the other novices by doing a little show jumping. Alex and Claire took their holiday at this quiet time and I was looking forward to mine.

Over Christmas I was going to spend three and a half weeks in Kenya with Angela Robley, my old school friend who had helped me with the horses for a while. Her parents are tea farmers in Kericho and she had asked me to go and stay there with her as long ago as when I was about twelve! Looking after my horses and competing had taken up so much of my time that I had been unable to accept her invitation until now. We were going out in the middle of December and coming back after New Year; Angie and I flew out with James Humphrey, a great friend of Fergus, Angie's brother, who would follow us a week later. A friend of Angie's met us at Nairobi with a pick-up truck we were to use to drive to the coast, where her parents were spending a week's holiday.

It was a 500-kilometre drive and took seven hours, on a straight road full of potholes through mile after mile of bush, and the three of us had to take it in turns to sit in the back of the truck where the sun beat down fiercely. Our destination was a village called Msambweni, about an hour's drive from Mombasa; Tom and Mary Robley were staying nearby in a villa on a lovely white beach which was deserted most of the time, and was also safe for swimming because a reef quite far out kept the Indian Ocean sharks away.

We spent the first few days getting used to the sun and having a complete rest, and then went on to visit a friend of Angie's, Ian Leckie, who lives right on the cliff edge surrounded by 500 acres of his own land. There were no houses in sight and the view across the sea was simply wonderful. We spent most of our time sunbathing, reading books, swimming, even playing the odd energetic game of tennis—despite the heat!—and going to the beach bars in the evening. On the coast we were not pestered by mosquitoes or flies, as there was always a good breeze.

One morning we left at six to make the long drive to the Robleys' tea plantation, again sharing turns in the back of the pick-up, reaching Nairobi at about 1pm where we met friends for lunch before driving on. There were some breathtaking views of the Rift Valley from a height of 11,000ft,

where it was pleasantly cool, and giraffe, zebra and Thompson's gazelle could be seen just off the road; we arrived at 6pm. The temperature had dropped as we neared Kericho and the country grew greener, thanks to the rain in that area—it falls nearly every afternoon, which is why the tea grows so well. I felt very much at home in the Robleys' house; everything was so English and the temperature was similar to that of an English summer—we used to have a log fire at night, wear a jumper in the evening and sleep under a blanket, but during the day it was very hot.

For me Christmas Day was unusual . . . It seemed very odd to be wearing sundresses and enjoying drinks on the veranda at this season!'

Angie, Mary and I used to ride for a couple of hours every morning at about seven, around the plantations where the tea-pickers were already at work, returning for breakfast when James and Fergus (who had come out on the 23rd) were just thinking of getting up. Mary had six horses, most of which she competes on, and I enjoyed schooling a couple of them, too. Kenyan horses do not have as much bone as most British horses and are really like small Thoroughbreds. There were numerous parties in the neighbourhood as there are still a lot of British residents in Kenya and their children come out for Christmas; a crowd of us used to go to the Mara Mara Club to enjoy the swimming pool and the squash, tennis and badminton courts.

For me, Christmas Day was most unusual: after church on Christmas morning we had a Pimm's party at the Robleys' and it seemed very odd to be wearing sundresses and enjoying cold drinks on the veranda at this season! We had the traditional lunch, though, of roast turkey and a flaming plum pudding with brandy butter and cream.

On Boxing Day we observed another tradition by holding a meet: but there were no hounds and no quarry. Six of us hacked the Robleys' horses there and Tom Robley brought the port and glasses in his MG; after we had drunk our stirrup cup we dispersed.

The following day was an early start: we rose at 4.45am to go to the Masai Mara to look for game; we were meeting some friends and there were five cars in the party altogether. The rain here is unpredictable and in a very short time can turn the roads to mud—we had to push the cars at one stage. We saw giraffes, zebras, baboons and crocodiles but unfortunately for me no lions or elephants; Angie had always seen them here. However, I hope to return to Kenya some day and spend a few nights in the game park.

At 5am on 29 December Angie, James, Fergus and I set off back to the coast to stay at Ian's again and celebrate the New Year—we had a succession of Pimm's parties and barbecues. We returned to Kericho on 3 January. Angie's birthday was on the 5th but we couldn't have much fun celebrating it as we had to leave at 6am for Nairobi to catch our flight home; Angie's parents joined us in the evening and treated us to a delicious dinner at a smart hotel. At midnight we took off for London. We were all, I think, reluctant to leave such a fascinating country, and I in particular was very sad at having to end such a blissful holiday.

HOME AGAIN: SPRING 1989

Alex and Claire had taken perfect care of the horses for me. Piggy had been kept fit and I took him hunting two days after I got back. He behaved like a lunatic. Never having hunted before, he thought, at the age of four-

teen, that it was some new form of liberty and self-indulgence specially designed to allow him to gallop flat out and jump fences without a thought for anything else. It wasn't long before he found the fences a nuisance: all he wanted to do was gallop fast. He really should have been a racehorse, but he was enjoying it and as long as he did I was happy to hunt him. Alex had a day on him, too.

On 9 January Banny, Lofty and Murphy started walking; Louis and Troy had been jumping before Christmas so they were now on holiday. I took Banny to one team chase to get him back into gear for the season, and also took Piglet—it was his introduction to this sport and he thoroughly enjoyed it. I could guess what he must have been thinking: 'Why on earth did I have to do all that dressage when team chasing and hunting would have been all I wanted to do, if only I'd known about them?'

All the horses were soon fit for their first events, and Banny and one of the young horses, Solomon—a bay, 6yr old 16.1hh gelding—started the season well, in March, with a clear round at Crookham.

'... I took Piglet to Gatcombe for a unique occasion that the BBC had organised for television to raise money for the injured jockeys ...'

THE GATCOMBE CHALLENGE (1989)

A week later I took Piggy to Gatcombe for a unique occasion that the BBC had organised for television to raise money for the injured jockeys and the Mark Davies Fund. Six National Hunt jockeys were to ride event horses round Mark Phillips's Gatcombe course, and at a later date the eventers who owned or usually rode these horses were going to ride them round the Grand National course at Aintree. I had been asked to take part, paired with Steve Smith-Eccles, and as Piglet was fit and undeniably a good cross-country horse, I didn't hesitate to agree, quite sure that it should be interesting as well as good fun. Rodney was lending Pomeroy; Mark Phillips, Cartier; and Mark Todd, Mr Todd, which was Sante de la Roche's horse. Robert Lemieux was bringing After Dark, and Ian Stark, Mix 'n' Match. We met at Gatcombe on Sunday, the jockeys' only free day. I had taken Piggy to Wylye for a cross-country the previous day—he seemed tuned up, even though he obviously felt it a bit of a shock to be eventing again all of a sudden; but he thoroughly enjoyed it.

We all walked the course together, the eventers explaining to the jockeys how they should ride each fence. Mark had made some of the jumps easier than they were for a proper championship event, but they were still going to face several that were very difficult. Steve Smith-Eccles seemed very relaxed but I wasn't sure whether he really *was* unperturbed, or was concealing his anxiety. Before lunch we gave the horses a practice jump and the jockeys tried them over a jump or two. An astonishingly large number of spectators had turned out—mostly racing people, for eventers compete on Sundays.

The horses set off one at a time. Piggy and Steve appeared to get on well. They were rather speedy over the first couple of fences and when they turned to the walled drop at fence three Steve was certainly shifting on a bit; but Piggy saw the problem, put in a short stride, and jumped beautifully over the drop, then down the hill through the copse and out over the gate. The next fence, a lamb creep, was downhill and had a big drop on the landing side: Steve obviously saw a long stride into it and went for it, and Piggy, presumably thinking that if his rider thought that was all right then

Steve Smith-Eccles negotiating the water on Piglet at the Gatcombe Jockey/Event Rider Challenge

he would go for it too, stood well back and flew it. However, he just caught it with his stifles and had jumped so big that by the time he landed on the sloping ground the combination of the speed and the drop made him turn over. They managed to get back together, and carried on; Steve said he couldn't even remember the next three fences. But they completed the course and Steve found that by half-way round he had got the hang of it and was finding it good fun.

The jockeys really did a marvellous job. Richard Dunwoody on Cartier had been first to go and did a lovely clear round. Graham McCourt took the wrong line at a corner and fell, but carried on without further problems. Simon Sherwood on After Dark had two stops at the coffin, but went well apart from that, and Peter Scudamore went clear on Mix 'n' Match. But it was Brendan Powell on Pomeroy who went the fastest and won the competition.

INJURY AT ALDON

Because of Gatcombe I had missed the Aldon event, so on the following day Alex and I took Solomon, Aloaf, Murphy and Pharaoh (a hunter of Mum's) to school them on the cross-country course there. First I took the novices who went well, and then I rode Aloaf round the OI, which he did beautifully. Lastly I took Murphy round: at fence seven he misunderstood what the fence was and we had a heavy fall that broke my collarbone. Mum had come with us as she had been a bit worried about Solomon, as he had

been very strong on Saturday when competing there in the Novice, so she took me to hospital while Alex drove the horses home.

I needed at least three or four weeks off for my bone to heal—and in fact it took a much greater toll on me, both physically and mentally, than I had anticipated. That coming weekend we had the King's Somborne horse trials; it had rained during the preceding few days but the weather improved just in time and we ran the show over two lovely sunny days.

I was worried about Murphy not being prepared enough for Badminton on account of my injury, so Robert Lemieux kindly agreed to ride him, and also the novice Solomon, at the Portman horse trials. Both horses acquitted themselves handsomely in the cross-country and Robert consented to ride Murphy in the Advanced at Belton.

THE AINTREE CHALLENGE

'Becher's Brook, the most notorious fence in the world, did not in fact entail much of a drop: it is deceptive because the course curves to the left immediately after, and it almost has to be ridden on an angle which of course makes it bigger.'

I was upset at being unable to ride Piggy round the Grand National course. Madeleine Gurdon took my place with The Done Thing and Polly Lyon took Mark Phillips's place as he had already ridden round Aintree—I went on my feet, of course, to support my friends. Seagram, Ivan Straker and Barbour were sponsoring the event and stood us all dinner that night. What with all the jokes and party games, this went on until five the next morning.

Sunday was wet and miserable, but walking the course was a memorable experience as the fences are so wide and high. The first one to worry us was number three, the first of the ditches—we were astonished to find how huge it was, and if this was a simple ditch and looked like a canyon, it made us wonder how enormous the famous Chair would be. By the time we got there, however, we had become accustomed to the size of the fences and found that the Chair itself looks so vast only because it is narrower as well as slightly taller than all the others. Becher's Brook, the most notorious fence in the world, did not in fact entail as much of a drop as we thought: it is deceptive because the course curves to the left immediately after, and it almost has to be ridden on an angle which of course makes it bigger. Nor is the hedge very high; the difficulty lies in taking off at the right place to land safely.

Our six riders started on the near side of the Melling Road, and we followed them by car on the tarmac inside the track. Robert Lemieux and Polly Lyon rode together out in front, going superbly. Everybody jumped Becher's well. With only three more fences to jump, Polly's horse was so tired that he put in an extra stride at a fence and they had a nasty fall, but neither was hurt. Mr Todd seemed to take a lot of spruce off most of his fences but it didn't seem to upset his rhythm. The Done Thing and Mix 'n' Match were struggling along behind with Pomeroy, as the thoroughbreds stormed on in front. Coming down to the second last—the Chair—Robert had been on his own in front for a while and had eased the pace a bit. Mix 'n' Match seemed to have found his second wind and was hot on Mr Todd's tail, while The Done Thing and Pomeroy were tiring. The first three home flew the Chair, but The Done Thing only just made it. The water jump was their last fence, but Rodney and Pomeroy had a thumping fall at the Chair, and could not continue. Mark Todd, Ian, Madeleine and Robert, who completed the course, all enjoyed their rides and were delighted by the experience.

This Aintree challenge was not without its sad side: Pomeroy died that night of an internal injury. He had been a wonderful partner for Rodney and had been his top horse for many years. He had done two seasons' hunting since retiring in 1987, as enthusiastically and reliably as he had gone eventing, and was truly a great horse. It was a real shame to lose him.

SPRING EVENTS 1989

Our next event was at Belton, where Robert rode Murphy and had the most wonderful ride across country. I had resumed riding but did only dressage and show jumping, because another fall would have been a serious setback for my healing collarbone. There were two more events to go before Badminton, so I thought that as I would be fit to ride at the next weekend, Aloaf would be fine to do Brigstock and Brockenhurst and then go for the fourth 'B': the biggest one.

'I had never ridden in a point-to-point, and I have never been so nervous …'

My luck seemed to be all bad that season: on the Thursday night Brigstock was cancelled because of the wet. However, I had entered Piglet in the members' race at the Portman point-to-point and as I was now not eventing on the Sunday, I thought I would take him there. I had never ridden in a point-to-point, and have never been so nervous as I was before that first one! Not only do racehorses go much faster than event horses, but you also have all the other runners to worry about, instead of going round on your own. There were only six of us in the race and Piggy was in the lead when we landed over the first fence. I couldn't understand why and assumed that the others wanted me to go out in front. Anyway, I let Piglet carry on because he seemed happy at that pace. He took the first five fences easily, cruising along in front, but then another horse (ridden by Mouse Tory—her first point-to-point, too!) came up alongside and Piggy thought this really *was* fun, so he accelerated. I was trying to persuade him that we were going fast enough, but didn't have much choice about our speed as Mouse Tory was on a very good horse that happened to be a front runner and wanted to lead the field. Piglet, even though he had never raced before, is very much a front runner too and didn't like someone else coming level: we carried on over the next five fences jumping side by side and leaving the other four behind.

When we passed the start and were beginning our second circuit we really had got a bit of pace on; I was only too aware that we still had a mile to go and that it was uphill, so I tried to get Piglet more under control so he didn't wear himself out before the finish. I managed to do this but Mouse was just half a stride in front of me as we came to the open ditch for the second time. I could see that we were on rather a short stride and that Piggy would have to put one in. But disaster struck again: Mouse took off, so Piggy thought is was time for him to do the same. We therefore took off a stride early, and hit the top of the fence to have a thundering fall, the worst of my life. Nothing was broken, and Piglet carried on without me. It had been a most thrilling experience and I had enjoyed every minute! I hope to ride a point-to-point again, but at sixteen Piglet will perhaps be past it by next year.

I was preparing for Brockenhurst, where I was going to run Murphy and Aloaf. Then unbelievably, bad luck frustrated me yet again: the Brockenhurst event was cancelled because of an outbreak of a virus infec-

tion, Rhinopneumonitis. The virus has been present in this country for many years; there are three types and there had been a few occurrences that spring: type A affects pregnant mares causing them to abort or absorb the foetus; type B affects the respiratory system and resembles influenza; type C has a paralysing effect. Understandably the organisers of the Brockenhurst event were worried that the New Forest ponies would be caused to absorb foals; but their decision to cancel did not help our preparations for Badminton, as there were only two weeks left.

The only other event that I could possibly do was Bicton, which would be far from ideal because it was only two days before we were due to go to Badminton. I still felt a glimmer of hope, though, and took Aloaf for a cross-country school around our King's Somborne course. However, he didn't go particularly well. For one thing, it is always difficult to ride at home, and for another, all the flags had been taken down so the jumps didn't look much like a course and there was no atmosphere of competition to make a horse do his utmost. Having not had the best of rides, I felt that Aloaf still needed another run. Murphy had had a good run at Belton, and as I was now physically fit I hoped that if I had two good rides at Bicton I might get to Badminton.

However, it was at about this time that I realised my broken collarbone had taken a greater toll than I thought. I found that I had lost a lot of my nerve on cross-country, and wasn't riding even the novice horses very well. I have hardly ever been nervous before a cross-country, but after I broke my collarbone I found that I had a tendency to caution rather than boldness. Apparently this is a common phenomenon after a bad accident and everybody goes through it. Nevertheless, full of optimism that I would quickly recover my nerve, I went to Bicton.

Local Yokel learning all about it

More dogs than horses! Alex at work, spring 1989

Mum lending a hand at Lanhydrock in Cornwall

BICTON 1989

The ground had been quite hard, but rain had fallen and made the course very slippery; nonetheless I felt it was imperative for me to run. I was sitting in the lorry before riding Murphy in the cross-country feeling very nervous, which was totally out of character. I went out telling myself that I had just got to ride as I had always ridden and try to get rid of this nervousness. As horses do, Murphy sensed that I was nervous and we had an abominable ride. I was either pulling him or kicking him too much, so he became tense and worried because he did not know what I was going to do next. We ended up by falling into the water.

With my dressage on Aloaf due in half an hour, we decided to call it a day and go home, for I knew I was not in a fit state to ride him properly. In consequence of this I had to withdraw from Badminton. Good fortune really seemed to have deserted me that spring of 1989.

After much discussion we concluded that it was Murphy who had made me nervous and that I was not going to recover my old form riding cross-country if I had to do it on him. So we thought we should sell him. It was a very sad decision to make, as I did believe that he was extremely talented. But he and I didn't seem to get on any more; I had grown too nervous to ride him properly and he was too good a horse for me to spoil. This was proved when in July he won the two-star CCI in Luhmühlen with Robert Lemieux after he had bought him from me.

Mason Gallery
Paintings
n Event Team

'... my back had been very painful: I had it X-rayed and it was found to be twisted ...'

Looking ahead, I intended to ride Aloaf at Bramham at the end of the spring season, and Banny at Windsor. At home I had a lovely six-year-old grey gelding whom we named Local Yokel; he was 16.1hh and by Hill Farmer, and earned his name because Mike lightheartedly refers to his friends and neighbours the local Exmoor farmers as 'local yokels'. As a stable name, we called him Charlie.

Charlie and Solomon were going well and Troy, who had done his first event, was showing great promise. I also had a good-looking five-year-old called Alderman Brown, which Mum had bought from Cutcombe cattle market on Exmoor the previous autumn; his stable name was Bruno. And of course there was Tangle Louis—or just Louis—whose warts were being treated and who had shown a lot of promise show jumping during the winter. Aloaf and Banny had good runs at Tidworth, then Aloaf won the OI at Ragley at the end of May; so things were beginning to look up.

I was not, however, entirely out of the wood as my back had been very painful: I had it X-rayed and it was found to be twisted, which necessitated treatment by a chiropractor in Winchester. This was on the Tuesday before Windsor, so it was important I should be fit by the weekend.

WINDSOR 1989

The cross-country course at Windsor was demanding, and after walking it I felt that this was going to be a big test for Banny; there were numerous big combinations, and enormous ditches under many of the plain fences.

All the dressage at Windsor is held on a Friday, and my test was in the late morning. Banny tried his best and did everything I asked him to. There was a welcome quiet atmosphere and the weather was sunny and warm, so we had nothing to worry about; unlike at Waregem the previous year with all the rain and wind and flapping flags. Immediately it was over, I hurried back to Winchester to have more treatment for my back.

On the Saturday we had ample time to watch all the juniors go round. I had walked the course twice already, and walked it a third time with Claire Mason. On my first two walks I had decided each time on the same line to take for each fence. But on the third walk, watching the juniors actually on the track and seeing them taking the fences so easily, I nearly changed my mind about one fence towards the end of the course: because they were jumping it so well, I contemplated taking the shorter way instead of the longer one.

Two fences before, there was a combination where a corner was the quickest route. I had chosen the slower alternative which involved two parallels with one stride between them. However, both these fences came late in the course, so I thought I would wait until I found out how Banny was going in the early part before finally making up my mind about them. At the corner fence I had decided that the corner might not be a good idea as he had once had a problem at one, and I thought he might have frightened himself; taking this corner would therefore be a risk.

Alex saw me off on phase A. Mum and Mike were on holiday on David and Vicky Mason's boat, so Lucy had kindly agreed to come and help Alex in the ten-minute box. The steeplechase at Windsor was moved in 1988 and is better than it used to be—it is now a lovely course of four fences. A lot of work had been done on the hard ground to ensure soft take-offs and landings so that the horses would not be punished. I was feeling much more confident than at the beginning of the season, so set off round Windsor Great Park for phase C in a happy mood.

Banny was full of running, and after our rest in the ten-minute box he set off on the cross-country brimming with confidence. He jumped the early fences better than I had expected, showing brilliance at the coffin and not looking suspiciously at the big ditches as I had thought he would. Another fence that worried me was a corner-type obstacle with a rail in front, over a ditch, and a hedge behind on an angle to make a corner; but he cleared it unhesitatingly which thrilled me. After a brilliant ride through the first water we came to the corner that I was worried about and where I had intended to take the long route over two parallels. However, because of the way he was going, I was so convinced that he would jump it that I changed my mind at the last instant and chose the short way: he came into it on a good stride and the line was right, but when he saw the back rail he stopped dead—he did not run out, just slammed on the brakes. He obviously remembered the corner we had jumped at Aldon which had frightened him. We took the double of parallels instead.

Two fences later we came to the Pimple fence, the other combination where I had not been sure which line to take. I had seen some juniors take the quicker of the two possible routes successfully so, as I had already had a stop and was not going to win anything, I tried to emulate them. But this fence involved a bounce and was as I found out technically too difficult for Banny, and he did not jump high enough: we fell, but went on to complete the course.

'It seemed that nothing was going right for me that 1989 season, and the harder I tried the worse matters became.'

He coped well with the rest of the course and I think he would have had no trouble with the Pimple fence if I had gone the route I had originally intended, as it would have given him more room. There was a lot to learn from that Windsor cross-country course. At Crookham Banny had jumped a right-hand corner easily; the hedge corner at Windsor was also a right one, but the second one was left-handed, so perhaps it is only the latter sort that he doesn't like.

I had wrenched my back when I fell, and it was giving me a lot of pain which kept me awake that night; by the time we show jumped it was hurting almost unbearably. Friends who were watching noticed that I was riding stiffly, and that was probably why Banny had two fences down after jumping the first part of the course competently. I had more treatment for my back that evening.

Misfortune seemed to pursue me relentlessly. I was looking forward to a good ride on Aloaf at Bramham the following week. But on Tuesday morning when I was having a dressage lesson with Paul Fielder I had to stop half-way through because my back was causing me so much pain; Paul rode Aloaf for the rest of the lesson and I went straight back to see the chiropractor for further manipulation. On Wednesday morning I felt much better, so Alex and I drove the G-Wagon and the lorry to Bramham. That afternoon I lunged Aloaf, but when I tried to get up on him to school him I could not sit in the saddle, let alone do a rising trot—I could only canter out of the saddle.

It seemed that nothing was going right for me that 1989 season, and the harder I tried the worse matters became. If I had taken a lot of pain-killers I might have been able to ride, but I would certainly have needed a long rest

Pages 186–7: Banny and me at Windsor three day event 1989, showing confidence after our fall

54

Some of our youngstock on Exmoor

afterwards; and if I had another fall I could have done myself permanent damage. So I was forced to withdraw from the event.

This was a great disappointment for us all, and especially for David Mason as MacConnal Mason Gallery was sponsoring the event. However, Claire still had her two rides, and Robert Lemieux was going to ride Ballymurphy under the MacConnal Mason name. But, unbelievably, as he was working him before his dressage test Murphy started to go unlevel, every tenth stride or so. We found that he had an infection in a back fetlock, so he had to be withdrawn too.

It made me very unhappy to tell David Mason that I was obliged to pull out both my horses, but I could not have had a better sponsor. He totally understands the sport of horse trials and appreciated that I could not ride with an injured and painful back, and Murphy was too lame to go into the dressage arena. Mum and Mike had arrived with the caravan on the morning of the dressage and naturally shared my disappointment. However, Bramham is one of our favourite events so we stayed on to give our support, especially as David Mason was sponsoring it.

I gave myself two weeks' complete rest at home to get over my back problem. Aloaf was fit and Alex hacked him every day, and I was going to France at the end of June to compete in a one day event at Chantilly with him.

CHANTILLY, FRANCE 1989

My disappointment at being unable to ride at Bramham was not the last of my troubles for the season, and to a certain extent my ill-fortune followed me even to France. I thought Aloaf had performed well in the dressage, and so did a lot of people who were watching him. Instead of praying that he wouldn't explode, I had gone into the arena full of confidence, really

rode every movement and Aloaf had done a very forward-going, active test. Two of the judges liked it, and one didn't like it at all. Each movement is marked out of ten: I had got sevens and eights from one judge, and twos and threes from another! We simply could not understand the difference in marks. There is often a disparity in judges' opinions, which is why there are always three of them, but this time the variance was extreme and impossible to comprehend. It sounds ludicrous, but I was placed third overall by one judge and *fifty-seventh* by another! Admittedly I was only twelve marks behind the leader as our scores had been very close, but in this particular one day event even just one mark made a significant difference. I suppose I was lucky that this was only the first or second time that it had happened to me.

'It sounds ludicrous, but I was placed third by one judge and fifty-seventh by another!

I put the dressage out of my mind and went forward to the cross-country not worrying any more about what had happened. Aloaf felt right on top form and gave me a brilliant ride—he was one of twenty-four horses to go inside the time, which pulled us up to sixteenth place. I had been lacking in confidence at the beginning of the year, but after finishing this round it was fully restored. Despite one unfortunate mistake in the show jumping we moved up to fifteenth in the final placings, a fine result. After Aloaf's cross-country performance I am looking forward to what I hope will be a great autumn season with him.

THE FUTURE

Everybody who rides in horse trials must expect to have patches of misfortune and I trust that my recent one is over now. The future is promising: I have plenty of support from Mum and Mike and my sponsors. I won't ride Aloaf at Burghley this year, but if all is well I may take him to Badminton in 1990; he may retire after that, as he is already thirteen. I have the two lovely six-year-olds, Solomon Grundy and Local Yokel, and the three five-year-olds, Tangle Louis (whose warts have been removed), Glentroy and Alderman Brown. Mum has several horses on Exmoor which are a possible future source of supply, and is still buying young horses two years old and under.

I also look forward to riding Friday's babies. She is now in foal and we hope to have her first progeny next spring—with any luck it will be skewbald; and maybe I'll have a string of skewbald event horses, as Friday's sister is skewbald too, and is also a brood mare. She has had her first foal, a beautiful bay colt—we would have preferred that one to have been coloured, and are hoping that her next one will be.

IN CONCLUSION

In this highly competitive sport there are many good riders who experience falls, or difficulties, or adverse fortune, and disappear for ever. But I remember someone saying that the difference between the good rider and the great is that where the good gives up, the great keeps coming back whatever the odds. The future looks bright and I sincerely hope that whatever it brings, my dedication to succeed in this challenging sport of horse trials will remain unshaken, and that I will be one of those that keep coming back, as enthusiastic and determined as ever.

Page 190: Friday at Horsens Bridge, Badminton 1988

Index

Note: Horses' names are in *italics*